AMERICAN
ECONOMIC
HISTORY ★ A
Garland
Series

Edited by
STUART BRUCHEY
Columbia University

THE ST. LOUIS FED'S MONETARY MODEL ★ When It Came How It Thrived 1970–1983

Donald A. Elliott

Garland Publishing, Inc.
New York & London ★ 1985

Library of Congress Cataloging in Publication Data

Elliott, Donald A. (Donald Allan), 1917–
The St. Louis Fed's monetary model.

(American economic history)
Bibliography: p.
1. Federal Reserve Bank of St. Louis. 2. Chicago school of economics. 3. Monetary policy. I. Title.
II. Title: Saint Louis Fed's monetary model.
III. Series.
HG2613.S784F434 1985 332.4′6′0724 84-45425
ISBN 0-8240-6668-5

All volumes in this series are printed on acid-free, 250-year-life paper.

Printed in the United States of America

THE ST. LOUIS FED'S MONETARY MODEL:

WHENCE IT CAME - HOW IT THRIVED, 1970 - 1983

BY

DONALD ALLAN ELLIOTT

ACKNOWLEDGMENTS

I wish to acknowledge and express my thanks to Keith Carlson and Professor Thomas Mayer who read this manuscript in its early stages and made many helpful comments, without implying in any way their endorsement of either the methods of analysis or the conclusions.

I would also like to thank Professors James Green and David Kamerschen of the University of Georgia, who have been especially supportive as this project has matured. Marlene Herman also deserves an especial thanks for her technical assistance.

It is a pleasure to dedicate this book to my wife Grace, who understood my long-held ambition to do economic research and who supported and encouraged me during this most interesting phase of our lives.

TABLE OF CONTENTS

TABLE OF TABLES

TABLE OF CHARTS

CHAPTER ONE

INTRODUCTION

> Money is not, properly speaking, one of the subjects of commerce but only the instrument which men have agreed upon to facilitate the exchange of one commodity for another. It is the oil which renders the wheels more smooth and easy.
>
> David Hume [1]
> 1752

When the Federal Reserve system was established in 1913, Congress, fearing a concentration of power in Washington which could mean a lack of concern for regional needs, created twelve individual Federal Reserve Banks, rather than the one central bank that was typical of most countries. Moreover, it was felt that every member commercial bank should be within an overnight railway ride of a branch of the system, so that if a bank feared a 'run', it could readily discount its notes with that branch and have currency available to meet the demands of its customers for liquidity.

The Federal Reserve Bank of St. Louis is one of those regional banks, set up to serve the central Mississippi valley with branches in Louisville, Kentucky; Memphis, Tennessee; and Little Rock, Arkansas. Since the early 1960's, it has become famous among professional economists as a centre of monetarist thought.

Professor Milton Friedman, formerly of the University of Chicago, is the best-known monetarist. In 1969, in a dialogue with Professor Walter Heller, Heller described the Federal

Reserve Bank of St. Louis as "the official arm of the Chicago School." To which, Friedman responded, "We ought to have one out of twelve anyway." [2]

To one interested in the history of contemporaneous economic thought, it is this statement which makes the Federal Reserve Bank of St. Louis, (better known amongst economists as the St. Louis Fed) a fascinating subject. Four questions immediately spring to mind:

1. How did the St. Louis Fed come to adopt Monetarism as its basic economic philosophy?

2. How has the St. Louis model (the econometric expression of its Monetarist philosophy) changed over the period 1970 - 1983?

3. Is the St. Louis Fed truly monetarist?

4. What contributions has the St. Louis Fed made to monetary theory and policy?

This book is concerned with the answers to those questions.

REFERENCES

1 David Hume, Philosophical Essays on Morals, Literature and Politics (Philadelphia, Penn.: Edward Beale 1817), p. 299.

2 Milton Friedman and Walter Heller, Monetary v. Fiscal Policy (New York, N.Y.: W.W. Norton, 1969), p. 60.

CHAPTER TWO

THE FEDERAL RESERVE BANK OF ST. LOUIS REVIEW

> According we find, that, in every kingdom into which money begins to flow in greater abundance than formerly, everything takes a new face, labour and industry gain life, the merchant becomes more enterprising, the manufacturer more diligent and skilful, and even the farmer follows his plow with great alacrity and attention.
>
> David Hume [1]
> 1752.

While the above quotation demonstrates that David Hume appreciated one of the basic tenets of Monetarism, it seems only fitting that the first use of the term should have occurred in an issue of the Federal Reserve Bank of St. Louis Review - specifically in a guest article by Karl Brunner entitled, "The Role of Money and Monetary Policy", which was published in the issue of July, 1968. [2]

It is in the pages of the Review, first printed monthly and now ten times a year, that the St. Louis Fed speaks its mind. During the period 1960 - 1983, each issue of the Review contained from two to four different articles on economic subjects, most of which were concerned with subjects important to monetarists, while others dealt with topics important to the residents of the central Mississippi valley.

As an example, during the year 1975, the Review contained thirty-three articles, of which some twenty were related to Monetarism. Most are prepared by economists on the staff of the Research Department of the Bank, but others are contributed by Visiting Scholars to the Bank. The St. Louis Fed does not invite nor publish papers submitted to it from outside sources. On occasion, however, professional economists will be invited to speak at seminars held for research personnel on matters of interest to them and their papers will be subsequently published in the Review. It is to be noted that during the 1960 - 1983 era, when the content did not coincide with the Bank's views, a disclaimer was printed in a footnote.

In the issue of July/August, 1983 and continued in subsequent Reviews, notice was given of a change in this policy. Now, "the views expressed are those of the individual authors and do not necessarily reflect official positions of the Federal Reserve Bank of St. Louis or the Federal Reserve System." This statement marks the end of an exciting and interesting era when the St. Louis Fed and the other Reserve Banks could speak out for themselves as individual entities. It seems rather sad, somehow, that they should lose their standing as independent sources of economic theory.

From time to time, the Review also published the speeches of Darryl R. Francis and Lawrence K. Roos, who were the presidents of the Bank during the period under review. Their addresses were given to various professional and academic audiences and they reflect not only the economic thought of the Bank's professional economists but also the St. Louis Fed's monetarist view of the world in which they lived.

Presidents Francis and Roos enthusiastically supported and agreed with the work of their staff. This was extremely important because there was no real meeting of the minds between the St. Louis Fed and the Federal Reserve Board in Washington. In a speech in London, England, on May 10, 1979, Roos said:

> ... it is only fair to admit that my viewpoint is neither reflective of the prevailing opinion within the Federal Reserve System nor does it enjoy the enthusiastic support of all opinion-holders within the United States. While this lack of widespread acceptance occasionally generates a degree of frustration for me and my colleagues at the Federal Reserve Bank of St. Louis, it does not diminish our concern that current monetary policymaking practices are not achieving the goals for which they are intended.[3]

Thus a great deal of credit is due to the St. Louis Fed for espousing the monetarist cause, particularly during the 1960's when it conflicted with the mainstream Keynesian position then taken by most professional economists. It is largely through the efforts of Milton Friedman, Karl Brunner and Allen Meltzer and those associated with their monetarist philosophy, of which not least is the St. Louis Fed, that Keynesian economists have changed their thinking from 'Money never matters", to "Money also matters" even if none would agree with monetarists that "Money is all that matters".

REFERENCES

1 David Hume, Philosophical Essays on Morals, Literature and Politics (Philadelphia, Penn.: Edward Beale 1817), p. 299.

2 Attributed by Professor Thomas Mayer in The Structure of Monetarism (New York, N.Y.: W.W. Norton, 1978), p. 1.

3 Lawrence K. Roos, "Monetary Targets -- Their Contribution to Policy Formation", The Federal Reserve Bank of St. Louis Review, (May, 1979), p. 12.

CHAPTER THREE

THE MONETARY ROOTS OF THE ST. LOUIS MODEL

> ... though the high price of commodities be a necessary consequence of the increase of gold and silver, yet it follows not immediately upon that increase; but some time is required before the money circulates through the whole state, and makes its effect felt on all ranks of the people. At first, no alteration is perceived; by degrees the price rises, first of one commodity, then of another; till the whole at least reaches a just proportion with the new quantity of specie which is in the kingdom. In my opinion, it is only in this interval or intermediate situation; between the acquisition of money and rise of prices, that the increasing quantity of gold and silver is favourable to industry.
>
> David Hume [1]
> 1752.

In 1963, Lionel Robbins set the tone for the work of the economists at the Federal Reserve Bank of St. Louis when he wrote that:

> a substantial number...of our political judgments are made in ignorance of consequences ...economic analysis by pointing to the results of action rather than action considered intrinsically...can make a contribution to rational action. [2]

In the early 1960's, the Research Department of the St. Louis Fed was doing just this by issuing a barrage of statistics concerning the economic situation of the American economy. As Exhibit "A" indicates, these statistics included weekly financial data, monthly monetary trends and national economic trends - all with tables, charts and analytical comments. This research stressed the importance of monetary aggregates and by charting them, illustrated their relationships to the state of the U.S. economy.

Nevertheless, as we shall see, the management of the St. Louis Fed was calling for more guidance, with an especial emphasis on the need to be able to project the effects of changes in the money supply on such key economic variables as nominal GNP, prices, employment and long and short term interest rates.

With this motivation, in the late 1960's, staff members led by Michael Keran, Leonall Andersen and Jerry Jordan began to use regression techniques in order to measure the empirical relationships between monetary and fiscal data and economic activity as illustrated by nominal GNP. Subsequently when Leonall Andersen and Keith Carlson decided to expand this work and create a mathematical model which could explain the major features of economic activity in the United States, they had a data base of excellent statistics to work with.

Every student of econometrics - defined as the study of the application of statistical methods to the analysis of economic phenomena - is advised of the first rule, namely; "garbage in means garbage out." Andersen and Carlson had solid data to work with. There are two other requirements for good econometrics:

1. correct statistical methods and
2. sound economic theory.

As we shall note, the statistical methods which they have used have been important in assessing the results which they have achieved.

It goes without saying that the economic theory which stands behind any econometric equations, if it is to be generally accepted, must be considered to be a reasonable portrayal of the way that the economy works. As Milinvaud has written:

> The art of econometrics consists in finding the set of assumptions which are both sufficiently specific and sufficiently realistic to allow (the econometrician) to take the best possible advantage of the data available. [3]

As our quotation from David Hume at the beginning of the chapter illustrates, even in 1752, it was recognised that there were lags in the operation of monetary policy between the initial increase of the stock of money and it's ultimate effect on the economy. These lags can be accommodated in econometric equations. For example, by using as one independent variable the past values of the variable to be predicted, an econometrician can usually improve the prediction, but it provides few insights into how the underlying mechanism works. Which emphasizes again that good theory must provide the framework for good econometrics.

Thus we can appreciate the difficulties that Carlson and Andersen encountered in setting up the detailed exposition of the St. Louis Model, outlined in the April 1970 Review. Carlson gives great credit to Professor William Yohe of Duke University, then a Visiting Scholar at the Bank, for his assistance. It was his knowledge of the history of economic thought which provided the background for the relationships which they were seeking to express in econometric language. As Carlson has said: "At all times the experience of economic history should be kept clearly in perspective."[4]

In order to understand and evaluate the theoretical foundation on which the St. Louis Model has been constructed, we must take a short look at economic history, and in particular, see how monetary theory developed from the thought of the Classical Economists of the early nineteenth century. Their ideas were extended into the algebraic expression $MV \equiv PT$ in the early 1900's in the work of Irving Fisher. In turn this equation of exchange was expanded into the quantity theory of money by the "Chicago School", Professors Jacob Viner, Frank Knight, Lloyd Mints, and Henry Simons during the Great Depression of the 1930's in order to formulate the governmental policies which they recommended should be undertaken to overcome it.

Their work was to be overshadowed by John Maynard Keynes and the theories which he developed in his famous book, the General Theory of Unemployment, Interest and Money, published in 1936. After World War II, Milton Friedman, also a professor at the University of Chicago, was almost solely responsible for the revival of interest in monetary theory, and as we shall see, his influence played a large part in the development of the St. Louis Model.

THE MONETARY PROBLEM

The relation between money, prices and the state of the economy has been the subject of increasing interest in every country since World War II, and we now see features in the financial pages of our daily newspapers concerned with the state of the money supply as set out in the weekly figures supplied by the Federal Reserve System in Washington and their effect on the financial markets. But the problem is not new - the Roman Empire had inflation problems which the Emperor Diocletion tried unsuccessfully to manage by instituting price controls. The hyperinflation that occurred in Germany subsequent to World War I illustrated graphically that too much money could have disastrous effects on the economy as it wiped out the savings of the middle class.

It goes without saying that a money economy is much more efficient than a barter economy. One does not have to search for someone who has the goods you wish to trade for - and in turn - who desires the very things that you wish to give in exchange. But once we enter into a monetary economy, we recognise that - since we can exchange money for goods - that choice need not be made immediately. It can lead to difficulties.

Think of a simple agricultural community where a worker receives his pay in the products of the fields where he toils. If he wishes to save part of his income, he does so in his own root cellar, barrels or bins. Demand for his employer's products is unchanged. However, as soon as wages are paid in the form of money, then this money represents a claim on goods which the worker can present at any time in the future. In saving some part of his income, there is an immediate decrease in the total demand for goods. Unless such savings are invested in some form, inventories increase and unemployment or reduced working time must follow until those inventories are returned to normal. Again and again we shall see reference to the problem which occurs when money is used as an asset rather than as a medium of exchange.

Professor George Shackle describes the situation neatly and elegantly in the aphorism which commences Chapter 6:

> Money opens the the Pandora's box of expectation and uncertainty, the limitless field of imagination is brought into view and determinacy must evaporate.[5]

THE FIRST ECONOMISTS

The monetarization of the economic system has been the source of much economic controversy over the years. In England, the bullionist controversy of 1796 - 1821 following the suspension of specie payments during the Napoleonic Wars and the Currency versus Banking School debate of the 1840's revolved around how the size of the note issue should be determined and the economic effects of changing the supply of money. It is interesting to note that the English one pound note, first issued in 1797, is to be replaced on January 1, 1985, by a coin.

History tells us that as far back as 1569, a Frenchman, Jean Bodine, had given five reasons for the rise in the general level of prices in Western Europe during the sixteenth century. He considered that the most important factor was the increase in stock of gold and silver brought into Europe from the newly-discovered American mines.

In 1752, David Hume, as set out in the quotation at the beginning of this Chapter, described how, in the short run (which is hardly ever given a specific term by economists) the level of economic activity depended upon the quantity of money and its velocity. However, he concluded that it was only in the interval between the acquisition of more money and the final response of prices, that an increasing supply of gold and silver is favourable to industry. During that period of time, the price of all products rise, expanding the output and profits of all entrepreneurs at the expense of recipients of fixed incomes. But as the pace of industry quickens, wages, rent and interest rates will rise as well. This will cause expectations of profit to decline and the economy will reach equilibrium again at a higher level of prices. When that occurs, money will once more function only as an 'oil', smoothing the wheels of industry.

It is interesting to note that Hume went on to say:

> From the whole of this reasoning, we may conclude that it is no manner of consequence,

> with regard to the domestic happiness of the state, whether money be in greater or less quantity. The good policy consists in keeping it, if possible, still increasing; because it keeps alive a spirit of industry in the nation, and increase the stock of labour, in which consists all real power and riches.[6]

As we shall see, after the debate between David Ricardo and Thomas Malthus, early in the nineteenth century, economic theory held money to be merely a 'veil', hiding the trade in goods and services which its exchange represented. The effect of money on the pace of industry disappeared from Classical Theory until it was revived by the 'Chicago School' during the Great Depression of the 1930's.

This occurred because accepted economic theory from Adam Smith's Wealth of Nations in 1776 to Keynes' General Theory of 1936, held that left to itself and given time, the economic system of any free enterprise nation would quickly find its equilibrium with all, or nearly all, of its willing workers employed. Government intervention of any kind would only interfere with this process. Money was considered to be unimportant in economic activity, because, with full employment, prices would provide the linkage to the stock of money, regardless of the amount involved.

THE CLASSICAL ECONOMISTS

Adam Smith (1723 - 1790) was the first of the classical economists and he, with David Ricardo and J.S. Mill dominated economic thought from the publication of Smith's great work The Wealth of Nations, in 1776 until the 1890's. Like Andersen and Carlson, Smith desired to explain how the market system worked and the influences which would increase England's wealth, or output of goods and services. It is interesting to note that the complete title of his book is, An Inquiry into the Nature and Causes of the Wealth of Nations.

This book was a reaction against the doctrines of eighteenth-century mercantilists who thought that a country's wealth could be augmented by increasing its stock of precious metals - by plunder or by a policy of running an export surplus.

As far as the stock of money is concerned and it's influence on the wealth of a nation, Smith had very little to say. Rather he emphasized that economic development depended on the accumulation of capital, that is to say, plant, machinery, inventory and sufficient moneys to support labour until the final product was sold. Such capital would allow for the specialization of labour and the proportion of the work-force engaged in productive labour. As he put it:

> In the midst of all exactions of government, this capital has been silently and gradually accumulated by private frugality and good conduct of individuals, by their universal, continual and uninterrupted effort to better their own condition.[7]

Thus he said "Capital are increased by parsimony, and diminished by prodigality and misconduct."[8] Moreover, individual self-interest would see to it that such capital was always allocated optimally in the market place.

> Every individual is continually exerting himself to find out the most advantageous employment for whatever capital he can command. It is his own advantage, indeed, and not that of society, which he has in view. But the study of

> his own advantage naturally, or rather necessarily leads him to prefer that employment which is most advantageous to the society.[9]

The ideas of Adam Smith were adopted and refined by David Ricardo (1772 - 1823) and set out in his Principles of Political Economy and Taxation. Thomas Malthus (1766 - 1834), who is noted for his work on population, was also very interested in Political Economy, and their mutual interest developed into a very strong friendship. But this did not keep them from disagreeing on principles.

Their debate on the effect of savings in the economy has been made famous by Keynes' statement, "if only Malthus instead of Ricardo, had been the parent- stem from which 19th-century economics proceeded, what a wiser and richer place the world would be today".

What was their debate about? [10]

Their dispute was concerned with the problem as to whether or not consumers would always have both the funds and the desire to buy back at profitable prices, all that was produced. Malthus said this would not necessarily occur, while Ricardo insisted that it would.

Mathus writes to Ricardo as follows:

> We see in almost every part of the world vast powers of production which are not put into action, and I explain this phenomena by saying from the want of a proper distribution to the actual produce, adequate motives are not furnished to continued production...I distinctly maintain that an attempt to

> accumulate very rapidly which necessarily implies a considerable dimunition of unproductive consumption by greatly impairing the usual motives of production, must prematurely check the progress of wealth.[11]

Ricardo replies:

> Mr. Malthus talks of "an economy of consumption and a discouragement to the indulgence of those tastes and wants which are the very elements of demand". The whole matter in dispute is centred in these fine words. Mr. Say, Mr. Mill and I say there will be no economy of consumption, no cessation of demand.[12]

Ricardo was referring to the proposition which we call Say's Law, named after the French economist Jean Baptiste Say (1767 - 1832), which, simply put, states that "Supply creates its own demand". Ricardo expressed it as follows:

> Productions are always bought by productions or services, <u>money is only the medium by which exchange is effected</u>. Hence the increased production being always accompanied by a correspondingly increased ability to get and consume, there is no possibility of overproduction.[13] Emphasis added.

Since Ricardo sees money only as a medium of exchange, his view of Say's Law rests on the assumption that all income is spent and none is hoarded. One can appreciate that Ricardo, as a former broker in the money markets of the day, would deem this to be self-evident. As he said:

> It appears to me that no man would willingly lock up his money, he would endeavour to make it as productive as possible; he would not purchase commodities if he expected a fall of commodities, but he would be glad to lend his money at interest, during the interval it was necessary for him to keep it. 14

While classical economists denied that there could be general overproduction, they were aware that changes in the extent of the market for products or in consumers' tastes, would leave individual producers with goods which they could not sell at a profit. Thus they had to be able to explain how such a problem would not escalate into what they called a 'general glut'.

Their explanation was that if one producer was unable to dispose of his output profitably, then there must be others who were enjoying an unusually large demand for their products, thereby obtaining higher than normal prices and profits. By making the assumption that capital and/or labour was relatively mobile, these resources would be re-allocated from the sectors of the economy that were not doing well to those enjoying abnormal demand. These adjustments would take time, but in the long run (however long that might be), they would bring about equilibrium at what we would now call "full" or "high" employment.

But Mathus was not convinced by this argument - for he was very much aware of the recession which followed the end of the Napoleonic Wars. As he wrote:

> From the harvest of 1815 to the harvest of 1816, there cannot be a doubt that the funds for the maintenance of labour were unusually abundant. Corn was particularly plentiful, and no other necessaries were deficient; yet it is an

> acknowledged fact that great numbers were thrown out of employment, partly from the want of power, and partly from the want of will to employ the same quantity of labour as before. How is this fact to be accounted for?[15]

It is interesting to note that Malthus had a Keynesian solution to the problem.

> ... altogether I should say that the employment of the poor in roads and public works and a tendency among landlords and persons of property to build, to improve and beautify their grounds, and to employ workmen and menial servants, are the means most directly calculated to remedy the evils arising from the disturbance in the balance of production and consumption. [16]

Ricardo would not agree, writing:

> I would not make a protest against an increase of consumption, as a remedy to the stagnation of trade, if I thought as you do, that we are now suffering from too great savings. As I have already said, I do not see how the stagnation of trade can rise from such a cause ...and in my opinion, increased savings would alleviate rather than aggravate the sufferings of which we have lately had to complain.[17]

Ricardo is saying that more savings, rather than less, would provide the capital to furnish the goods which must be in great demand, since those then available were overstocked. He is thus repeating his oft-quoted criticsm, "Mr. Malthus never appears to remember that to save is to spend, as surely as what he exclusively calls spending."

Ricardo and Malthus also had different thoughts about the position of money in the economy. As we have seen, for Ricardo it was but a 'veil' - serving only as a medium of exchange. But Malthus also saw it as a store of value, and as such, it could be troublesome.

> Theoretical writers in Political Economy from the fear of attaching too much importance to money have perhaps, been too apt to throw it out of their consideration in their reasonings. It is an abstract truth that we want commodities, not money. But, in reality, no commodity for which it is possible to sell our goods at once, can be an adequate substitute for a circulating medium, and enable us in the same manner to provide for our children, to purchase an estate, or to command labour and provisions a year or two hence. [18]

Despite their differences, their friendship continued, each recognising their different points-of-view. Thus, Ricardo writes to Malthus:

> If I am too theoretical (which I really believe is the case) you, I think are too practical. There are so many combinations and operating causes in political economy that there is great danger in appealing to experience in favour of a particular doctrine, unless we are sure that all causes of variation are seen and their effects duly estimated. [19]

This last sentence sets out the basic problem which troubles all econometric models.

John Stuart Mill (1806 - 1873) simplified Malthus' argument in a little-known essay entitled "On the Influence of Consumption upon Production". Mill writes, "When two persons perform an act of barter, each of them is at once a seller and a buyer. He cannot sell without buying". But he points out, "If, however, we suppose that money is used, these propositions cease to be exactly true."[20]

Mill is pointing out the usefulness of money as something other than a mere medium of exchange:

> The effect of the employment of money and the utility of it, is, that it enables this one act of interchange to be divided into two separate acts or operations; one which may be performed now, and the other a year hence or whenever it shall be most convenient. [21]

Now during periods of 'glut', every individual

> ...delays selling if he can, keeping his capital unproductive in the meantime, and sustaining the consequent loss of interest. There is stagnation to those who are not obliged to sell, and distress to those who are. [22]

Thus, an economic recession was caused by the fact that;

> ...persons in general expectation of being called upon to meet sudden demands, liked better to possess money than any other

> commodity. Money, consequently was in request and all other commodities were in comparative disrepute ...with the result that <u>all commodities fall in price or become unsaleable</u>.[23] Emphasis added.

Jean Baptiste Say, in a letter to Malthus in 1820, confirms that just such situations had come about in France:

> Mr. Ricardo insists that, notwithstanding taxes and other charges, there is always as much industry as capital employed, because interest is not suffered to be lost. On the contrary, many savings are not invested, when it is difficult to find employment for them, and many which are employed are dissipated in ill-calculated undertakings. Besides Mr. Ricardo is completely refuted, not only by what happened to us in 1813, when the errors of government ruined all commerce, and when the interest of money fell very low, for want of good opportunities of employing it; but our present circumstances, when capitals are quietly sleeping in the coffers of their proprietors. The Bank of France alone possesses 223 millions of specie, which is more than double the amount of notes in circulation, and six times what prudence would consider necessary to reserve for the ordinary course of payments. 24

As has been said, Ricardo remained unconvinced, continuing to believe that these disequilibrium effects were fleeting and unimportant - mere qualifications to long-run equilibrium analysis. John Stuart Mill, in his <u>Principles of Politicical</u>

Economy, published in 1848, did not mention his earlier qualification concerning the demand for money.

However, let it be noted that there can be no question but that supply creates a potential demand. What is crucial is whether or not that potential demand is transmuted into effective demand. A newly produced automobile which is to sell for $10,000.00, puts almost all of that $10,000.00 worth of monetary purchasing power into the hands of labour, lessors and lenders in the form of wages, rent and interest paid for raw materials, parts and services. The remainder is wrapped up in the potential profit which is made by the car-dealer only when the automobile is sold. Assume that his normal profit is $500.00 - where does that sum come from? We know that most automobile purchasers finance some part of the price, and thus it is extremely important that the financial community be able to provide the funds to purchase such consumer durables. If the automobile cannot be sold for a high enough price to produce a normal profit, it will erode the car dealer's confidence and his ability to continue in business.

The same is true for the economy as a whole. But the question remains, - how can there be any assurance that all of this monetary purchasing power will be used immediately?

To the extent that this purchasing power is not exercised, it remains in the hands of its holders as savings and there can be no doubt but that such savings make available real resources - labour and the means of production - which can be used for investment and thereby increase effective demand. But as has been illustrated and as we shall see again, the mechanism breaks down when confidence fails and expectations of profit falter.

This is the income-expenditure approach to short-run economic fluctuations and is based on the fact that one person's expenditure is another's income. This approach holds that the thrust of economic policy must be to maintain and expand expenditures. As we shall see, this concept was used by John Maynard Keynes to explain the Great Depression of the 1930's and thereby provide a fresh outlook on an old problem.

One cannot conclude this section without agreeing with Prof. Corry that:

> The way in which the Classical economists tended over the years to shed its conditioning clauses and forget the vital analysis of non-equilibrium situations must remain as a salutary reminder - ever necessary for the economist - that conditions change. We do not live in a static world and, therefore, the assumptions from which the deductions proceed, have to be kept continually under review, in the light of testing against real-world data.[24]

So it was to be for the St. Louis Model!

THE QUANTITY THEORY

Irving Fisher (1867 - 1947) was an American Monetary reformer and a pioneer mathematical economist. As such, he is considered to be the 'father' of the equation of exchange. As he put it, "One of the normal effects of an increase in the quantity of money is an exactly proportional increase in the general level of prices."[24]

This is the expression of the equation of exchange, but it is meant to apply in the long-run, when the economy has attained a hypothetical position at full employment. The reason that this was held to be true in such a circumstance is described by Fisher:

> As inflation in the currency cannot increase the production of farms and factories, nor the speed of freight trains or ships. The stream of business depends on natural resources and technical conditions, not on the quantity of money. The whole machinery of production, transportation and sale is a matter of physical capacities and techniques, none of which depend on the quantity of money.[27]

It must be emphasized again, that Fisher's proposition was to be applicable only on the assumption that there was continuous full employment. He assumed that there would be 'transition periods' which would last ten years on the average.[27] During these periods the level of real output and the velocity of the circulation of money would change. Moreover he assigned a critical role to the difference between the money rates and the real rates of interest, about which we shall have more to say later. Fisher wrote much more extensively about the monetary changes necessary to mitigate the economic problems of these "transition periods", than on the long-run proportionality of prices to money. However, it is for his equation of exchange that he is best remembered.

The Quantity theory of money is based on the Fisherian equation of exchange, which is a mathematical identity that relates the flow of money expenditures to the flow of economic transactions. The flow of money expenditures in any period, say, one year, is depicted by MV, where M is the stock of money and V is the velocity at which the supply of money turns over during the year. The value of economic transactions during a year is depicted by PT , where T represents the physical volume of transactions and P the average price of each transaction.

Since total money expenditures MV must equal the total volume of goods and services on which that money has been spent, PT, it follows that:

$$MV \equiv PT$$

Since V is not a directly observable variable, it can be measured only as V = PT/M. At full employment, the level of transactions T and the level of velocity V were considered to be stable. This means, mathematically that if the money supply M increases, then the price level P must rise proportionally. This, then, is the 'transactions' quantity theory of money and can be expressed mathematically as:

$$M\bar{V} = P\bar{T}$$

where V and T are held to be constants.

Actually, classical economists never considered V to be constant in the sense of unchangeable. They recognised the effects of interest rates and price expectations on velocity; however they felt that such factors were relatively unimportant in the long run. As we have seen the same was true for transactions - there could be partial 'gluts' when some markets did not clear, but these situations were not important in the long view.

Unfortunately, the concept of the demand for money does not emerge clearly in the 'transactions' formulation of the Quantity theory. However, by merely substituting 1/k for V, the equation becomes M =kPT and it is known as the Cambridge cash-balance equation. Algebraically the two equations mean the same thing. But there is a fundamental difference between the analyses which underlie each which we have endeavoured to emphasize previously, namely:

> The central question in...transactions analysis is how rapidly money is spent. The central question in cash-balances analysis is why holders of cash haven't spent it yet. 29

The Cambridge 'k' implies that money is a utility-yielding asset and the demand for it, like the demand for any commodity, is a matter for individual decision. The problem was that the 'k' ratio was treated as a numerical constant - yet one would expect a rise in interest rates to cause a fall in 'k' as individuals substituted income bearing securities for cash. Similarly one would expect falling interest rates to cause a rise in 'k'.

In the formulation MV = PT, there is ambiguity about the meaning of 'transactions'. Not only are new goods and services included, but also capital goods, intermediate goods and factor services. Thus an automobile that changed hands three times in one year would be the equivalent of three automobiles. As well, where do we find the "general price level" for such transactions?

The development of national accounting has stressed income transactions and the GNP implicit deflator. Thus the equation of exchange can easily be restated as:

$$\dot{M} + \dot{V} = \dot{P} + \dot{X} = \dot{Y}$$

where X is the real level of new output of goods and services or more familiarly, GNP, measured in constant dollars, P is the GNP (implicit) deflator, which when combined with X, gives Y as the nominal level of current GNP. The dots over the variables indicate changes in percentage terms and recognise that velocity and real output do vary over time.

This is known as the 'income' Quantity theory and the St. Louis model was developed in order to quantify the relationships between these variables.

The transactions Quantity Theory was the extent of 'macroeconomics' as taught in the early 1930's. The famous Swedish economist, Knut Wicksell, (1851 - 1926) felt thwarted by the inadequacy of the theoretical structure of this concept because it failed to explain "why the monetary or pecuniary demands for goods exceeds or falls short of the supply of goods in given conditions". [30]

It was this same difficulty which led Keynes to his famous statement about the 'long run' in economic theory:

> ...this long-run is a misleading guide to current affairs. In the long-run we are all dead. Economists set themselves too easy, too useless a task if in tempestuous seasons they can only tell us that when the storm is long past, the ocean is flat again. [31]

This problem was to come to a head during the Great Depression. The classical economists had never visualized the possiblity of a 'general glut' whereby prices, output and employment would be reduced by as much as twenty-five percent in a short time and remain at depressed levels for several years. When this did occur, they turned to the transactions Quantity Theory of money for an explanation and for guidance in developing policies that would bring the economies of the world out of their ghastly malaise.

THE CHICAGO SCHOOL

The Economics staff at the University of Chicago, during the 1930's and since, has been famous amongst professional economists, for its interest in Money and Banking - with special emphasis on the Quantity theory of money. John Maynard Keynes, on the other hand, is noted for his expenditure model of the economy. In 1931, he had just finished publishing a two-volume work entitled Treatise on Money which had appeared in December 1930. In this work, Keynes abandoned the Quantity theory for an income approach which examined the savings-investment process and laid the groundwork for his famous General Theory of Money, Interest and Employment, to be published in 1936.

In order to appreciate their theoretical and practical approach to the problems of the Great Depression, it is interesting to note that Keynes met with some members of the Chicago School when he came to the University to participate in the 1931 Harris lectures.[32] The subject that year was 'Unemployment as a World Problem".

We have seen that for the classical economists, unemployment was felt to be only a 'transitional' problem. Thus the general sentiment of the economists of the day was that governments should do nothing to alleviate the problems - indeed any action that they might take would only exacerbate the difficulties. This was the so-called British Treasury view, which held that public works simply diverted savings from the private sector to the government and failed to increase total activity.

It was only when Keynes expounded the theory of the Multiplier in his General Theory, that the benefits of government spending were recognised amongst economists.

Moreover, since the Treasury view must mean that during a recession there were profitable projects available, one could ask why private enterprise had not discovered them. Again it would take the General Theory to illustrate how 'liquidity preference' prevented the rate of interest from falling to the level that would make private investment payable, and with renewed optomism, raise the "animal spirits" of entrepreneurs to the point that they were willing to take the risks of new investment. All of that was to come.

At this time, Professor R.G. Hawtrey was espousing a different view, one which Milton Friedman was to largely bring into the mainstream of economic theory and for which the St. Louis Model was to provide empirical endorsement, namely, if one expanded public works without expanding bank credit, one did not add to employment; if one expanded bank credit, one could add to employment without public works.[33] But this too was to come later.

In 1931, the general feeling amongst economists was that the depression and unemployment were the result of prices being much too low, and these prices in turn generated business losses and the reduction of output. The need, therefore was to raise prices above costs and thereby increase profits.

Keynes saw the solution in Wicksellian terms - the central bank's policy should be to reduce the rate of interest below the 'natural rate' which equated savings and investment. When interest rates were below the expected rate of return of new investment, entrepreneurs would act. This would raise demand and with it the price level relative to costs and thereby generate business profits. Higher profits, in turn, would stimulate more output and employment.

The problem with such a policy, with the gold standard of the day, was that a central bank could not, on its own, reduce the rate of interest in its country below that of other countries. If it did so, it would cause an outflow of gold as investors sought the higher interest rates that would be prevailing abroad - causing a loss of international reserves. This, in turn would require lower wages and employment in the country that did so in order to reduce the price of its exports and enable it to regain those reserves. In such a case, Keynes advocated 'public works' as the means of reducing unemployment.

At the Harris lectures, Keynes put it this way:

> The cure of unemployment involves improving business profits. The improvement of business profits can come about by an improvement of new investment relative to saving. An increase of investment relative to saving must also, as an inevitable by-product, bring a rise of prices, thus ameliorating the burdens rising out of monetary indebtedness. The problem resolves itself, therefore, into the question as to what means we can adopt to increase the volume of investment. 34

He set out three 'lines of approach':

> 1. Restore confidence - about which not much could be deliberately done.
>
> 2. "Carry out a program of public investment which has the practical drawback; it is not easy to devise at short notice schemes which are wise and efficiently conceived and which can be put rapidly into operation on a really large scale."
>
> 3. Lowering the long-run rate of interest by a vigorous central bank policy of open-market purchases of debt instruments because an increase in the price of bonds and debentures causes the rate of interest to fall.

Since the United States was only marginally concerned with international trade, he suggested:

> I think in this country deliberate public works should be regarded much more as a tonic to change the state of business conditions, but the means of getting them back to a state of equilibrium should be concentrated on the rate of interest. That condition not being so in Great Britain, one had to lay stress on public programs, but in this country it should operate on the rate of interest. [35]

During the 1931-1936 period, the Chicago school, using the Fisherian MV = PT approach, advocated similar governmental policies, but for very different reasons. It held that the major cause of the business cycle was the instability, not of investment, but of the velocity of circulation V. Professors Simons and Mints therefore recommended that the government make the changes in M which would offset those changes in V and thus maintain a constant level of what Simons called the "total turnover of MV."[36]

It is interesting to note that Milton Friedman contends that Simons' belief in the instability of velocity was based on a theoretical view of the Great Depression and that if Simons had then known "the facts" which we now know and he did not, [37] he would have chosen a policy rule stated in terms of changes in M rather than V. Patinkin disputes this statement, suggesting that Simons would have been well aware of the empirical changes in the stock of money. [38]

The Chicago school also agreed that one of the causes of the Great Depression was the low level of prices or P. Thus, its members also advocated increasing M when P tended to fall and decreasing

M when it tended to rise. The necessary variations in M were to be generated by open-market operations or by Federal budgetary deficits financed by money creation. The latter were to be preferred because open-market purchases:

> ...increase the cash reserves of the banking system, and therefore, it is hoped, to give the banks the desire to put their idle funds to work. But the bankers have learned in recent years, not how to make money by lending, but that under certain circumstances the rate at which they lose money is less if they stop lending, so it is conceivable that the banking system would welcome the additional liquidity and would not increase its loans or investments. 39

It is important to appreciate that the Chicago school, while advocating federal budget deficits engendered by increasing either government expenditures or decreasing taxes, required that deficit expenditures be balanced over the business cycle, rather than annually. This, of course, required that there be budgetary surpluses during business booms.

Later Simons and Mints began to express a definite preference for generating deficits by means of reducing taxes; both because it was a more flexible procedure which could subsequently be reversed, and because it involved less governmental activity than did increasing Federal expenditures.

INTEREST RATES

To this point in our story, little has been said about the theory of interest rates. This is because the classical economists had little to say about them. If we go back to David Hume we find that he regarded profits and interest to be interdependent. "The low profits of merchandise induce the merchants to accept more willingly of a low interest". On the other hand, "no man will accept at low profits, where he can have high interest"; a business boom that brought greater competition and lower profits would also lower the rate of interest. [40]

Adam Smith agreed that the rate of interest was determined by the rate of profits. "...wherever a great deal can be made by the use of money, a great deal will commonly be given for the use of it", [41] and vice versa. This presupposed that there was a supply of saving (thrift), while demand came from entrepreneurs, and the strength of that demand depended on the rate of return on capital.

Irving Fisher regarded the so-called 'real' rate of interest as a reflection of time-preference. Individuals were held to prefer satisfaction now rather than later. Thus they had to be paid a 'reward for waiting' which would then enable them to purchase additional real goods at some future date. Unless individuals preferred more future and fewer present goods, there would be no supply of savings. The rate of return on capital, what Keynes called the 'marginal efficiency of capital' represented the demand for these savings.

Except in the short term, classical economists held that there was no connection between the interest rate and the money supply. But Fisher did single out another factor which brings the Quantity theory of money into play. This is the distinction between the real rate of interest and the nominal rate of interest. If the nominal rate of interest is 10% per year at the beginning of the year and prices increase by 5% during that year, then the real rate of return to the lender is 10% - 5% = 5%. However, what matters for the market is not the ex post yield which is realized after the event, but what people anticipate will happen. Thus individuals who intend to buy securities or loan money will look at the real rate of return which they expect to get and the anticipated rate of inflation. They will add that rate to the real rate to obtain the nominal rate they desire. Thus in our illustration, if the lender had anticipated that the price level would rise by 5% during the year that his money was at risk, he would have demanded a nominal rate of 15% to ensure he received a real return of 10%. We shall see how this idea is incorporated into the St. Louis Model.

Nevertheless one must ever keep in mind Irving Fisher's conclusion:

> We have found evidence, general and specific...that prices do, generally and perceptibly, affect the interest rate in the direction indicated by a priori theory. But since forethought is imperfect, the effects are smaller than the theory requires and lag behind price movements, and in some periods, very greatly. [42]

Keynes saw a different role for the money stock and brought it back into a dynamic role in the economic process by asserting that economists must think about the demand for money as an asset, rather than the quite different demand for loanable funds. For him, interest was the price that must be paid to people to forego willingly the advantages of liquidity - the old concept of hoarding. Instead of individuals being paid interest to reward them for saving - Keynes held that savings increased and decreased with the level of income. Interest therefore was the payment necessary to prevent individuals from hoarding.

As he put it:

> The fundamental psychological law, upon which we are entitled to depend with great confidence both a priori from our knowledge of human nature and from the detailed facts of experience, is that men are disposed, as a rule and on the average, to increase their consumption as their income increases but not by as much as the increase of income. [43]

Since saving is the difference between income and consumption, Keynes was saying that saving increased at a proportionately larger rate, as incomes rose. As Milton Friedman was to complain, Keynes had very little statistical support for this law. Other consumption functions have been constructed and it now appears that U.S. consumers will spend between 92 and 96 percent of additions to their disposable income. That is, the marginal rate of savings is positive and varies between 4 and 8 percent.

The problem with Keynes' theory is that the interest rate cannot be determined until the level of income is known, and the level of income cannot be determined until the level of the interest rate is known. To overcome this difficulty, J.R. Hicks first and then Alvin Hansen later, proposed the famous IS/LM framework as a way to bring together the four elements involved, namely, investment demand, saving, the demand for money and the quantity of money. The IS/LM paradigm shows how these four variable jointly determine national income and the rate of interest.

However, there is a disadvantage with the Hicks-Hansen IS/LM model, namely, it uses a diagram to illustrate its static equilibrium format. It is therefore not ideally suited to deal with the dynamics of disequilibrium processes wherein economic variables evolve and interact <u>over time</u>.

The modern loanable funds theory of interest says that the components of the supply of loanable funds are:

1. Gross saving out of current income - plus

2. New money created by banks (or minus money destoyed) - plus

3. Dishoarding - lending of funds saved in previous years but hoarded then (or minus hoarding).

The components of demand for loanable funds are:

1. Business demand to enable the purchase of capital goods. (investment). - plus

2. Government demand to finance deficit spending (or minus any government tax surplus) - plus

3. Consumer demand to finance consumer purchases on credit - plus

4. Financial demands made for bond, stock and commodity trading.

The equilibrium rate of interest is determined where the demand for loanable funds from business, government, consumers and the markets equals the supply of loanable funds made available by savers, dishoarders and the banks.

We shall see how the St. Louis Model combines elements of these theories to produce equations which forecast interest rates, both short and long term.

KEYNES' GENERAL THEORY

To return to our review of economic history, we note that shortly after Keynes' trip to Chicago, England went off the gold standard, and as has been stated, in 1936 he published his famed General Theory of Unemployment Interest and Money. In that book he pointed out that a stable equilibrium could exist, not at full employment but rather with high unemployment, with no natural forces tending to correct it. In particular, he said that a fall in wages would not restore profitability to business by lowering costs relative to prices, since competition would lead to falling prices and expectations of further decreases. This would discourage investment and the fall in the money value of assets would reduce the availability of credit.

Keynes held that output, and therefore employment, is determined by 'effective demand' which in turn depends upon the economy's propensity to consume and invest. Given that the propensity to consume utilizes a relatively constant proportion of a nation's output, one can appreciate that in a depression, an increase in investment coming about, for example, as the result of a great new invention (the steam engine, the motor car, etc.) would increase employment. Simultaneously a multiplier would come into effect as the newly-employed purchased more consumer goods, which, in turn, would add employment. This would have an accelerator effect which would increase the demand for investment to satisfy this extra consumer spending.

Since spontaneous increases in private investment do not occur when most needed, Keynes pointed out that governments could relieve unemployment by schemes of public investment (dams, roads, etc.) which would not have otherwise been undertaken. These would be every bit as effective as private investment since they too would increase consumption and investment through the multiplier and accelerator effects. Always, of course, provided that the necessary funds were obtained by borrowing, rather than raising taxes. Simply put, this theory says "Demand creates its own supply".

Thus for Keynes, the purpose of a government deficit was to increase aggregate demand directly, by increasing government expenditures.

This hypothesis was expanded by post-Keynesian economists and set out in the algebraic equation so well-known to first-year economic students:

$$Y = C + I + G + (X - M)$$

where:

Y = Gross National Product

C = Consumption expenditures

I = Investment expenditures

G = Government expenditures

$(X - M)$ = Exports - Imports = Net exports (plus or minus)

The Department of Commerce now accumulates and publicizes the quarterly values of these variables and we know them as the national income accounts. One can see that as the size of the variables on the right hand side of the equation increase or decrease - then Y or Gross National Product is increased or decreased by a similar amount. With increasing Y, employment also increases until 'full' or 'high' employment is reached.

Patinkin sums up the differences between Keynes and the Chicago School when he points out that both saw the economy as unstable in the short run and both chose discretional government policy to deal with the instability. The Chicago School chose the price level as its target level and Keynes, the level of employment.

Keynes was, of course, not unaware of the value of increasing the money supply as an alternative to government expenditures during times of depression. Thus his famous illustration:

> If the Treasury were to fill old bottles with bank-notes and bury them at suitable depths in disused coal-mines which are then filled up to the surface with town rubbish and leave it to private enterprise on well-tried principles of laissez-faire to dig the notes up again...there need be no more unemployment...It would, indeed, be more sensible to build houses and the like; but if there are political and practical difficulties in the way of this, the above would be better than nothing. [44]

In this connection, Keynes makes the point which is basic in the St. Louis model, namely, as monetary expansion increases effective demand, it will expend itself partly in raising prices and partly in increasing output. The problem is, how will these variables vary over time? As Keynes says, it will depend on where the economy is in the business cycle. Thus:

> It is probable that the general level of prices will not rise very much as output increases, as long as there are available efficient unemployed resources of every type. But as soon as output has increased sufficiently to reach the 'bottlenecks', there is likely to be a sharp rise in the price of certain commodities.[45]

Keynes continues:

> Up to this point (of true inflation), the effect of monetary expansion is entirely a question of degree, there is no previous point at which we can draw a definite line and declare that conditions of inflation have set in. Every previous increase in the quantity of money is likely, in so far as it increases effective demand, to spend itself partly increasing the cost-unit and partly in increasing output. [46]

We shall see how the St. Louis model incorporates these ideas of demand pressure and potential output into its econometric equations for prices, interest rates and nominal output.

Just three years after the publication of the General Theory World War II began and brought with it seening proof of Keynes theories. Expand government demand, even though it be for tanks and fighter aircraft rather than houses and universities. At the same time, let the central bank arrange to increase the stock of money in line with the expanded demand - and the unemployment problem was resolved. But it must be noted that the surge of prices and wages had to be controlled by rationing and wage and price controls. The price of 'full' employment was very tight government regulation.

During World War II, Federal government economists used the Keynesian structure and the pioneering work of Simon Kuznets to quantify total output, calculating what could go to civilian consumption and investment, and therefore, what was available for military purposes. As Robert Lekatchman has put it:

> VJ Day had ended the first war conducted on Keynesian principles...the war agencies analyzed needs and resources within the national income framework constructed by

> Keynes and accorded statistical serviceability by our own Department of Commerce. [47]

It was but a small step to recognise that in peacetime, the same calculations could show what output and employment were possible, what savings would occur from the resulting income and what spending would be required to offset those savings and thereby ensure full employment. John Kenneth Galbraith describes the situation as World War II was ending:

> The early drafts of the Full Employment Act, as it was first called, proclaimed the sovereign and indefeasible right of every American to a job. And the Government was called upon each year to specify and ensure the investment, public and private, that (offsetting estimated savings at full employment) would ensure such a level of employment. In any one year when private investment did not supply the requisite total, the Federal Government would be instructed to borrow and spend whatever was necessary to make up the difference. Initially the legislation named the investment that most likely would be required - a round $40 billion.[48]

But this was going too far for many organizations. As an example, the National Association of Manufacturers concluded that such legislation would enhance government control, destroy private enterprise, unduly increase the powers of the Federal Executive, legalize Federal spending and pump-priming, bring socialization, be unworkable and impractical, promise too much and be open to ridicule. [49]

In the end, Congress passed the Employment Act of 1946, declaring it to be the policy of the United States government,

> ...to use all practicable means... with the assistance and cooperation of industry, agriculture, labour and state and local governments, to coordinate and utilize all its plans, functions and resources for the purpose of creating and maintaining, in a manner calculated to foster and promote free competitive enterprise and the general welfare, conditions under which there will be afforded useful employment, for those able, willing, and seeking work, and to promote maximum employment, production and purchasing power. 50

In terms of the income quantity theory of money where $\dot{Y} = \dot{P} + \dot{X}$ - this amounted to a policy of stabilizing nominal GNP (Y) at 'maximum' employment, without the term 'maximum' being defined. Fortunately, the period between 1946 and 1962 was largely one of 'good times' in terms of prices, output and unemployment.

In the few mild recessions that occurred during this post-war period, the Federal government was constrained by what James Buchan and Richard Wagner have called the unwritten fiscal rule; namely: the Federal budget should be in surplus in all but exceptional periods of war and severe depression, and in normal times the Federal debt incurred for those purposes should be repaid. 51 This was the position which had been taken by the Chicago School and was still influential as can be seen in President Eisenhower's 'State of the Union' message of January 7, 1960, when he said:

> Personally, I do not feel that any amount can be properly called a surplus as long as the nation is in debt. I prefer to think of such an item as a reduction on our children's inherited mortgage.

Despite President Eisenhower's views, 1959, was to mark the largest peace-time Federal deficit up to that point.

THE KENNEDY-JOHNSON ADMINISTRATION

January 1961, saw the inauguration of President Kennedy who had campaigned on a promise "to get the country moving again." He had not challenged the orthodox principle of a balanced budget during his election campaign, rather he criticized President Eisenhower for allowing a budget deficit of $12 billion during fiscal 1959. In January 1962, although six percent of the labour force was unemployed (a high figure for those times), he remained true to this principle by proposing a balanced budget.

However, in the spring of 1962, the economy turned down and American peacetime economic policy moved in a new direction with President Kennedy's commencement address at Yale University in June, when he said:

> The myth persists that Federal deficits create inflation and budget surpluses prevent it ...Obviously deficits are sometimes dangerous - and so are surpluses. But honest assessment plainly requires a more sophisticated view than the old and automatic cliché that deficits automatically bring inflation ...What we need is not the labels and clichés but more basic discussion of the more technical question

> involved in keeping a great economic machine moving ahead. 52

Behind this philosophy was Professor Walter Heller, then Chairman of the Council of Economic Advisers and his theory of the full-employment budget and the concept of 'fiscal drag'. Heller stressed that though the Federal budget was then in deficit, the progressive nature of the tax system would produce a budget surplus as aggregate nominal income approached the level of full employment.

This was a refinement of Keynesian aggregate demand doctrine and implied that this surplus was a 'drag' on economic expansion which was threatening to plunge the economy into an unnecessary recession. The theory of 'fiscal drag' leads to the conclusion that in order to keep the economy growing, fiscal 'dividends' should be regularly paid in the form of increased government spending or reduced tax rates. In a mixture of metaphors, one could justify a tax cut on the basis that it would loosen the brake which was slowing the expansion and 'a rising tide would raise all boats'...everyone would become more prosperous.

In August 1962, President Kennedy announced that he would propose a substantial tax reduction in January, 1963. The passage of the Act was delayed in Congress and it was not signed by President Johnson until February 1964. This 'inside lag' of some eighteen months illustrates the kind of difficulty that faces any President who wishes to 'fine-tune' the economy by the use of fiscal policy.

The tax reductions contained in the Revenue Act of 1964 were the largest fiscal action ever undertaken by the Federal government in peacetime, cutting individual income tax liabilities almost one-fifth and corporate tax bills by one tenth. Unlike the U.S. tax reductions of the 1920's, late 1940's and 1954, the 1964 action was taken in a period marked by a federal budget deficit and rising federal expenditures.

The results exceeded the most optomistic expectations. By the spring of 1965, unemployment had dropped from 6% to 4.7% and Arthur Okun has estimated that $30 billion was added to the Gross National Product by the end of 1965. [53]

The Federal budget, which has been in deficit at the yearly rate of $1.7 billion at the end of Quarter I of 1963, showed a surplus of $4.3 billion at the end of Quarter II of 1965. At the same time, consumer spending forged ahead as individuals spent most of their added income for goods and services. The accelerator effect of these purchases encouraged a boom in business investment as businessmen rejoiced in rising profits.

Just as encouraging was the fact that wholesale prices rose only 0.5% in 1964 and 0.6% in the first half of 1965, while unit labour costs were below their level of a year earlier. Consumer prices went up by just 1.5% per year. The only concern was the continuing deficit in the U.S. balance of payments.

The stimulus to the economy also reflected the partnership between fiscal and monetary policy. As we have noted, most economists of this period considered fiscal policy to be the active mover while, as in World War II, monetary policy was considered to be passive - merely accommodating the growth of real output. [54] The Federal Reserve therefore allowed the demands for liquidity and credit which were being generated by the expanding economy, to be met at stable interest rates by increasing the quantity of money.

The question as to whether or not it was the 1964 tax cut or the concomitant expansion in the money stock which fueled the recovery will be considered a little later. At the time, Keynesian policies were given the credit for the result and the apogee of Keynesian theory came on December 31, 1965, when Time magazine put the picture of John Maynard Keynes on its cover as Man of the Year.

For Keynesians during the 1946 - 1965 era, fiscal policy was considered to have a much greater ability to stabilize the economy and achieve full employment than monetary policy. There were three reasons for this belief:

1. One could illustrate on a blackboard, how, if monetary policy was geared to maintain interest rates in the IS/LM paradigm, the movement of the IS (Investment - Saving) schedule, was all important in the variance of GNP.

2. Even if monetary policy was not accommodative, Keynesians felt that rising incomes would increase savings, and as well, rising interest rates would draw funds from hoards and/or speculative balances, thereby increasing the velocity of money. Thus, the savings rate and the rate of velocity were considered to be flexible enough to provide the money needed to finance new investment.

3. World War II and the 1964 tax cut demonstrated that Federal fiscal policy, by directly and immediately altering the disposable income of consumers and the profitability of investors, had a faster impact than monetary policy, which Keynesians held acted in an indirect fashion through its effect on interest rates.

What Keynesians were saying was that the variables in the income Quantity theory of money should be reversed so that it is written

$$\dot{GNP} = \dot{P} + \dot{X} = \dot{M} + \dot{V}$$

because, in general, causality runs from $\dot{P} + \dot{X}$ to $\dot{M} + \dot{V}$, and the central bank would normally accommodate an increase in $\dot{P}$ +

$\dot{X}$ by an increase in M. However, if monetary policy held M constant, then V would increase sufficiently to pick up the slack in M. Thus velocity V was considered to be very flexible.

THE MONETARIST COUNTER-ATTACK

A counter-attack against the dominance of fiscal policy during this 1946 - 1965 era was lead by a few hardy economists amongst whom one must mention Lloyd W. Mints,[55] Clark Warburton [56] and Milton Friedman. Friedman was a professor at the University of Chicago, appointed in 1948, and was to become the best- known 'Monetarist'. In 1956, in his introductory essay in the book, Studies in the Quantity Theory of Money, Friedman described the Quantity theory of money as:

> A theoretical approach that insisted that money does matter - that any interpretation of short term movements in economic activity is likely to be seriously at fault if it neglects monetary changes and repercussions, and leaves unexplained why people are willing to hold the particular quantity of money in existence. [57] Emphasis added.

In the short term, he presents the Quantity theory of money as a theory of the demand for money. The problem is how a theory of the demand for money becomes a theory of prices and output. Friedman does this, as we shall see, by stipulating that the demand for money represented by V, though not a stable number, is a stable function of a few key variables. If the demand for money is stable, then "substantial changes in prices or nominal income are almost invariably the results of changes in the nominal supply of money". [58] This is the case because, if the nominal quantity of money supplied is greater than the nominal supply of money demanded, then the "discrepancy will be manifested primarily in attempted spending, thence in the rate of change of nominal income' [59]

We can illustrate this theory in simple mathematical terms, where:

$$\dot{M} + \overline{V} = \dot{P} + \dot{X}$$

We note that V is expressed to be constant. Thus, the sum of $\dot{P}$ + $\dot{X}$ varies proportionately with $\dot{M}$ because monetarists hold that causality runs from money to nominal income.

In part, to demonstrate empirically the independent causal role played by the money stock in U.S. business cycles, Friedman and Mrs. Anna Schwartz, compiled their monumental Monetary History of the United States, 1867 - 1960, which was published in 1963. They showed that there was a consistent relationship between fluctuations in the money supply and national income over this period. When they also concluded that a one-third decline in the money supply between 1929 and 1933 was primarily responsible for the severity and duration of the Great Depression, they caught the attention of the economics profession. Their findings were:

> Changes in the money stock are therefore a consequence as well as an independent source of change in money income and prices, though once they occur, they produce in their turn still further effects on income and prices. Mutual interaction, but with money clearly the senior partner in longer run movements and in major cyclical movements, and more nearly an equal partner with money income and prices in shorter run and milder movements - this is the generalization suggested by our evidence. [60]

In summarizing the lags which he and Mrs. Schwartz had ascertained, Friedman wrote:

> We have found that, on the average of 18 cycles, peaks in the rate of change in the stock of money tend to precede peaks in general business by about 16 months and troughs in the rate of change of money precede troughs in general business by about 12 months...For individual cycles, the recorded lead has varied between 6 and 29 months at peaks and 4 to 22 months at troughs. 61

It is from this evidence that Friedman has concluded that monetary policy, involving changes in the growth rate of the money stock, acts with so long and variable a lag, that using it to 'fine-tune' the economy might just as easily aggravate as dampen cyclical movements in the private sector. Moreover, because he believes that central banks tend to overreact to current problems of inflation and/or employment, he has advocated a steady rate of growth of the money stock (which he considers to be best represented by M2) as the surest method of minimizing booms and recessions.

One notes that the results of "A Monetary History of the United States" were expressed in general terms. Despite the depth of their research, several reviewers were critical because Friedman and Mrs. Schwartz had not stated any economic theory to support their findings.

In order to compare his Quantity theory approach with the Keynesian doctrine, Friedman, in 1963, collaborated with David Meiselman and they published a statistical evaluation which assessed, as indicated by the title, "The Relative Stability of

Monetary Velocity and the Investment Multiplier in the United States."

Friedman and Meiselman argued that Keynesian concepts had become popular at the expense of monetary theory on the basis of very little empirical evidence. Their objective was to correct this deficiency by a statistical comparison of the two theories, which they outlined as follows:

> The view that the quantity of money matters little is typically held for either of two reasons; one, because the quantity of money is regarded as adapting to the 'needs of trade', and hence is regarded as a passive element in the system, determined by and responsive to other economic and non-economic factors, but incapable of being a source of disturbances; the other, because the ratio of money to assets is regarded as variable and pliable, and hence the economic effects of changes in the quantity of money does matter and for three reasons; one, because the quantity of money is capable of being controlled fairly accurately by deliberate policy; two, because changes in the quantity of money can produce substantial changes in the flow of income, prices and other important variables; three, because the relationships between the stock of money and other assets are relatively stable and dependable. 62

To compare the economic validity of the two theories would be an extremely complex undertaking, so Friedman and Meiselman chose to contest the Keynesian view that autonomous expenditure, whether investment, government spending or net exports, rather than the quantity of money, was the chief determinant of income.

Each of these two hypotheses was represented by one simple equation. Regression analysis was done using quarterly data covering the period 1897 - 1958. The velocity of money was found to be consistently more stable than the Keynesian multiplier - with the exception only of the period of the Great Depression in the early 1930's.

Since their empirical work demonstrated that the velocity of money exhibited a greater regularity than did the autonomous expenditure multiplier, they argued that stable relationships between these changes and income changes as postulated by the Keynesian model do not exist. Moreover, since the velocity of money is the more stable relationship, money becomes very significant, for it means that we can better explain changes of aggregate income and employment from changes in the quantity of money than from changes in autonomous expenditures.

These propostions were considered to be so important that the September 1965 issue of the American Economic Review devoted 100 pages to the critics of Friedman and Meiselman, a reply by them and rejoinders by the critics. There was much dispute about the reliability of their results. Indeed, Albert Ando and Franco Modigliani objected that they had grossly misspecified the Keynesian model, making their statistical results "essentially worthless". 63

As one can appreciate, this debate was followed closely by the Research Department at the Federal Reserve Bank of St. Louis and stimulated the regression analysis which led to the St. Louis model.

Clearly the early 1960's was a period of economic ferment - both theoretically and empirically. That ferment also pervaded the Board of Governors of the Federal Reserve System in Washington.

THE FEDERAL RESERVE SYSTEM

The goal of the seven members of the Board of Governors of the Federal Reserve System is to manage the nation's monetary policy in the best interests of the country. Whereas we now accept that the goals of monetary policy should be full employment, economic growth and stable prices, the framers of the original Federal Reserve Act in 1913 made no mention of them. The Act was intended, as set out in the preamble, "...to furnish an elastic currency, to afford means of rediscounting commercial paper, to establish a more effective supervision of banking in the United States, and for other purposes."

This preamble, providing for the extension of Federal Reserve credit by rediscounting commercial paper when presented to it by member banks, served notice that Congress had accepted the Banking School's 'real bills' doctrine, which asserts the impossibility of note overissue as long as banks restrict their loans to self-liquidating commercial or agricultural paper.

It is interesting to note that the Federal Reserve banks were also given the power to purchase U.S. securities, though this was thought of primarily as a measure to permit them to earn income. The vastly more important effects of security purchases on member bank reserves, interest rates and the money supply, were simply not recognised at the time.

It is the twelve member Federal Open Market Committee which has the sole responsibility for determining the direction and extent of the System's open market operations. Known as the FOMC, its membership consists of the seven members of the Board of Governors plus five presidents of Federal Reserve Banks. The president of a the Federal Reserve Bank of New York is a permanent member, and the four remaining positions are rotated among the presidents of the other eleven Federal Reserve Banks.

Meetings of the FOMC are held approximately every five or six weeks. All of the presidents of the twelve Reserve banks attend and are free to speak, although only the five members vote. Each Reserve bank has a research department which briefs their president before he goes to these meetings. Moreover, some staff members will attend with him, in order to advise him as necessary during the meeting. Thus, it is essential that the president and his staff be ad idem - there must be trust and confidence flowing both to the president from his staff and vice versa.

THE FEDERAL RESERVE IN FERMENT

When active countercyclical monetary policy first got under way after the Accord of 1951, the Federal Reserve faced a new situation and new objectives for which the experiences of earlier periods offered little guidance. One of the main objectives was to dampen the swings of the business cycle. This meant 'tightening' the money supply when expansion threatened to become unsustainable and 'easing' it when the economy became soft.

This was originally handled by the pure Keynesian theory of money and its velocity, as illustrated by the statements of Chairman Martin in 1957 and 1961. In August 1957, he said:

> I think we have a responsibility for (economic) growth. We should increase the money supply to provide for that growth. [64]

When asked what the Federal Reserve was doing to curb inflation, he expanded this answer by saying:

> We are looking at the growth factor in the economy and we think that growth factor should be in the neighbourhood of three or four percent. In excess of that, is, we think, too much. We have let the balance of the two percent of our three percent growth take place out of the velocity of money. 65

By this, Chairman Martin meant that interest rates were allowed to rise in order to draw funds from 'hoards' to transactions balances, thus dampening any tendency to inflation.

On March 7, 1961, Chairman Martin summed up Federal Reserve policy in his classic statement to the Joint Economic Committee:

> The flexible monetary policy that has been in effect now for a full decade...as I have capsuled it before in the shortest description I have been able to devise, is one of the leaning against the winds of inflation and deflation, with equal vigor. 66

During the 1950's, it was pretty much the FOMC practice to guide open-market policy in response to money market conditions. These were the combination of (a) the interest rate on Federal funds; (b) net reserves - the difference between the excess reserves balances of banks and the total amount banks borrow from the Fed through the discount window; and (c) at times, the interest rate on three-month Treasury bills, together with (d) something that one can only call the general atmosphere of the money markets.

Monetary policy was said to be 'easing' or 'easy' when short-term interest rates were falling or low and to be 'tightening' or 'tight' when these rates were rising or high. But interest rates can give off misleading signals of policy's impact at crucial junctures in the business cycle, with movements in rates reflecting not the effect of monetary policy but of cyclical developments in the economy itself.

Thus, early in 1960, the economy went into recession and interest rates fell even though bank reserves and the money supply contracted until the middle of the year. In these circumstances, it didn't seem right to describe monetary policy as 'easy', simply because interest rates were falling.

These kinds of considerations led the House Committee on Banking and Currency to request Professors Karl Brunner and Allen Meltzer in 1964 to conduct a study of how the Federal Reserve arrived at decisions and conducted monetary policy. Their report stated that they could find no logical theory or model in use at the Fed, or any desire to explain or measure what was happening.

At the same time, a sub-committee of the FOMC raised questions such as; How should monetary policy be analyzed? How should it be measured? and How specific should the FOMC be in its public statements? These matters caused considerable controversy within the FOMC and as a result, no change in procedures were made.

In 1965, Chairman Martin conceded that the Board of Governors could regulate the growth of bank reserves "in accordance with some set formula', but it preferred to use human judgment to assess current economic needs. "With this approach" he stated, "the growth of bank reserves reflects in part market factors, which depend in turn on the strength of credit demands within the economy." 67 Even when all the demand factors have been taken into account, the effect of policy changes,

> ...are not subject to exact scientific determination and so, remain a matter of judgment, and one on which judgments may differ. I am stressing these limits to our knowledge in order to explain why central banking remains an art rather than a science. 68

Which prompted Senator Proxmire to say:

> I have the greatest respect for your ability and I think that you are an outstanding and competent person and when you try to come down and discuss this in meaningful specific terms, it is like nailing a custard to the wall...and frankly, Mr. Martin, without specific goals, criteria, guidelines, it is impossible to exercise any Congressional oversight over you, and I think you know it. 69

The problem that existed at this time was carefully elucidated by Federal Reserve Governor Maisel when he said:

> Money market conditions cannot measure the degree to which markets should be tightened or how long the restraint should be retained. There was no direct or known relations between money market conditions and spending; nor theory to show how much tightening was necessary or when conditions ought to return to normal. It was known that a lag exists between

> monetary action and spending but money market conditions did not measure lags any more than magnitudes. [70]

However, the professional staff at the St. Louis Fed soon produced a model which they believed would give empirical guidance to policymakers about these matters.

REFERENCES

1 David Hume, Philosophical Essays on Morals, Literature and Politics (Philadelphia, Penn.: Edward Beale 1817), p. 303.

2. Lord Robbins, Politics and Economics, Papers in Political Economy, (London, Macmillan, 1963) p.22.

3 E. Milinvaud, Statistical Methods of Econometrics, (Amsterdam, North Holland, 1966) p. 514.

4 Leonall Andersen and Keith Carlson "St. Louis Model Revisited" International Economic Review p.323.

5 G.L.S. Shackle, "The Harvest", History of Political Economy, (1972) p. 601.

6 David Hume, Philosophical Essays etc., Op. cit. p. 303.

7 Adam Smith, An Inquiry into the Nature and Causes of the Wealth of Nations, edited by Edwin Canaan (New York, Modern Library, 1937) pp. 328 - 329.

8 Ibid., p. 321.

9 Ibid., p. 421.

10 The following draws heavily on Prof. B. Corry's Money Investment and Saving in English Economics, 1800-1851. (London: MacMillan & Co. 1962) pp. 68-72.

11 Letter dated July 21, 1821, Works and Correspondence of David Ricardo, ed. P. Sraffa, Notes on Malthus, Op. cit., 2:311.

12 P. Sraffa, Notes on Malthus, Op. cit., 2:311.

13 David Ricardo, Principles of Political Economy, Op. cit., 2:362.

14 David Ricardo, Minutes of Evidence taken before the Secret Committee on the Expediency of the Bank resuming Cash Payments, Op. Cit., 5:339.

15 Thomas Malthus, Principles of Political Economy, Op. cit., 2:386.

16 Ibid. p. 395

17 P. Sraffa, Notes on Malthus, Op. cit., 2:449.

18 Thomas Malthus, Principles of Political Economy, Op. cit., 2:324.

19 P. Sraffa, Notes on Malthus, Op. cit., 6:295.

20 B. Corry, Money, Investment and Savings, etc., Op. cit. p.68.

21 Ibid., p.70.

22 Ibid., p.71.

23 Ibid., p.72.

24 J.B. Say, Letters to Mr. Malthus, p.49, quoted in Prof. Hollander's "Malthus and Depression", History of Political Economy, 1975, p. 319.

25 B. Corry, Money, Investment and Saving, etc., Op. cit., p.153.

26 Irving Fisher, The Purchasing Power of Money, (New York Macmillan, 1911) p.183.

27 Ibid., p. 155.

28 Ibid., pp.55-73, 159-161.

29 A.G. Hart and P.B. Kenan, Money, Debt and Economic Activity, 3rd ed. (Prentice-Hall, 1964), p.244.

30 Knut Wicksell, Lectures on Political Economy, (London, Routledge and Kegan Paul) II:160.

31 J.M. Keynes, A Tract on Monetary Reform, (London, Macmillan, 1936) p.65.

32 The following draws on Don Patinkin, "Keynes and Chicago" The Journal of Law and Economics (1979) pp.213 - 232.

33 R.F. Harrod, The Life of John Maynard Keynes, (London Macmillan, 1951) p.352.

34 Don Patinkin, "Keynes and Chicago", Op. cit., p.217.

35 Ibid., p.218.

36 Ibid., p.221.

37 Ibid., p.222.

38 Ibid., p.223.

39 Ibid., p.230.

40 D. Hume, Essays on Moral, etc. Op. cit., pp.320-330.

41 Adam Smith, Wealth of Nations, Op. cit., I.91.

42 Irving Fisher, The Theory of Interest. (New York, Macmillan, 1930) p. 451.

43 J.M. Keynes, The General Theory of Unemployment, Interest and Money, (London, Macmillan, 1936) p.96.

44 Ibid., p.129.

45 Ibid., p.300.

46 Ibid., p.303.

47 Robert Lekatchman, The Age of Keynes, (New York, Random House, 1966) p.176.

48 J.K. Galbraith, Money, Whence it Came, Where it Went, (Boston, Houghton, Mifflin, 1975) p.263.

49 Ibid., p.264.

50 Ibid., p.265.

51 James Buchanan and Richard Wager, Democracy in Deficit, the Political Legacy of Lord Keynes (New York: Academic Press, 1977), p. 14.

52 Public papers of the Presidents of the United States, John F. Kennedy, 1962, (1963), pp. 472-473.

53 Arthur M. Okun, "Measuring the Impact of the 1964 Tax Reduction," in Walter W. Heller, ed., Perspectives on Economic Growth (New York: Random House, 1968), p.47.

54 See for example, the 1962 Report of the Council of Economic Advisors.

55 Lloyd W. Mints, Monetary Policy in a Competitive Society (New York: McGraw- Hill, 1951).

56 Clark Warburton, Depression, Inflation and Monetary Policy, Selected Paper s, 1945-1953 (Baltimore: The Johns Hopkins Press, 1966).

57 Milton Friedman, ed., Studies in the Quantity Theory of Money (Chicago: University of Chicago Press, 1956), p.3.

58 Milton Friedman, "A Theoretical Framework for Monetary Analysis" in Milton Friedman's Monetary Framework ed. R.J. Gordon (Chicago, University of Chicago Press, 1974) p.51.

59 Ibid.,

60 Milton Friedman and Anna Schwartz, A Monetary History of the United States (Princeton, New Jersey: Princeton University Press, 1963), p. 695.

61 Milton Friedman, A Program for Monetary Stability (New York: Fordham University Press, 1960,) p.87

62 Milton Friedman and David Meiselman, "The Relative Stability of Monetary Velocity and the Investment Multiplier in the United States: Commission on Money and Credit, Stabilization Policies (Englewood Cliffs, New Jersey: Prentice Hall, 1963), pp.166-167.

63 Albert Ando and Franco Modigliani, "The Relative Stability of Monetary Velocity and the Investment Multiplier", American Economic Review (September, 1965), p.694.

64 U.S. Congress, Senate Committee on Finance: Hearings on the "Investigation of the Financial Condition of the United States: (Part Three, 1957), p. 1301.

65 Ibid., p.1307.

66 Quoted from Sherman Maisel, Managing the Dollar (New York: W.W. Norton, 1973), p. 63.

67 The Federal Reserve Board Bulletin (September 1965). p.1238.

68 Ibid.

69 Quoted in John Culbertson, Full Employment or Stagnation? (New York: McGraw-Hill, 1964), pp.154-155.

70 Sherman Maisel, Managing the Dollar, Op. Cit., p.82.

CHAPTER FOUR

THE ST. LOUIS PEOPLE AND THEIR ORIGINAL EQUATIONS

> The recent successes of Keynes' theories have given a new stature and luster to the men who practice what Carlyle called "the dismal science." Economists have descended in force from their ivory towers and now sit confidently at the elbow of almost every important leader in government and business, where they are increasingly called upon to forecast, plan and decide. ...The job of maintaining expansion without inflation will require not only their present skills but new ones as well.
>
> *Time* Magazine
> December 31, 1965

At this juncture in time, the seeds of ferment in economic theory and Federal Reserve policy were floating throughout the whole Federal Reserve System. Why, then, did the monetarist seeds fall on fertile soil at the St. Louis Fed to be nurtured and grow strong? One answer lies in the fact that Darryl R. Francis was appointed president of that bank in January 1966. Anyone who has had anything to do with the Civil Service will appreciate that a strong, independent research staff, willing to experiment and try new ideas, is only possible with the forceful and dedicated backing of the man at the top. In President Francis the St. Louis Fed had that man.

Darryl Francis grew up on a poor farm in northeast Missouri. To get to agricultural school, he was given a steer calf by his uncle, fattened it and with the $140.00 which it brought, he went off to the University of Missouri at Columbia. When he was running short of funds, he received an assistantship in the agricultural economics department - which persuaded him to graduate in 1936 as an agricultural economist.

After working on a research project at the University, he was employed by the St. Louis Fed as an agricultural specialist in the Research Department. After five years there, and a stint with commercial banks in Memphis and St. Louis, he was appointed a Vice President of the Bank and manager of the Memphis Branch, then First Vice President in 1959 and President in 1966 at age 53.

With his background in price theory and as a true son of the "show-me" state, Francis was enthusiastic about the new turn towards Monetarism. As he has said, "My time at the Bank was my post-graduate work."[1] His staff recall that he was extremely interested in their research and would often call them into the conference room to discuss it. He, himself, is very proud of their professional abilities and achievements and thoroughly enjoyed his and their position in the economic world.

In a speech given on February 23, 1972, Francis outlined how his own economic philosophy has been formed:

> For a number of years, I have accepted the description of economic behaviour which is summarized by the "monetarist tradition" and, since my appointment to the presidency of the St. Louis Federal Reserve Bank in 1966, I have advocated stabilization policies consistent with this tradition. I would like to emphasize that my stance is not merely a belief, but an outgrowth of empirical observation and testing. This does not mean that I necessarily accept all the tenets or all the pronouncements of monetarists. But the work and research that has been done at our Bank for the past thirteen

> years has produced overwhelming evidence which has helped to confirm my views of the functioning of our economy and of the proper conduct of economic stabilization efforts.[2]

As a long-time executive of the Bank, Mr. Francis had had the opportunity to become acquainted with and influenced by a remarkable economist, Homer Jones, who had come to the Bank in 1958 at age 52 as Vice President in charge of research, and was to retire in 1971 as Senior Vice President. It was undoubtedly Dr. Jones' influence on the St. Louis Fed's monetarist views that caused Professor Heller to refer to the St. Louis Fed as an arm of the Chicago School. Originally Homer Jones was from Iowa, where he attended the University of Iowa and was a student of Dr. Frank Knight whom we have previously encountered as a member of the Chicago School. Also on the staff was Henry Simons who like Professor Knight, was to go to Chicago to teach and become a member of the 'School.' Homer Jones soon followed them to the University of Chicago for graduate work although he did not obtain his doctorate until after World War II.

In 1930 he taught for a year at the University of Pittsburgh and then in 1931 he went on to Rutgers University. At Rutgers, Dr. Arthur Burns was also a member of the staff, and he, on January 31, 1970, was to succeed William McChesney Martin as Chairman of the Board of Governors of the Federal Reserve system. Jones at age 24, taught insurance and statistics and one of his students was a junior, 18 year old Milton Friedman, who then intended a career as an insurance actuary. When offered a graduate scholarship in mathematics at Brown University and an economic scholarship at the University of Chicago, Friedman chose Chicago - and gives Homer Jones the credit for influencing him to make the decision.[3]

Shortly after, Homer Jones also returned to the University of Chicago for post-graduate work and there he collaborated with Friedman, George Stigler and Allen Wallis as editors of The Ethics of Competition,[4] a collection of the writings of Frank Knight. But this was not to be the end of their relationship. After Chicago, Jones went to Brookings and then spent a decade at the Federal Deposit Insurance Corporation. There Rose Director worked for him as a graduate assistant and was shortly to become Mrs. Milton Friedman.

After World War II, Milton Friedman gained his Ph.D. at Columbia University and then in 1948, returned to teach at the University of Chicago, where he was on the committee which passed Jones' Ph.D. dissertation in 1949. As a result, they became both personal and professional friends and it is not surprising that Milton Friedman would send his 1967 Presidential address to the American Economic Association to Homer Jones for comments and that he and Mrs. Friedman would attend Jones' retirement dinner in 1971. That Homer Jones holds Milton Friedman's ideas in high respect was impressed on the author, when in a conversation about this manuscript, Jones stated that "if Milton Friedman said it, then it is correct."

His continued interest in monetarism is illustrated by the fact that at age 76 he was a member of the Shadow FOMC, a group of Monetarist economists who comment on the policies formulated by the Federal Reserve System's FOMC.

Homer Jones' attitudes came not only from having been educated in the "Chicago School," but also from his deep interest in Money and Banking and his desire to see that every facet of their relationship was explored, theoretically and empirically. To this end he was constantly bombarding the Bank's professional staff with pencilled notes on yellow paper suggesting lines of thought for their exploration and overwriting their papers with pencilled ideas, until the staff-member viewing the final result, was at a loss to decide how much was his own and how much was Jones'.

Jerry Jordan, a former Senior Vice President in charge of Research at the Bank and in 1981-1982 a member of the Council of Economic Advisors, describes the contributions of Homer Jones and Darryl Francis to the St. Louis Fed as follows:

> Homer's great strength to me was that he was simply an agnostic - he was always questioning and always pushing the staff to prove it. Where's your evidence? Spell out your theory. Show me! And at the time he was just as critical of ideas thrown out by Milton Friedman and Karl Brunner as he was by those thrown out by the liberal Keynesian economists.
>
> He was never satisfied with any article that we wrote when it went to press - it always could be improved upon if we only took a little more time or if we only did a little more research and had a little more data. Of course, he also recognised that we had schedules and deadlines to meet. But he always felt that our articles could have been improved upon if we had just worked a little harder and a little faster - he pushed us very hard.
>
> Darryl Francis was trained in economics under Harry Gunnison Brown at the University of Missouri and understood good price theory and was from the 'show me' state. The background fitted well with Homer's agnosticism - prove it - where are the facts? Between the two of them

> they simply made a very strong combination of that independent streak of let's find out what we think to be true and tell it like we see it, and then if somebody has a better idea, let them come back at us.[5]

Jones' strength was not only his desire for perfection - but his insistence that since the Bank dealt with numbers, they should be made available to the public and be incorporated into staff articles. This was done - in the form of charts, bar charts, box charts, triangles and where appropriate by mathematical appendices - so that a reader could readily see the relationships which existed between them. Appendix A indicates the publications which were available - free! Little wonder that the staff of the St. Louis Fed were known by their colleagues in the Federal Reserve System as the 'money-nuts.'

From the beginning of Jones' tenure at the St. Louis Fed the stress was on the need for charts to show the association for example, between the monetary base and the money stock, or between the money stock and prices, nominal and real output. He felt that if these relationships were demonstrated often enough, they would eventually be picked up - if only by the private sector - as business economists used that information to forecast business trends to the financial advantage of their companies.

One is reminded of John Maynard Keynes' letter to George Bernard Shaw of January 1, 1935, when he was responding to a suggestion by Shaw that he interest himself in something on, or by, Karl Marx, he wrote:

> To understand my state of mind, you have to know that I believe myself writing a book on economic theory which will largely revolutionize - not, I suppose at once but in the course of the next

> ten years - the way the world thinks about economic problems.[6]

So it developed for Keynes and in a different way for Jones, as well. While his name is not as well-known - there are no specific books or articles for which Jones is famous - nevertheless by inspiring his professional colleagues Homer Jones also has been instrumental in changing the way the world thinks about economic problems. Milton Friedman, writing in 1976, describes his influence:

> For the first time, a bank publication, The Review of the Federal Reserve Bank of St. Louis began to be cited regularly in the academic journals...Homer's insatiable curiosity about the facts, and his belief in the power of repeated exposure to the facts to erode illusion, led to the publication by the Bank of its now famed series of weekly and monthly collection of statistics. They preached no explicit doctrine. They simply presented numbers. Yet the appearance, week after week, of these clearly drawn charts of the money supply did more than any other thing, in my opinion, to bring about the change that has occurred from almost exclusive concentration on monetary policy interest rates and the esoteric 'tone and feel of the market' to stress the quantity of money. The shift is not yet complete, but without Homer, I doubt that it would have occurred to anything like the extent it has.[7]

At the same time that Homer Jones commenced his work with the St. Louis Fed, a young economist on the staff, James Meigs, was writing his disseration for the University of Chicago under Milton Friedman. It was considered to be of such high calibre that it was published by the University of Chicago Press in 1962 under the title of Free Reserves and the Money Supply. It is a measure of Homer Jones as a teacher and an economist that Meigs says: "It would never have been written without the help of Homer Jones."[8]

Friedman wrote a very graceful introduction. A part of that work was developed through regression analysis and served to introduce econometrics to the Bank. Jones has indicated to the author that he was influenced by and found intellectual support in Meigs' ideas. But Meigs left soon after receiving his doctorate, and the new members of the staff were those whose names we have come to know through their publications in the Review; articles which have done so much to publicize Monetarism and the St. Louis Model.

Interestingly enough, three of them came from Professor Heller's own University of Minnesota. Leonall C. Andersen was the first, having been taught by Dr. Heller and coming in 1962 from a small college in Minnesota where he, himself, had been teaching. Joining him in 1963 was Keith Carlson, who is affectionately known as the "Keeper of the Model" by his colleagues, and who also had been teaching at the same college with Andersen.

Michael Keran was the third Minnesotan to arrive at the St. Louis Fed. He came in 1965 after working in Japan to obtain the material to complete his dissertation on "Monetary Policy and the Business Cycle in Post War Japan" The importance of his work is not so much that it became part of the St. Louis Model, but rather that it influenced Andersen and Carlson - brought up in the Keynesian tradition - to believe that there was something to be said for the impact of monetary policy on aggregate demand. This was confirmed, as Keran pointed out in subsequent Review articles not only in Japan but also in post-war Great Britain, France, Italy and Germany.[9] Moreover this monetarist view was verified - not by bar charts, but mathematically - using simple reduced form equations.

The final member of our cast is Jerry Jordan, who teamed up with Leonall Andersen to produce the 1968 article which was to brand the St. Louis Fed as Monetarist. Jordan came in 1967 as junior economist, working on the dissertation which gave him his doctorate from the University of California at Los Angeles in 1969. At that University he had studied under Armen Alchian and Karl Brunner, and indeed Brunner had recommended him to Andersen as a prospective employee of the Bank.

The Andersen-Jordan partnership began with an article entitled "Money in a Modern Quantity Theory Framework" carried in the Review of December 1967. The first part consisted of putting Milton Friedman's new demand for money into layman's language. In doing so, they make the point that there is a difference in the demand for money as an asset and the demand for credit. In 1978, Friedman confirms the importance of this distinction:

> I believe an important distinction between Keynesian and monetarist views is one that I have not myself stressed sufficiently but that comes out in the course of your comments. This is the distinction between money and credit and most particularly what one regards as the price of money. The Keynesian approach invariably regards the interest rate as the price of money whereas the quantity approach regards the interest rate as the price of credit and the inverse of the price level as the price of money.

> This is extremely important in connection with the way in which the demand curve for money is used.[10]

Andersen-Jordan used this distinction to suggest a model of the transmission process of a change in the stock of money. Thus a Federal Reserve open-market purchase of government securities leads to the following sequence of events:

1. Government security dealers are induced by higher prices (lower interest rates) to exchange securities for demand deposits. They repay debt or rebuild their inventories with other securities, thus spreading the untaxed cash balances throughout the country until new equilibrium interest rates are reached in every securities market.

2. Since banks now have more reserves than they desire, they make new loans and investments, exchanging them for new demand deposits. Spending units are willing to borrow as long as the interest rates are less than the expected yields from hiring labour and purchasing real and financial assets, so they now spend their borrowed funds and increase aggregate output.

Andersen-Jordan stressed that changes in the stock of money instituted by the monetary authorities who they assert, control its supply, cause changes in interest rates, which, in turn, cause changes in spending and prices.

In three short years, the St. Louis Model revised this hypothesis and expressed interest rates as a result of the adjustment process rather than a crucial link in the process, and thus they were related directly, rather than inversely to changes in the money stock.

Andersen-Jordan went on to assert that "growth in the output of a country is determined primarily by growth in population and technology, together with people's time preferences and attitudes toward uncertainty".[11] As has been noted, in Fisherian terms, time-preferences determine the supply of savings in the community and attitudes toward uncertainty determine the demand for funds to be used for investments.

Thus they conclude: "Money is not the only possible indicator of monetary actions, and it is certainly not the only potential source of disturbance to stable growth".[12] One could infer that autonomous disturbances which affected consumption and/or investment might destabilize the economy, requiring government intervention in the form increased fiscal expenditures as set out in Keynesian theory. But very shortly thereafter Andersen-Jordan, as a result of their own research, were to uphold the efficacy of changes in the money stock and references to autonomous disturbances largely disappeared from the Review, embedded in the constant and coefficients of the 1970 St. Louis spending equation.

One reason for this change in attitude was the empirical success of the economic forecasts contained in the research papers published in the Reviews of this period. They emphasized the relatively close but lagged relationship between the level of the money stock and the price level as illustrated by the GNP deflator. Thus in December, 1966, the St. Louis Fed suggested that despite the restrictive monetary policy of the last eight months of 1966, the so-called "credit crunch" when the money supply was held virtually stationary, the lagged effects of the rapid monetary expansion of late 1965 and early 1966 would cause inflation to continue. This view proved to be prophetic.

By the first quarter of 1967, the implicit GNP deflator was up by 2.6 percent. This accurate forecast gave President Francis the confidence to enunciate what he then called 'a monetary view' at FOMC meetings. Thus the report of the May 23, 1967 meeting states:

> Mr. Francis expressed the view that monetary policy had been highly stimulative thus far in 1967, that fiscal policy was providing an increasing stimulus and the economy was responding relatively quickly. On the grounds that a marked increase in demands for goods and services was likely later in the year and that monetary policy actions had their main effects after some time lag, he thought some firming in the money market should be sought now to guard against the development later of excessive demands and associated inflationary pressures.[13]

But President Francis was not satisfied with such phrases as "firming in the money market", which he had used at this meeting. As he put it in a speech to the Money Marketeers in New York City on October 30, 1968, in which one can sense the influence of Homer Jones:

> Rational economic stabilization policy requires that its operations be conducted in terms of specified and measurable changes in strategic variables. Vague concepts such as "easier," "tighter," or "more restrictive" carry little operational content for money management. If the FOMC directive contained truly quantified instructions, those responsible for its implementation would receive

> definite rather than impressionistic instuctions. Under these conditions money managers at all levels could be held accountable for the success or failure of their actions.
>
> The ideal of quantification is not out of reach. ...Since World War II much research has pointed to the possibility of improving the precision of economic stabilization. Statistical analyses and econometric procedures have been applied to a wide variety of economic problems. ...It is time that scientific methodology and modern quantitative analysis be used to a greater extent in developing appropriate procedures for monetary and fiscal management.[14]

The same issue of the Review which carried the report of Mr. Francis' speech, also contained an article entitled "Monetary and Fiscal Actions: A Test of Their Relative Importance in Economic Stabilization" by Leonall Andersen and Jerry Jordan. This article will be described in detail later; it is sufficient to say that its econometric equations indicated that economic activity was dominated by changes in the money supply rather than governmental receipts or expenditures and demonstrated the quantities involved. It was to be the genesis of the St. Louis Model.

DISCONTENT WITHIN THE FEDERAL RESERVE SYSTEM

Among members of the Board of Governors of the Federal Reserve System a similar discontent was growing, largely as a result of the policy measures taken on December 3, 1965. On that date, the Board of Governors, without prior consultation with the Johnson Administration, decided that 1966 was to be the year when monetary policy would halt the inflationary rise of aggregate demand. This was to be accomplished by raising the discount rate from 4 to 4.5 percent, which was then considered to be an extraordinarily high figure since it marked the highest rate since March 1930.

Moreover, interest rates on Treasury Bills and commercial paper had risen and were impinging on those allowed to be paid by the commercial banks, so the Board raised the interest rate which they could pay on time deposits from 4.5 to 5.5 percent, leaving the rate for savings and loan institutions at 5 percent. This increase of one full percentage point was considered necessary in order that the free market could allocate savings to their most efficient uses, particularly as between housing and industrial investment.

Disintermediation immediately occurred, sucking funds out of the savings and loan institutions to the higher rates offered by the commercial banks and financial securities with the result that housing starts feel from an annual rate of 1,770,000 in December 1965 to 850,000 by October 1966. The housing industry was called upon to make the major sacrifice in the fight against inflation, while the remainder of the economy was reaching new highs in income and profits.

By September, Congress rushed through new legislation, allowing the Board of Governors to vary interest rates with the size of time deposits. On the same day the legislation was passed, the Fed cut interest rates on time deposits under $100,000 from 5.5 percent to 5 percent, and this with other actions, resolved the crisis. But it led Governor Maisel to agree with President Francis:

> In the debate surrounding the events of 1966, I joined those who felt that poor measurement and

> lack of an analytical framework prevented the System from determining the proper amount of reserves. ...To formulate policy on the intangible basis of tone and feel of either the economy or the financial markets, was to invite serious mistakes.[15]

THE FIRST REDUCED-FORM EQUATIONS

But which route would the St. Louis Fed take to develop the information which President Francis desired? It could create a large structural model of the economy or it could use a smaller reduced form model. The die was cast when Andersen and Jordan (hereinafter called AJ) decided to test three commonly held propositions concerning the relative importance of monetary and fiscal actions in implementing stabilization policy. These propositions were that:

> The response of economic activity to fiscal actions relative to that of monetary actions is (I) greater (II) more predictable and (III) faster.[16]

As they state:

> As a step toward analyzing the three propositions ...empirical relationships between the measures of fiscal and monetary actions and total spending are established. These relationships and developed by regressing quarter to quarter changes in the money stock (M) and in the various measures of fiscal actions; high-employment budget surplus (R-E) high-employment expenditures (E) and high-employment receipts (R). Similar equ-

> ations were estimated where changes in the monetary base (B) were used in place of the money stock.[17]

The results surprised both Keynesians and Friedmanites; they brought fame and controversy to the St. Louis Fed and set it even more firmly on the path of Monetarism. Moreover, their use of small reduced form equations was adopted by Andersen and Carlson to create the St. Louis Model.

With a single equation approach, it is important that both the monetary and fiscal variables be correctly specified and that they are independent of, (exogenous) i.e. that they are not determined by economic activity. If this is the case, they will capture the direct and indirect impact of monetary and fiscal actions on nominal GNP irrespective of the transmission channels.

Thus, for example, it was not good enough for Andersen-Jordan to merely look at the national accounts and accept government expenditure as the figure they needed for the years in which they were interested. The reason is that government expenditures include payments that are made as a result of economic activity. If the economy is in a recession, government expenditures will include payments for unemployment insurance, as an example, which are much greater in the recession than they would be in a boom - they are dependent on the state of economic activity - not divorced from it. Being endogenous, they would bias the equation.

As an example, we note that unemployed workers were paid $4.5 billion in 1977 as compared with $16.8 billion in the recession year of 1976.[18]

Thus, it is important to to look at how AJ classified the market variables of the U.S. economy and to appreciate that the dependent variables are determined by the interplay of market forces which result from changes in the independent variables.[19]

CLASSIFICATION OF MARKET VARIABLES

Dependent Variables

Prices and quantities of goods and services.
Prices and quantities of factors of production.
Prices (interest rates) and quantities of financial assets
Expectations based on:

a. movements in dependent variables
b. expected results of random events
c. expected changes in fiscal and monetary policy.

Independent Variables

Slowly changing factors:

a. preferences
b. technology
c. resources
d. institutional and legal framework.

Events outside the domestic economy:

a. change in total world trade
b. movements in foreign prices and interest rates

Random events:

a. outbreak of war
b. major strikes
c. weather

Forces subject to control by:

a. fiscal actions
b. monetary actions

It is interesting that AJ make no mention of changes in the velocity of money which one would expect to be included, at least under 'Slowly changing factors'.

Moreover, this classification illustrates the monetarist hypothesis that the private sector is stable since no mention is made, even under 'Random events', of the possibility of autonomous changes in consumption, investment and/or net exports. A Keynesian economist would, of course, include such expenditures among the independent variables.

The extent of the testing and the significance of the coefficients can only be appreciated by looking at the results that Andersen and Jordan achieved - using a stream of taxicabs to rush their regressions to McDonnell-Douglas computer in St. Louis since the computers at the Bank could not handle them (See Appendix B.)

A typical equation

$$GNP = \beta_0 + \sum_{i=0}^{3}\beta_{1i}\ \Delta M_{t-i} + \sum_{i=0}^{3}\beta_{2i}\ \Delta E_{t-i} + \sum_{i=0}^{3}\beta_{3i}\ \Delta R_{t-i}$$

regresses quarter to quarter changes in nominal GNP on current and three lagged quarter to quarter changes in the money supply (M1), high employment expenditures E (Expenditures on goods and services adjusted to remove cyclical unemployment benefits) and high-employment receipts (R) defined as tax receipts adjusted to high-employment income.

The empirical results were

$$GNP = \underset{(1.88)}{2.10} + \underset{(6.57)}{5.84}\ M_{t-i} + \underset{(.13)}{.07}\ E_{t-i} + \underset{(.23)}{.23}\ R_{t-i} \qquad \begin{array}{ll} R^2 & = 0.58 \\ S.E. & = 4.11 \\ DW & = 1.80 \end{array}$$

("t" statistics shown in parentheses)

and even more startling were the quarterly coefficients.

QUARTERLY COEFFICIENTS

	M	E	R
t	1.51	.36	.16
t-1	1.59	.53	-.01
t-2	1.47	-.05	-.03
t-3	1.27	-.78	.11

These results mean:

1. A $1 billion dollar increase in M1 would raise nominal GNP by $5.84 billion in four quarters and approximately 25 percent or $1.51 billion, would occur in the first quarter. These results upset Keynesian theories. For comparison, we note that experiments made in 1971 using the large Keynesian type Federal Reserve Board - MIT model indicated that a $1 billion dollar increase in the money stock, other things being equal, would only produce a $0.3 billion increase in nominal GNP in that quarter and approximately $3.2 billion after twelve quarters.[20]

2. Milton Friedman and Anna Schwartz hold that business cycle research illustrates that money affects income with long and variable lags. As we have seen, in summarizing work that he had done with Mrs. Schwartz, Friedman wrote:

> We have found that on the average of 18 cycles peaks in the rate of change in the stock of money precede peaks in general business by about 16 months and troughs in the rate of change in the stock of money precede troughs in general business by about 12 months...For individual cycles, the recorded lead has varied between 6 and 29 months at peaks and between 4 and 22 months at troughs.[21]

The AJ results say that the linkage is rapid, and judging from the significance of the estimated coefficients, reliable. This would support the use of monetary policy as a flexible instrument, contrary to Friedman's call for a fixed rate of growth of the money stock.

3. The effect of high-employment tax receipts (R) was not found to be statistically significant and AJ suggested omitting that variable altogether on statistical grounds. Theoretically they then state this means that financing expenditures, whether by taxes or borrowing, has the same effect.[22]

4. On the other hand, they suggest that the quarterly changes in the high-employment expendituures (E), varying as they do from .36, .53 -.05, -.78 through three lagged quarters and summing only to .07 are consistent with the analysis of John Culbertson who points out:

> ...In a financially constrained economy (i.e. no monetary expansion to finance Government expenditures), expenditures by the Government in the debt markets in competition with private expenditures can very possibly "crowd out of the market an equal (or conceivably even greater) volume that would have financed private expenditures." He asserts that it is possible to have a short-lived effect of government spending on total spending if the financial effects lag behind its positive effects.[23]

5. Current and lagged values of M explained between 50 and 60 percent of the variance in GNP changes and other autonomous influences including velocity, autonomous consumption, weather, wars and autonomous investment are contained in the constant term 2.10 which is found to be "quite large and statistically significant."[24]

A criticism by Blinder and Solow, concerns the use of the constant term which they express as follows:[25]

> AJ argue that we need not specify a complete structural model of the economy to know that the reduced form for income will be;
>
> (24) $$Y_t = f(G_t, R_t, M_t, Z_t)$$
>
> where G, R and M have been described and Z is a vector of "all the other forces that influence total spending." If G, R, and M are specified properly as exogenous variables this will indeed be a "true" reduced form, from which it follows that changes in income are given by:
>
> (25) $$dY_t = a_1dG_t + a_2dR_t + a_3\ dM_t + a_4dZ_t + e_t$$
>
> where we have now added an independent stochastic term e_t indicating exogenous "shocks" that affect the system but are not captured by any variables in the model. Now AJ wish to drop the last set of variables from the regression. Why? Because they cannot specify correctly a complete macro model of the economy that would tell them what to include in the vector.

At this point Blinder and Solow add, "this inability is not to be interpreted as a criticsm of Andersen and Jordan. We are not convinced that anyone is capable of doing this correctly" They go on:

> AJ seem to think they can avoid this difficulty by replacing the a dZ term in equation (25) by a constant a_o. They suggest interpreting the constant as the "average" value of a_4dZ_t over the period. This is simply illegitimate. If

(25) is the "true" model and they estimate instead:

(26) $$dY_t = a_o + a_1dG_t + a_2dR_t + a_3dM_t + v_t$$

they will have misspecified the equation and so impounded a dZ into their error term:

$$v_t = e_t + a_4dZ_t - a_o$$

Unless dZ_t is uncorrelated with dG_t, dR_t, and dM_t, ordinarily least squares in (26) will, as is well known, yield biased and inconsistent estimates of the parameters of (25).

There were other criticisms, largely having to do with the exogenity of both (M) and (E) and thereby the bias of the equations, which will be developed later. While AJ expressly stated that they did not intend to "develop evidence bearing directly on any causal relationships implied by such theories", there has been much said in the economic literature on that account as well.[26]

6. The possibility that money is passively supplied in response to demand generated by economic activity, or indeed fulfils the demand for loans on which an upturn in activity depends, is a Keynesian objection to the monetarist position called 'reverse causation'. In the Treatise on Money (1930) Keynes insisted that money "comes into existence along with debts" - in other words, the supply of money is related to expenditure contracts and any debts which they necessitate.

Contrary to this view, the research work which had previously been done at the St. Louis Fed had found a strong relationship between the supply of money M and the monetary base B. Since R is a monetary variable which is controlled by the Federal Reserve then M is held to be exogenous - unrelated to economic activity.

To test this hypothese, AJ also estimated an equation, substituting B for M. (See Equation 1.4, Exhibit B). This relationship continued to explain about one-half the variation in the changes in GNP with no significant assistance from the fiscal variable E. (The money multiplier was greatly increased, having a much smaller base to begin with.)[27] The problem is that establishing responsibility for increasing the base does not ensure the exogenity of the variable. Reserves and through them, money, while controlled by the authorities, may be supplied according to the demand.

Andersen went on to offer other empirical evidence against reverse causation for the period 1953 - 1968.[28] The relevance of his test was challenged by Smith and Waud.[29]

7. It is to be noted that this is a seemingly mechanical process - one need only prime the economic pump with money and thereby one can automatically increase the flow of goods and services. No consideration is given to the state of Keynes 'animal spirits' of entrepreneurs which he held must be nurtured towards optomism - since the expected yield of any future investment could only be a hazardous guess at best.

8. Andersen-Jordan also point out that "Market interest rates are not used in the article as strategic monetary variables since they reflect to a great extent fiscal actions expectations and other factors which cannot properly be called monetary actions."[30]

Thus they were swinging to the view that interest rates were the result - not a link in the expenditure process. Keith Carlson feels that this overstates their position somewhat. Thus he says:

> I don't think this denies that interest rates are a link - rather with other factors affecting interest rates, they are not reliable as monetary indicators.[31]

THE ST. LOUIS MODEL IS DEVELOPED

In April 1967, the St. Louis Fed had predicted that the restrictive monetary action of late 1966 would cause a decline in output in late 1967, while the rapid monetary expansion of early 1967 would put additional fuel into inflation in 1968. The rate of growth in output declined from 4.4 percent in the middle of 1967 to a 2.8 percent rate in the last quarter of 1967. The rate of increase in the price level accelerated to 5.3 percent per annum in the fourth quarter of 1968 from 2.2 percent in the second quarter of 1967.

In September 1967, the St. Louis Fed forecast that the rapid monetary expansion of 1967 would cause inflation to continue unabated even if the proposed surtax were adopted. The surtax went into effect in July 1968, and inflation averaged 4.7 percent throughout 1968.

The Andersen-Jordan equations gave statistical verification of this domination of the U.S. economy by changes in the money stock. It was therefore time to construct a model - that, given a proposed change in the growth of M1 and high-employment governmental expenditures - would be able to predict not only nominal income, but prices, real output, unemployment and interest rates. If this could be done then President Francis' wishes could be satisfied. This is how he put it:

> It is not sufficient for an economist to tell us that a slower growth in money will eventually result in a slower rate of price increase. As a policymaker, I would like to have a better information as to the specific open market transactions that would achieve, with a high degree of probability, a desired growth of money. I am also vitally concerned with the

> time distribution to be expected with regard to changes in prices and output for a given change in the growth rate of money. Then I want to know how soon tangible results can be expected with regard to prices and output, and how the pattern will appear in the data subsequently reported.[32]

There were three challenges inherent in the development of the St. Louis model.

1. As indicated above, such a model would assist in the development of stabilization policies by illustrating the responses to changing monetary and fiscal actions. In fact, if such forecasts could be accurately made, the Board of Governors of the Federal Reserve System could seemingly 'fine-tune' the economy by changes in the money stock on its own.

2. Large Keynesian-type econometric models were being developed which were disputing the empirical statements of Monetarists. These models looked at the various sectors of the economy, aggregating the impact of monetary and fiscal actions in each sector to arrive at nominal income. Rather than try and reform the Keynesian orthodoxy, the St. Louis Fed recognised the crucial point. It would take a system to beat a system.

3. It was necessary to provoke other economists of the 'monetarist' persuasion to join the fray as Keynes had done with his <u>General Theory</u>, in order, as Keynes put it in the aphorism which opens Chapter 8, "to raise a dust, because it is only out of the controversy that will arise, that what I am saying will be understood."

Jerry Jordan had been promoted to Vice President, Computers, so Andersen now asked Keith Carlson to work with him to achieve such

CHART I

Flow Chart of the St. Louis Model

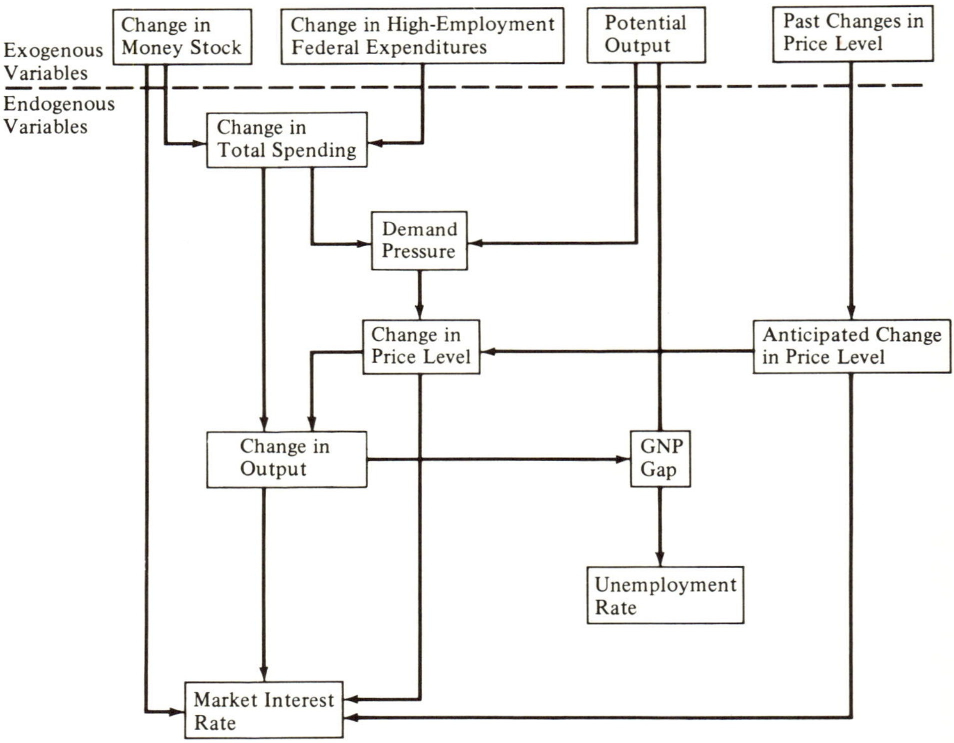

SOURCE: Leonall Andersen and Keith Carson, "A Monetarist Model for Economic Stabilization," *Review* (Federal Reserve Bank of St. Louis) 52 (April 1970): 10.

a model. It is at this point that Carlson pays particular tribute to Prof. William Yohe, then a Visiting Scholar, for the assistance which he gave them in working out the relationships in the model.

These relationships are seen in the Flow Chart (Chart I) developed by Andersen and Carlson (or AC as we shall henceforth call them) to illustrate the linkages between the various variables of their Model.

As was the case in the Andersen-Jordan spending equation, nominal GNP is determined by monetary actions (M) and high-employment federal expenditures (E). AC adopted the Andersen-Jordan recommendation and dropped high-employment tax receipts from the spending equation. They also assumed the Friedman 'black box' because they say that "no direct information is provided as to how such actions affect spending". (Emphasis is in the original).[33]. Friedman believes that changes in the money stock affect expenditures in so many and such complicated ways, that it is useless to try and find them all. AC agree and the St. Louis model compares change in the money supply and high-employment government spending without trying to trace through the particular channels by which they affect income.

Contrary to Keynesians for whom interest rates are the dominant factor in new investment and aggregate spending, AC are agreeing that "the impact of changes in money on any specific interest rate is both too weak to be captured statistically or identified as a strategic variable in the transmission process".[34]

THE ST. LOUIS EXOGENOUS VARIABLES

The top line of the flow chart consists of three exogenous variables, which, in the eyes of AC are determined outside the Model. They are:

1. **The Money Stock** - which AC holds is best represented by M1 differing here from Milton Friedman - who prefers M2. The money stock, as we have noted, is considered to be exogenous because it is closely related to the monetary base which is directly under the control of the Federal Reserve.

2. **High-Employment Government Expenditures** - Again as has been described, the only adjustment that is made to the federal government's actual spending is that paid for unemployment compensation. Thus, high-employment benefits are calculated for the level of high-employment which is considered the norm for the period, as set out in heading 3 below dealing with potential output.

High-employment government expenditures are considered to be exogenous because they are directly under the control of the Federal government. But unemployment expenditures, along with others like those for food stamps and welfare, are known as 'built-in' stabilizers, crafted by the government to expand in recession and decrease in boom. Such payments maintain aggregate expenditure during recessions in the U.S. economy and therefore they may be a problem.

For as L.R. Klein says:

> ...let me point out that non-monetarists should not agree that induced (non-exogenous) actions of the Treasury have no significant causal effects on real income. I believe that the built-in stabilizers are of enormous importance, quietly doing their own work and keeping fluctuations in bounds. They can be as important as the exogenous effects studied in the paper at hand.[35]

Milton Friedman has been associated with the St. Louis Model since its earliest conception and is one of a number of economists whom AC thanked for their comments on earlier drafts of their 1970 article. However, it is problems such as that enunciated by Lawrence Klein which led him in 1976 to comment:

> ...In general, I believe much too sharp a distinction has been drawn between "transfers" and "expenditures on goods and services." ...I have long been impressed with the empirical ambiguities in the application of the Keynesian apparatus - most of the controversy surrounding the paper that I wrote some years ago with Meiselman centred on how to define autonomous expenditures, almost none on how to define money. The similar growing ambiguity about what "government expenditures" means reinforces my scepticism about using the value of these concepts to analyse the determinants of aggregate income and the price level, or the division of changes in aggregate income between changes in real income and in prices.[36]

3. **Potential Output**: is measured by estimating real output consistent with a "full-employment unemployment rate" which was originally set at four percent. Subsequently it was changed to measure "the lowest rate of unemployment attainable, under the existing institutional structure, that will not result in accelerating inflation" - which was deemed, for example, to be 5.4 percent in 1978, by the Council of Economic Advisors.[37] Potential output is considered to be exogenous because it grows only with the increase of the labcur force, resources and productivity.

TABLE I

MODEL IN ALGEBRAIC FORM

(1) **Total Spending Equation**
$\Delta Y_t = f_1(\Delta M_t \ldots \Delta M_{t-n}, \Delta E_t \ldots \Delta E_{t-n})$

(2) **Price Equation**
$\Delta P_t = f_2(D_t \ldots D_{t-n}, \Delta P^A{}_t)$

(3) **Demand Pressure Identity**
$D_t = \Delta Y_t - (X^F{}_t - X_{t-1})$

(4) **Total Spending Identity**
$\Delta Y_t = \Delta P_t + \Delta X_t$

(5) **Interest Rate Equation**
$R_t = f_3(\Delta M_t, \Delta X_t \ldots \Delta X_{t-n}, \Delta P_t, \Delta P^A{}_t)$

(6) **Anticipated Price Equation**
$\Delta P^A{}_t = f_4(\Delta P_{t-1} \ldots \Delta P_{t-n})$

(7) **Unemployment Rate Equation**
$U_t = f_5(G_t, G_{t-1})$

(8) **GNP Gap Identity**
$$G_t = \frac{X^F{}_t - X_t}{X^F{}_t}$$

Endogenous Variables

ΔY_t = change in total spending (nominal GNP)
ΔP_t = change in price level (GNP price deflator)
D_t = demand pressure
ΔX_t = change in output (real GNP)
R_t = market interest rate
$\Delta P^A{}_t$ = anticipated change in price level
U_t = unemployment rate
G_t = GNP gap

Exogenous Variables*

ΔM_t = change in money stock
ΔE_t = change in high-employment Federal expenditures
$X^F{}_t$ = potential (full-employment) output

*Other than lagged variables.

Source: Leonall Andersen and Keith Carlson, "A Monetarist Model for Economic Stabilization" Federal Reserve Bank of St. Louis Review, April 1970, p.9.

4. **Past Changes in the Price Level**: The role of past changes in the price variable reflects the new interest in 'adaptive' expectations, which says that people expect prices to continue in the same direction as those in the past. Thus it is considered to be an exogenous (independent) variable and past changes of the price level then give rise to anticipated changes in the price level, which becomes an endogenous variable. These anticipated changes, in turn, affect two other endogenous variables, the price level and the rate of interest.

GENERAL FORM OF THE MODEL

The equations of the St. Louis Model are presented in algebraic form in Table I. The details of the estimation procedure were set out by AC as follows:

> Each of the equations is estimated by ordinary least squares. Lag structures, with one exception, are estimated by the Almon lag technique. The reported relationships reflect considerable experimentation with the number of lags and the degree of the polynomial. The sample period starts with 1953 for the spending equation and with 1955 for all the others. The data is quarterly and, with the exception of interest rates, is seasonally adjusted.
>
> Criteria used in the selection of the equations were minimizing the standard error of estimate and eliminating serial correlation in the estimated residuals. In addition, the signs and statistical significance of the estimated coefficients received consideration, along with the pattern of the lag distribution.

> Since these criteria frequently could not be satisfied simultaneously, an element of subjectivity was present in selecting the "best" equation.[38]

THE TOTAL SPENDING EQUATION

The total spending equation is set out in algebraic form in Equation 1 of Table 1. The economic theory behind this equation goes back to David Hume, namely, that a change in the rate of monetary expansion will, in the short-run, influence real output and the price level, the combination of which gives the nominal GNP. The changes in total output will then influence employment.

In the long-run, output and employment depend on the growth of natural resources, the capital stock, the labour force and productivity. Once the high-employment level of production is reached, further expansion of the money stock serves only to increase the price level. This last statement is one where Keynesians and Monetarist do agree!

Nevertheless, in order to test the Keynesian position that changing government expenditures are an extremely important influence on output and employment, AC specify that the change in total spending (ΔY) is a function, not only of current and post changes in M1 (ΔM), which is the total of demand deposits and currency held by the non-bank public, but also current and past changes in high-employment Federal expenditures (ΔE). AC then leave it to the size and significance of the estimated parameters to determine whether the data conforms more closely to Keynesian or Monetarist theory. (see Table II)

As in the Andersen-Jordan equations, the pattern of the coefficients in Table II indicates a large and rapid influence of

TABLE II

TOTAL SPENDING EQUATION

Sample Period: I/1953 - IV/1969

Constraints: 4th Degree Polynomial

$(m_{-1} = e_{-1} = 0;\ m_5 = e_5 = 0)$

$$\Delta Y_t = \underset{(3.46)}{2.67} + \sum_{i=0}^{4} m_i \Delta M_{t-i} + \sum_{i=0}^{4} e_i \Delta E_{t-i}$$

$R^2 = .66$
S.E. $= 3.84$
D-W $= 1.75$

$m_0 =$	1.22	(2.73)	$e_0 =$	.56	(2.57)
$m_1 =$	1.80	(7.34)	$e_1 =$	.45	(3.43)
$m_2 =$	1.62	(4.25)	$e_2 =$	.01	(.08)
$m_3 =$	.87	(3.65)	$e_3 =$	−.43	(−3.18)
$m_4 =$	.06	(.12)	$e_4 =$	−.54	(−2.47)
$\Sigma m_i =$	5.57	(8.06)	$\Sigma e_i =$	.05	(.17)

Symbols are defined as:

ΔY_t = dollar change in total spending (GNP in current prices) in quarter t

ΔM_{t-i} = dollar change in money stock in quarter t—i

ΔE_{t-i} = dollar change in high-employment Federal expenditures in quarter t—i

Note: "t" statistics appear with each regression coefficient, enclosed by parentheses. R^2 is the percent of variation in the dependent variable which is explained by variations in the independent variables. S.E. is the standard error of the estimate. D-W is the Durbin-Watson statistic.

Source: Leonall Andersen and Keith Carlson, "A Monetarist Model for Economic Stabilization" Federal Reserve Bank of St. Louis Review, April 1970, p.11.

monetary actions on total spending relative to that of fiscal actions.

The monetary coefficients indicate that an increase of the money stock of $1.00 in a quarter would increase total GNP after five quarters by $5.57 as seen in the expression $\sum M_i = 5.57$. On the other hand a similar increase of government spending of $1.00 would increase nominal GNP by .56¢ in that quarter, and thereafter, .45¢ in the first quarter and 01¢ in the second quarter and then cause decreases of .45¢ and .54¢ in the next two quarters. After five quarters, an increase of spending of $1.00 by the Federal government would only increase nominal GNP by .05¢ as seen in the expression $e_i = \sum .05$. The fiscal multiplier is thus only .05.

As Milton Friedman has said:

> One way to characterize the Keynesian approach is that it gives almost exclusive importance to the first-round effect. This leads it to attach importance primarily to flows of spending rather than stocks of assets.
>
> Similarly, one way to characterize the quantity-theory approach is to say that it gives almost no importance to first-round effects. The empirical question is how important the first-rounds effects are compared to the ultimate effects.[39]

And we can see in the St. Louis Model the ultimate effects of high-employment government spending are miniscule.

This can be compared with Keynesian economists Alan S. Blinder and Robert M. Solow, who write, "...a fiscal planner will not often be led astray if he uses a multiplier of 2 in his back-of-the envelope calculations,"[40] or a difference of some 400 percent between the Keynesian and St. Louis Models.

Since the AC fiscal coefficients are very similar to those found by Andersen-Jordan, they conclude that fiscal actions, unaccompanied by changes in money, have little net effect upon GNP over five quarters. They explain this circumstance by saying that these results are "consistent with a 'crowding-out' theory of effects of government spending"[41]. Empirically, every extra dollar spent by government subtracts ninety-five cents worth of spending by the private sector - therefore Y increases by only five cents. This also must mean that if government spending decreases by one dollar, then the private sector will increase its spending by ninety-five cents, ceteris paribus.

Robert J. Gordon theorizes, however, that these results might mean:

1. The Federal government has stabilized Y by changing G expenditures to offset autonomous changes in the variables which have been left out of the spending equations, or

2. This result has occurred through coincidence.

This, of course, is the same type of criticism put forward by Blinder and Solow in connection with the Andersen-Jordan equations, and expanded on by Ando and Modigliani.[42]

However, Professor Gordon goes on to examine these propositions empirically by comparing a "true" model:

$$\Delta Y = a + \sum_{i}^{k} B_i \Delta M_{t-i} + \sum_{i}^{L} Y_i \Delta G_{t-i} + \sum_{i}^{N} n_i \Delta A_{t-i} + u_t$$

with the St. Louis equation:

$$\Delta Y = a + \sum_{i}^{k} b_i \; \Delta M_{t-i} + \sum_{i}^{L} c_i \, \Delta G_{t-i} + v_y$$

where A is a set of non-stochiastic left-out variables.

To focus the problem, Gordon introduces a "shock proxy" for A - which is equal to the sum of net exports, consumer expenditures on new automobiles and non-residential fixed investment. As he writes:

> Although this trilogy is by no means totally exogenous, its fluctuations over short periods of four to eight quarters are relatively independent of changes in the money supply and government spending, and are affected by the timing of changes in foreign demand, consumer expectations, tax rates and incentives and other excluded variables.[43]

Prof. Gordon adds that the Federal Reserve might destablize Y by:

> ...attempting to stabilize interest rates, leading to an automatic postive response of M to movements in A and u, if the latter represent shifts in expenditure functions rather than in the demand for money.

Five sample periods were used:

(i) 1958/ I - 1969/IV

(ii) the total post-Korean era (1953/I - 1974/IV)

and three sub-periods of (ii), namely

(iii) The Eisenhower years 1953/I - 1960/IV
(iv) Kennedy-Johnson 1961/I - 1968/IV
(v) Nixon-Ford 1969/I - 1974/IV

The procedure was to isolate these individual episodes and examine the shifts in the coefficients in the reduced form regressions in which the "shock proxy" was alternatively included and excluded and to investigate the simple correlations between the policy variable and the "shock proxy".

As Gordon says - "Overall, there is something in these results for everyone." Specifically:

1. There was coincidence - auto sales boomed in 1955 as post-Korean defence spending declined.

2. In 1958-59, government expenditures increased counter-cyclically during the 1958 recession and fell during the 1959 mini-boom.

3. 'Crowding out' occurred in 1966-67 as Vietnam expenditures increased dramatically.

4. Nixon-Ford government expenditures were destabilizing, contracting in 1969-70 and expanding during the boom of 1971.

5. The government expenditure coefficient, with the "shock proxy" excluded, reached 3.94 in the Nixon-Ford period and was 1.65 when the "shock proxy" was included, though Gordon notes that these figures are on 'the borderline of significance'.

6. Other than that instance, the monetary and fiscal coefficients pretty well mirror the results found by AC.

7. Overall, it appeared that the Federal Reserve allowed M to vary in order to stabilize interest rates and offset shifts in velocity.

Generally speaking, however, the data which Prof. Gordon obtained favours the Monetarist view and this is confirmed by his final word that:

> The MPS (Keynesian) model builders should take seriously the possibility that, in peering into the black box, they have not yet located all of the creeks, tributaries and rivers which lead from money to income.[44]

PRICES AND OUTPUT

Once we have the change in total spending the problem is to divide it between price and real output. This is done by firstly estimating price changes as a function of (a) current and past output i.e. demand pressure, and (b) anticipated price change.

Demand Pressure: - We have noted that Keynes made the point in his chapter on the Theory of Prices in the General Theory that the closer the economy came to full employment - the greater would be the pressure on prices. As he put it:

> Thus we must first consider the effect of changes in the quantity of money on the quantity of demand; and the increase in effective demand will generally speaking, spend itself in increasing the quantity of employment and partly in raising the level of prices. Thus...we have a condition of prices rising gradually as employment increases.[45]

We recognise that if there were no gap between potential output and current ouput, the economy must be at full employment and any increase in effective demand must spend itself totally in raising prices, since there are no resources available to increase production. On the other hand if there is a large gap between potential output and current output the so called "slack" in the economy - then real output is likely to increase more quickly than prices. This hypothesis, of course, underlies the Phillips curve. The question facing AC was how to express this demand pressure in mathematical terms. They did it with the equation:

$$D_t = Y_t - (X_t^F - X_{t-1})$$

where Y is the change in total spending in quarter t, X_t^F is potential full-employment real GNP in 1958 prices in quarter t, and X_{t-1} is real GNP in 1958 prices in the previous quarter. The figures for potential output were based on those then used by the Council of Economic Advisers. At that time, potential output was estimated to be rising at a 4.3 percent annual rate.

Meyer and Varvares point out:

> This specification of the demand slack variable may seriously bias upward the equations' estimate of the response of inflation to demand slack, inasmuch as it allows changes in nominal income associated with changes in the price level to "explain" changes in the price level.[46]

Keith Carlson graciously admits the point - saying "Including Y was criticized originally - adding apples (nominal output) and oranges (real output). But Meyer's criticism is also relevant."[47] The specification has been changed in the most recent St. Louis Model.

TABLE III

ANTICIPATED PRICE DEFINITION

(pi from Long-Term Interest Rate Equation)

$$\Delta P^A_t = Y_{t-2} \left\{ \left[\left(\sum_{i=1}^{17} p_i \frac{\dot{P}_{t-i}}{U_{t-i}/4} \right) .01 + 1 \right]^{1/4} - 1 \right\}$$

$p_1 = .02$	$p_7 = .08$	$p_{13} = .06$
$p_2 = .03$	$p_8 = .08$	$p_{14} = .06$
$p_3 = .04$	$p_9 = .08$	$p_{15} = .04$
$p_4 = .06$	$p_{10} = .08$	$p_{16} = .03$
$p_5 = .06$	$p_{11} = .08$	$p_{17} = .02$
$p_6 = .07$	$p_{12} = .07$	$\Sigma p_i = .96$

Symbols are defined as:

ΔPA_t = anticipated price change (scaled in dollar units) in quarter t

$\dot{P}_{t-i}$ = annual rate of change in GNP deflator (1958 = 100) in quarter t—i

$U_{t-i}/4$ = index of unemployment as a per cent of labor force (base = 4.0) in quarter t—i

Y_{t-2} = total spending (GNP in current prices) in quarter t—2

Source: Leonall Andersen and Keith Carlson, "A Monetarist Model for Economic Stabilization" Federal Reserve Bank of St. Louis Review, April 1970, p.12.

Anticipated Price Change - Ordinarily, one would expect decreasing prices to accompany increasing unemployment, as was the case in the early stages of the Great Depression. Recently, however, anticipated prices have become a part of economic theory based on the incidence of the so-called condition of 'stagflation' - defined as periods of rising prices during times of high unemployment. The theory of adaptive expectations has been used to explain this 'stagflation' by saying that led by strong unions, wage increases, and shortly thereafter, prices, are based on the inflation record of the preceding several years and the expectation that such inflation will continue even in periods when the demand for labour is decreasing.

Thus, for example, Otto Eckstein tells us that in a sense, the wage and price controls imposed by President Nixon in 1971 were an attempt to "brainwash" the public of their inflationary expectations.[48]

The degree to which price-setting behaviour is influenced by price expectations is difficult to measure because expectations are not quantitative. Ordinary common sense tells us that our expectations are based on past experience. But as has been noted, in an economic world, governmental and other policy changes can have a large influence on what we predict for the future.

Since such a variable is not observable, it has to be constructed and this AC do as illustrated in Table III. Although this Table was copied from the original AC article in the 1970 Review, it is the only one which omits the figures for R^2, S. E., and D-W.

As one would expect, anticipated prices are based on the percentage change of past prices. However, AC modify this figure by an index of unemployment on the basis that if unemployment is rising (falling), entrepreneurs will discount unemployment is rising (falling), entrepreneurs will discount (increase) the effect of past inflation on future prices. Thus the percentage of price change in each quarter is divided by the unemployment rate of the quarter. As a result of a specification search, the best prediction came after sixteen quarters - from t_1 to t_{17}.

But according to Fisherian analysis, there is another measure of price expectations which is contained in the long-term interest rate. Fisher held that this rate reflects an unvarying real interest rate plus a risk factor for expected inflation. Thus the coefficient p_i is obtained from the long-term interest rate equation and measures that risk factor.

The role of Y_{t-2} reflects Friedman's theory that the response of anticipated price changes is not felt until approximately two quarters after a change in the monetary stock. In his words:

> On the average, the effect on prices comes about six to nine months after the effect on income and output, so the total delay between the change in monetary growth and a change in the rate of inflation averages something like 12 - 18 months. That is why it is a long road to hoe to stop an inflation that has been allowed to start. It cannot be stopped overnight.[49]

Arranging the equation in this way allowed the anticipated price change to be scaled in dollar units.

THE PRICE EQUATION

The demand pressure and anticipated price change equations are then combined to give the price equation as illustrated in Table IV. This equation expresses the change in prices as the dollar change in total spending (GNP in current prices) due to the price change in quarter t.

TABLE IV

PRICE EQUATION

Sample Period: I/1955 - IV/1969

Constraints: 2nd Degree Polynomial

$(d_{-1} \neq 0;\ d_6 = 0)$

$$\Delta P_t = \underset{(7.07)}{2.70} + \sum_{i=0}^{5} d_i D_{t-i} + \underset{(8.55)}{.86} \Delta PA_t$$

$R^2 = .87$
S.E. = 1.07
D-W = 1.41

$d_0 = .02\ (2.63)$
$d_1 = .02\ (6.33)$
$d_2 = .02\ (6.63)$
$d_3 = .01\ (2.93)$
$d_4 = .01\ (1.86)$
$d_5 =\ *\ (1.38)$
$\Sigma d_i = .09\ (9.18)$

Symbols are defined as:

ΔP_t = dollar change in total spending (GNP in current prices) due to price change in quarter t

$D_t = \Delta Y_t - (XF_t - X_{t-1})$

ΔY_t = dollar change in total spending (GNP in current prices) in quarter t

XF_t = potential output in quarter t

X_{t-1} = output (GNP in 1958 prices) in quarter t—1

ΔPA_t = anticipated price change (scaled in dollar units) in quarter t

Note: "t" statistics appear with each regression coefficient, enclosed by parentheses. R^2 is the percent of variation in the dependent variable which is explained by variations in the independent variables. S.E. is the standard error of the estimate. D-W is the Durbin-Watson statistic.

*Less than .01

Source: Leonall Andersen and Keith Carlson, "A Monetarist Model for Economic Stabilization" Federal Reserve Bank of St. Louis Review, April 1970, p.13.

It is interesting to compare this theoretical framework with Keynesian price theory. That theory divides markets into two broad categories; competitive 'flexprice' markets where prices are determined by supply and demand (raw materials and primary foodstuffs) and 'fixprice' markets (manufactured goods) in which prices reflect both 'normal' production costs and the demand for retained profits to finance planned investment expenditures, given the firms dividend payout ratio.[50]

But in 'fixprice' markets the pressure of aggregate demand and inflationary expectations enter into labour costs as illustrated by the Phillips curve. Keynesians just don't emphasize these components of the St. Louis Price Equation.

DETERMINATION OF OUTPUT

Given ΔY_t as determined by the spending equation and ΔP_t from the price equation, the value of the change in real output, which we have previously defined as ΔX_t, can be derived from the following identity.

$$\Delta X_t = \Delta Y_t - \Delta P_t$$

ΔX_t will then be expressed as a dollar amount.

THE UNEMPLOYMENT RATE

We have seen how the unemployment rate is used to modify past price changes in the formation of the anticipated price equation. AC estimate it by regressing the unemployment rate on the current and lagged values of the real GNP gap, expressed as a percent of potential real GNP. This equation is estimated by unconstrained least squares, and is shown in Table V.

TABLE V

UNEMPLOYMENT RATE EQUATION

Sample Period: I/1955 - IV/1969

$$U_t = \underset{(72.50)}{3.90} + \underset{(1.10)}{.04G_t} + \underset{(6.80)}{.28G_{t-1}}$$

$R^2 = .92$
S.E. $= .30$
D-W $= .60$

Symbols are defined as:

U_t = unemployment as a per cent of labor force in quarter t

$$G_t = \frac{XF_t - X_t}{XF_t} \cdot 100$$

XF_t = potential output in quarter t

X_t = output (GNP in 1958 prices) in quarter t

Note: "t" statistics appear with each regression coefficient, enclosed by parentheses. R^2 is the percent of variation in the dependent variable which is explained by variations in the independent variables. S.E. is the standard error of the estimate. D-W is the Durbin-Watson statistic.

Source: Leonall Andersen and Keith Carlson, "A Monetarist Model for Economic Stabilization" Federal Reserve Bank of St. Louis Review, April 1970, p.14.

At full employment $X^F - X_t = 0$. If this should occur in quarter t, then U = 3.90%. This would measure frictional and institutional unemployment and would therefore be consistent with 'high' or 'full' employment which, at the time, was estimated by the Council of Economic Advisers at 4% per annum.

This equation is based on Arthur Okun's observation that increased output arises from an increased labour force, increased average hours worked, a reduction in the unemployment rate and/or an improvement in productivity that, in the short run, move together in a relatively stable manner. This makes for a simple relationship between output and employment. Okun developed a rule of thumb which in 1970 stated that for every 3 percent increase in real output, unemployment would decrease by 1 percent to a limit of 4 percent unemployment.[51]

It is to be noted that while the R^2 and S.E. statistics are excellent, the Durbin-Watson statistic is very low at .60. This suggests autocorrelation and serious misspecification - there are probably some omitted variables.

INTEREST RATES

In the Flow Chart of the St. Louis Model, interest rates are considered to be the final result of the economic process, that is to say, they do not influence other variables in the Model.

In Keynesian models, a change in the interest rate is the link between changes in the money stock and aggregate spending. Milton Friedman describes the transmission process succinctly:

> Consider how a Keynesian would describe the effects of an increase in the quantity of money. It would go:

TABLE VI

LONG-TERM INTEREST RATE EQUATION

Sample Period: I/1955 - IV/1969

Constraints: 2nd Degree Polynomial

$(x_{-1} \neq 0,\ p_{-1} \neq 0;\ x_{17} = p_{17} = 0)$

$$R^L_t = \underset{(5.20)}{1.28} \underset{(-3.53)}{- .06\dot{M}_t} + \underset{(11.01)}{1.42Z_t} + \sum_{i=0}^{16} x_i \dot{X}_{t-i} + \sum_{i=0}^{16} p_i \left(\frac{\dot{P}_{t-i}}{U_{t-i}/4}\right)$$

$R^2 = .92$
S.E. $= .28$
D-W $= .69$

x_0 = .02 (3.85)	x_6 = .01 (2.61)	x_{12} = .01 (1.38)
x_1 = .02 (4.35)	x_7 = .01 (2.27)	x_{13} = .01 (1.28)
x_2 = .02 (4.44)	x_8 = .01 (2.01)	x_{14} = * (1.20)
x_3 = .02 (4.08)	x_9 = .01 (1.80)	x_{15} = * (1.13)
x_4 = .02 (3.54)	x_{10} = .01 (1.64)	x_{16} = * (1.07)
x_5 = .02 (3.03)	x_{11} = .01 (1.50)	Σx_i = .20 (2.88)
p_0 = .02 (1.23)	p_6 = .08 (17.13)	p_{12} = .06 (9.29)
p_1 = .03 (3.05)	p_7 = .08 (14.49)	p_{13} = .06 (8.89)
p_2 = .04 (5.96)	p_8 = .08 (12.64)	p_{14} = .04 (8.57)
p_3 = .06 (10.82)	p_9 = .08 (11.37)	p_{15} = .03 (8.30)
p_4 = .06 (17.34)	p_{10} = .08 (10.47)	p_{16} = .02 (8.07)
p_5 = .07 (19.66)	p_{11} = .07 (9.81)	Σp_i = .96 (19.04)

Symbols are defined as:

RL_t = Moody's seasoned corporate Aaa bond rate in quarter t

$\dot{M}_t$ = annual rate of change in money stock in quarter t

Z_t = dummy variable in quarter t (0 for I/1955 - IV/1960 and 1 for I/1961 - IV/1969)

$\dot{X}_{t-i}$ = annual rate of change in output (GNP in 1958 prices) in quarter t—i

$\dot{P}_{t-i}$ = annual rate of change in GNP deflator (1958 = 100) in quarter t—i

$U_{t-i}/4$ = index of unemployment as a per cent of labor force (base = 4.0) in quarter t—i

Note: "t" statistics appear with each regression coefficient, enclosed by parentheses. R^2 is the percent of variation in the dependent variable which is explained by variations in the independent variables. S.E. is the standard error of the estimate. D-W is the Durbin-Watson statistic.

*Less than .01

Source: Leonall Andersen and Keith Carlson, "A Monetarist Model for Economic Stabilization" Federal Reserve Bank of St. Louis Review, April 1970, p.14.

> 1. Interest Rates fall.
> 2. Investment increases.
> 3. Output and real income increase.
> 4. Consumption increases.
>
> It is not clear when he would come to the statement "prices rise" but it would surely be late in his list.[52]

The channels through which Keynesians say that any change in interest rates is transmitted throughout the economy is elegantly illustrated in Chart II. This depicts the flow chart of the large Keynesian MPS model employed by the Federal Reserve. This is the 1969 version of the Model and in it, monetary policy affects income in three ways.

1. **The wealth effect** - interest rates fall, bond and stock prices rise, households feel wealthier and consume more.

2. **The cost of capital effect** - interest rates fall and all kinds of capital investment will rise.

3. **The credit availability effect** - as monetary policy expands available credit, more potential borrowers are able to obtain loans.

The differences between the ways Keynesians and Monetarists look at interest rates are extraordinary.

In the St. Louis Model, the long term interest rate equation is used to provide a coefficient in the formation of price anticipations. (Table VI) AC state that the long term interest

CHART II

First-Round Effects of Monetary Policy in the MPS Model

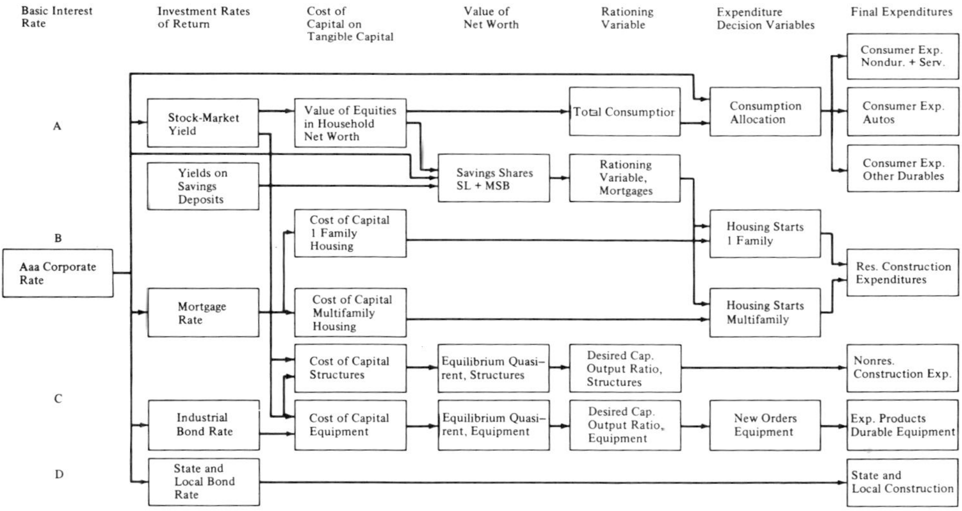

Note: This is the 1969 version of the model.
SOURCE: *Federal Reserve Bulletin,* June 1969, p. 484.

rate reflect's Milton Friedman's view that monetary expansion influences market interest rates in three stages - not channels! They are:

1. **The liquidity effect** - the purchase of government securities by the Federal Reserve from bond dealers in order to increase the monetary base will require it to pay a higher price than is then existing - thereby lowering interest rates minimally and momentarily.

2. **The spending effect** - total spending for goods and services (real output) increases and will cause prices to rise.

3. **The inflation effect** - rising prices will lead to anticipations of further inflation. Lenders will add a Fisherian inflation premium in order to offset the losses in real return which they foresee, thereby raising interest rates.

Thus AC specify that long-term interest rates depend on:

1. **The current rate of change in the money stock** (M). As illustrated in Table VII, an increase of 1% per annum in M will lower interest rates by .06%, ceteris paribus.

2. **Current and past rates of change of real output** (X). If real output increases by 1% per annum this will cause interest rates to rise by .20%, ceteris paribus.

TABLE VII

SHORT-TERM INTEREST RATE EQUATION

Sample Period: I/1955 - IV/1969

Constraints: 2nd Degree Polynomial

$(x_{-1} \neq 0,\ p_{-1} \neq 0;\ x_{11} = p_{11} = 0)$

$$RS_t = \underset{(-3.14)}{-1.13} \; \underset{(-6.36)}{-\ .17\dot{M}_t} + \underset{(5.03)}{.92Z_t} + \sum_{i=0}^{10} x_i \dot{X}_{t-i} + \sum_{i=0}^{10} p_i \left(\frac{\dot{P}_{t-i}}{U_{t-i}/4}\right)$$

$R^2 = .90$

S.E. $= .47$

D-W $= .69$

x_0	$= .08$	(8.10)	p_0	$= -.04$	$(-.91)$
x_1	$= .08$	(8.99)	p_1	$= .04$	(1.53)
x_2	$= .08$	(8.97)	p_2	$= .09$	(8.26)
x_3	$= .08$	(8.45)	p_3	$= .14$	(18.52)
x_4	$= .08$	(7.83)	p_4	$= .17$	(13.17)
x_5	$= .07$	(7.25)	p_5	$= .18$	(10.29)
x_6	$= .07$	(6.76)	p_6	$= .19$	(8.92)
x_7	$= .06$	(6.36)	p_7	$= .18$	(8.14)
x_8	$= .05$	(6.02)	p_8	$= .15$	(7.64)
x_9	$= .03$	(5.75)	p_9	$= .11$	(7.30)
x_{10}	$= .02$	(5.52)	p_{10}	$= .06$	(7.04)
Σx_i	$= .71$	(8.24)	Σp_i	$= 1.27$	(16.89)

Symbols are defined as:

RS_t = four- to six-month commercial paper rate in quarter t

$\dot{M}_t$ = annual rate of change in money stock in quarter t

Z_t = dummy variable in quarter t (0 for I/1955 - IV/1960 and 1 for I/1961 - IV/1969)

$\dot{X}_{t-i}$ = annual rate of change in output (GNP in 1958 prices) in quarter t—i

$\dot{P}_{t-i}$ = annual rate of change in GNP deflator (1958 = 100) in quarter t—i

$U_{t-i}/4$ = index of unemployment as a per cent of labor force (base = 4.0) in quarter t—i

Note: "t" statistics appear with each regression coefficient, enclosed by parentheses. R^2 is the percent of variation in the dependent variable which is explained by variations in the independent variables. S.E. is the standard error of the estimate. D-W is the Durbin-Watson statistic.

Source: Leonall Andersen and Keith Carlson, "A Monetarist Model for Economic Stabilization" Federal Reserve Bank of St. Louis Review, April 1970, p.15.

3. **Current and past changes of prices adjusted by an index of the unemployment rate.** If this figure rises by 1% per annum, this will cause interest rates to rise by .96%, ceteris paribus.

For completion, AC's short-term interest rate equation is illustrated in Table VII. The underlying theory is the same as that of the long-term interest rate equation - but the coefficients are slightly different. However, like the Unemployment and Long-term interest rate equations, while the R^2 and S.E. statistics are excellent, the Durbin-Watson statistics are very low and suggest autocorrelation.

Blinder and Solow comment:

> The interest rate equation has the property that if the annual rates of change of the money stock and real output are constant (and if price expectations are also given) the interest rate is determined **independently of the numerical values of these rates of change**. (emphasis in original.)[53]

They also note that AC 'use ordinary least squares throughout even though several equations contain contemporanious endogenous variables on the right side'.[54]

WHAT IS THE RESPONSE TO AN INCREASE IN THE MONEY STOCK?

If we suppose that the money stock is increased by $1.00 at any moment in time, what is the response as between the nominal output, the price level and real output?

CHART III

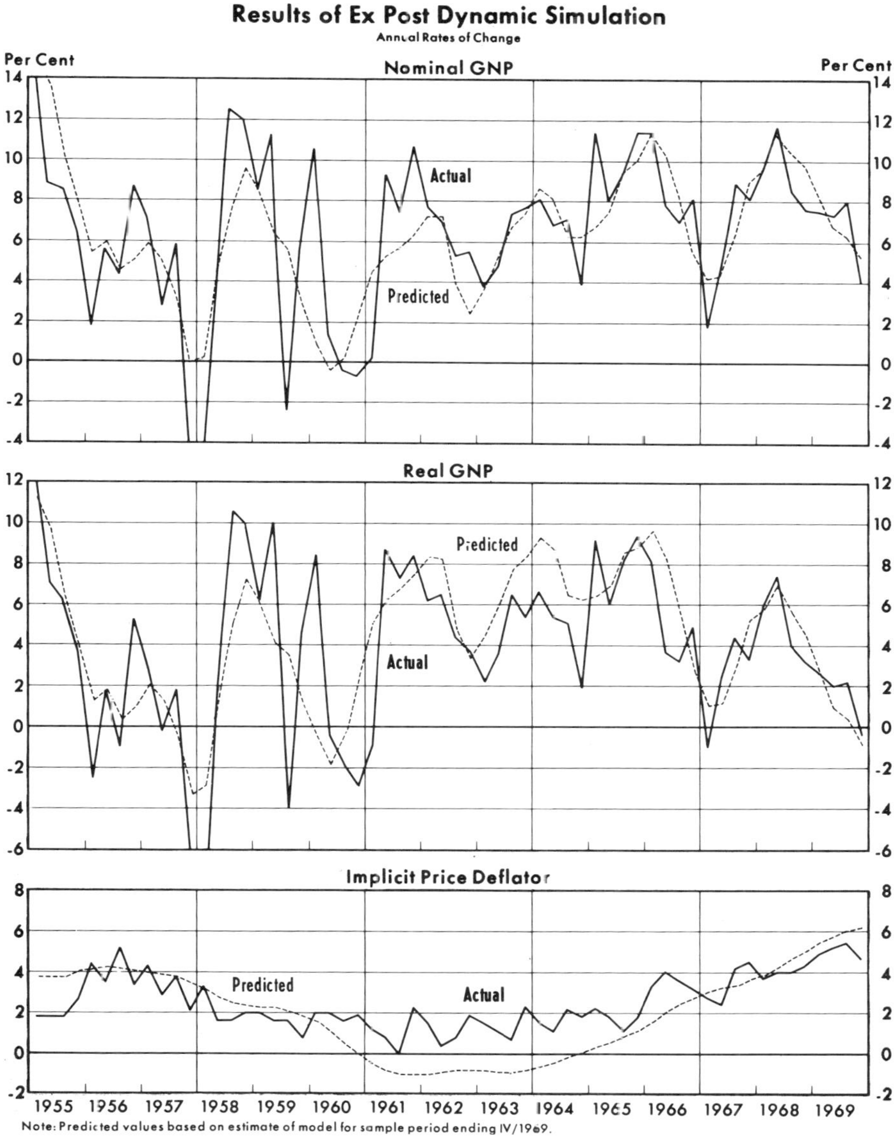

Source: Leonall Andersen and Keith Carlson, "A Monetarist Model for Economic Stabilization" Federal Reserve Bank of St. Louis Review, April 1970, p.14.

Using the percentage figures provided by AC, [55] one can draw up a tabulation which will illustrate, in approximate terms, how the St. Louis Model's spending, price and output equations would respond to this $1.00 stimulus.

Response to a $1.00 increase in the Money Stock
Expressed in Dollar Terms

	M	Y	P	X
t_0	$1.00	$1.22	$ 0	$1.22
t_1		$1.80	$ 0	$1.80
t_2		$1.62	$ .40	$1.22
t_3		$ .87	$ .43	$ .44
t_4		$ .06	$ .04	$ .02
	$1.00	$5.57	$ .87	$4.70

These results tell us that if the monetary authorities increase the money stock by $1.00, at the end of the subsequent 5 quarters, nominal GNP will have increased by $5.57, of which sum approximately 85% will be reflected in real output and approximately 15% in price increases.

In order to evaluate these equations, several experiments were performed and the result of one ex post simulation is illustrated in Chart III. Actual values for the current and lagged exogenous values were used, but only the initial actual values for the lagged endogenous values were employed. The model generates solution values for the endogenous variables in the first simulation period which are then used to generate solution values for the second period, and so on for each succeeding period.

AC feel that the tendency for the model to avoid diverging sharply from the actual path for extended periods provides a basis for trusting the tracking ability of the model over several quarters, even if on a quarter to quarter basis it may appear to be off the mark.

TABLE VIII

ALTERNATIVE EX POST SIMULATIONS: ACTUAL MINUS PREDICTED[1]

Comparison of Wharton and St. Louis Models for 1963-64

	Nominal GNP[2]		Real GNP[2]		Price Level[3]		Unemployment Rate[4]	
	Wharton	St. Louis	Wharton	St. Louis	Wharton	St. Louis	Wharton	St. Louis
1963: I	−4.6	0.4	−3.9	−0.4	−0.1	0.2	0.9	0.3
II	−0.2	0.3	0.4	−0.7	−0.1	0.2	0.7	0.1
III	1.3	1.5	2.5	0.6	−0.3	0.1	0.9	−0.1
IV	0.9	2.1	2.2	−0.4	−0.2	0.5	1.2	0.2
1964: I	0.9	1.7	2.7	−1.4	−0.3	0.6	1.4	0.2
II	1.1	0.1	2.3	−3.2	−0.3	0.6	1.4	0.2
III	1.5	1.7	4.0	−2.7	−0.5	0.8	1.6	0.2
IV	0	−1.7	2.2	−6.8	−0.4	0.9	1.2	0.2
Average Error	0.11	0.76	1.55	−1.88	−0.28	0.49	1.16	0.16
Root Mean Squared Error	2.00	1.49	2.92	3.09	0.33	0.60	1.28	0.21

[1]Sample period:
Wharton: 1948-1964
St. Louis: 1955-1969

Exogenous variables:
Wharton: 43
St. Louis: 3

[2]Billions of dollars.

[3]Computed from the level of implicit price deflator.

[4]Per cent.

Sources: M. K. Evans and L. R. Klein, *The Wharton Econometric Forecasting Model*, 2nd, Enlarged Edition (Philadelphia: University of Pennsylvania, 1968); and Federal Reserve Bank of St. Louis.

Source: Leonall Andersen and Keith Carlson, "A Monetarist Model for Economic Stabilization" Federal Reserve Bank of St. Louis Review, April 1970, p.16.

Another interesting test that was done was to compare the results obtained for the years 1963 and 1964 with those obtained by the Keynesian based Wharton model for that period. This comparison was of interest for two reasons, firstly, the Wharton model contained forty-three primary exogenous variables whereas the St. Louis model had only three, and secondly, this period included the 1964 tax cut which is of prime importance to Keynesian theory, but is given only minimal influence in the St. Louis model.

The results are illustrated in Table VIII, and they show that the St. Louis model did about as well as the Wharton model in this period. This is really not unexpected because the money supply was expanded with the expanding economy during this period. As Arthur Okun has said:

> Both preceding and following the enactment of the tax cut, (in 1964) monetary strategy was geared to provide the reserves needed to stabilize interest rates and the availability of credit.[56]

The question as to whether it was the reduction of taxes or the expanding money stock which was responsible for the growth of output and employment following the enactment of the tax cut in February 1964, was the subject of a subsequent dialogue between Milton Friedman and Arthur Okun to which reference will be made in Chapter VI.

USE OF THE MODEL FOR CURRENT ANALYSIS

Now that the St. Louis Fed had a model which did comparatively well in ex post simulation, it was time to try out its predictive powers and see how creditably it could provide the specific kinds of information desired by President Francis and Governor Maisel.

How did it do?

There are two issues of the Review which deal with the answer. The first is contained in Keith Carlson's article in the February 1972 Review, entitled "Projecting with the St. Louis Model - A Progress Report".

Carlson focussed on a six-quarter time period commencing January 1, 1970 and ending June 30, 1971. The period ended then because of the fact that President Nixon instituted price and wage controls in August 1971. As he says:

> The St. Louis model is small in size and not designed for quarter to quarter forecasting because many factors are known to influence short-run movements in economic activity.[57]

An example is the major automobile strike of quarter IV of 1970 and its subsequent settlement. Such influences are the reason that the coefficient of determination of the 1970 spending equation is $R^2 = 0.66$; meaning that movements of the variables M and E in that equation explain just two-thirds of the changes in Y. That such activities can influence nominal GNP can be seen in the changes which occurred in that variable at this time:

	1970 III	**1970 IV**	**1971 I**	**1971 II**
Percentage increase in nominal GNP from previous quarter	6.8	1.5	16.0	8.0

Thus Carlson goes on to say, "for this reason, the model's performance is examined for a six-quarter period as a whole rather than quarter by quarter".

Three simulations were done and each is compared to the actual results of that period. These simulations were:

1. **Ex post** - It was based on coefficients estimated with data for the variables of the model through the second quarter of 1971, and used observed values for money and Federal expenditures to drive the model in the simulation period.

2. **Ex ante A** - It was based on coefficients estimated from data through the fourth quarter of 1969 - then like the ex post simulation, it used actual values of the money stock and Federal expenditures to drive the model.

3. **Ex ante B** - It was based on the 1969 model and then used steady state growths of money - at the actual average rates of 6.5% for M and 8.6% for E during the period under review.

Error	**Defined as**
Actual minus ex post	Unexplained
Ex post minus ex ante A	Due to changing economic structure
Ex ante A minus Ex ante B	Due to steady rate assumption
Actual minus Ex ante B	Total error

These sources of error are outlined in Table IX and expressed in percentage terms. Carlson makes an interesting observation in this connection:

> Rates of change in total spending, real product and prices are emphasized because the part of the model relating to these variables is estimated in first difference form, reflecting greater confidence in the statistical reliability of first difference estimates in the GNP accounts than of levels.[58]

By 1978 this confidence in first difference estimates was to do a complete reversal when a statistical problem developed. Thereafter the model was to be defined in rates of change.

TABLE IX

SOURCES OF ERROR IN ST. LOUIS MODEL*

(Percent)

	1970				1971		Six-Quarter Average
	I	II	III	IV	I	II	
Total Spending							
Total error	−2.7	−1.7	−2.0	−6.8	5.5	−0.5	−1.37
Unexplained error	−1.6	−2.0	−0.5	−4.0	7.7	−1.5	−0.32
Error due to changing economic structure	−0.2	−0.3	−0.5	−0.3	0.5	0.5	−0.05
Error due to steady rate assumption	−0.9	0.6	−1.0	−2.5	−2.7	0.5	−1.00
Real Product							
Total error	−3.8	−1.2	−1.9	−7.7	4.7	0.2	−1.62
Unexplained error	−2.4	−1.1	−0.1	−4.7	7.1	−0.5	−0.28
Error due to changing economic structure	−0.6	−0.7	−0.9	−0.6	0.0	0.0	−0.47
Error due to steady rate assumption	−0.8	0.6	−0.9	−2.4	−2.4	0.7	−0.87
Prices							
Total error	1.5	−0.5	0.1	1.3	0.4	−0.7	0.35
Unexplained error	1.1	−0.9	−0.3	1.0	0.2	−0.9	0.03
Error due to changing economic structure	0.4	0.5	0.4	0.4	0.5	0.4	0.43
Error due to steady rate assumption	0.0	−0.1	0.0	−0.1	−0.3	−0.2	−0.12
Unemployment Rate							
Total error	−0.3	0.0	0.3	0.9	0.8	0.9	0.43
Unexplained error	−0.3	−0.1	0.1	0.6	0.3	0.2	0.13
Error due to changing economic structure	0.0	0.1	0.1	0.2	0.3	0.2	0.15
Error due to steady rate assumption	0.0	0.0	0.1	0.1	0.2	0.5	0.15
Corporate Aaa Rate							
Total error	0.7	0.8	0.8	0.3	−0.4	−0.2	0.33
Unexplained error	0.3	0.5	0.5	0.0	−0.5	0.0	0.13
Error due to changing economic structure	0.3	0.3	0.2	0.3	0.2	0.2	0.25
Error due to steady rate assumption	0.1	0.0	0.1	0.0	−0.1	−0.4	−0.05
Commercial Paper Rate							
Total error	1.5	1.1	0.6	−0.9	−2.5	−1.9	−0.35
Unexplained error	1.1	1.1	0.6	−0.8	−1.7	−0.5	−0.03
Error due to changing economic structure	0.1	0.0	−0.1	−0.2	−0.2	−0.1	−0.08
Error due to steady rate assumption	0.3	0.0	0.1	0.1	−0.6	−1.3	−0.23

*Total error = actual — ex ante B
Unexplained error = actual — ex post
Error due to changing economic structure = ex post — ex ante A
Error due to steady rate assumption = ex ante A — ex ante B

Source: Keith Carlson, Projecting with the St. Louis Model: A Progress Report", Federal Reserve Bank of St. Louis Review (February, 1972), p.22.

TABLE X

ST. LOUIS MODEL SIMULATIONS VS. ACTUAL
(Percent)

	1970 I	1970 II	1970 III	1970 IV	1971 I	1971 II	Six-Quarter Average
ACTUAL							
Annual Rates of Change in:							
Total Spending	3.4	5.3	6.3	2.0	13.8	7.7	6.42
Real Product	−2.9	0.7	1.2	−4.0	7.9	3.4	1.05
Prices	6.6	4.6	5.1	6.3	5.4	4.2	5.37
Unemployment Rate	4.2	4.8	5.2	5.9	5.9	6.0	5.33
Corporate Aaa Rate	7.9	8.1	8.2	7.9	7.2	7.5	7.80
Commercial Paper Rate	8.6	8.2	7.8	6.3	4.6	5.0	6.75
EX POST SIMULATION[1]							
Annual Rates of Change in:							
Total Spending	5.0	7.3	6.8	6.0	6.1	9.2	6.73
Real Product	−0.5	1.8	1.3	0.7	0.8	3.9	1.33
Prices	5.5	5.5	5.4	5.3	5.2	5.1	5.33
Unemployment Rate	4.5	4.9	5.1	5.3	5.6	5.8	5.20
Corporate Aaa Rate	7.6	7.6	7.7	7.9	7.7	7.5	7.67
Commercial Paper Rate	7.5	7.1	7.2	7.1	6.3	5.5	6.78
EX ANTE A SIMULATION[2]							
Annual Rates of Change in:							
Total Spending	5.2	7.6	7.3	6.3	5.6	8.7	6.78
Real Product	0.1	2.5	2.2	1.3	0.8	3.9	1.80
Prices	5.1	5.0	5.0	4.9	4.7	4.7	4.90
Unemployment Rate	4.5	4.8	5.0	5.1	5.3	5.6	5.05
Corporate Aaa Rate	7.3	7.3	7.5	7.6	7.5	7.3	7.42
Commercial Paper Rate	7.4	7.1	7.3	7.3	6.5	5.6	6.87
EX ANTE B SIMULATION[3]							
Annual Rates of Change in:							
Total Spending	6.1	7.0	8.3	8.8	8.3	8.2	7.78
Real Product	0.9	1.9	3.1	3.7	3.2	3.2	2.67
Prices	5.1	5.1	5.0	5.0	5.0	4.9	5.02
Unemployment Rate	4.5	4.8	4.9	5.0	5.1	5.1	4.90
Corporate Aaa Rate	7.2	7.3	7.4	7.6	7.6	7.7	7.47
Commercial Paper Rate	7.1	7.1	7.2	7.2	7.1	6.9	7.10

[1]Coefficients estimated through II/1971; actual money and expenditures used in simulation.
[2]Coefficients estimated through IV/1969; actual money and expenditures used in simulation.
[3]Coefficients estimated through IV/1969; money at 6.5 percent and expenditures at 8.6 percent in simulation period. (Averages of actual quarter-to-quarter rates from I/1970 to II/1971.)

Source: Keith Carlson, Projecting with the St. Louis Model: A Progress Report", Federal Reserve Bank of St. Louis Review (February, 1972), p.24.

Anyone who is sufficiently interested to have read this book this far, will want to know in detail, not only the results that were obtained but also the reasons given by Keith Carlson for the differences in the figures. For that reason it is important to repeat his words exactly. The next six pages will do so.[57]

Carlson commences by saying that: Unexplained error provides an indication of the overall reliability of the specification of the model. Error attributable to changing economic structure provides a measure of the stability of the coefficients over time, although with the addition of only six quarters of data, this is a very weak test of parameter stability. Finally, error attributable to the steady state assumption regarding the monetary and fiscal variables sheds light on the usefulness of the model as a guide to the formulation of policy.

The results of the three types of simulations...are summarized in Table X. As noted, the sources of error as defined above are shown in Table IX. The focus of discussion is the average error for each variable, i.e., the last column of Table IX.

Assuming steady growth of moneys and expenditures at the average rate that actually occurred (ex ante B simulation), the average annual rate of change of total spending would have been overpredicted by 1.37 percentage points. Of this overprediction, 0.32 is unexplained. In other words, using all available information, including observations in the simulation period, but retaining the fundamental specification of the St. Louis model, average projection error was 0.32 percentage points for this period.

The average error associated with changing economic structure is .05 percentage points. Updating the coefficients with six additional quarters of data improves the accuracy of the total spending projection by .05 percentage points, on average.

The average error for total spending attributable to the assumption of steady growth of the policy variables is the largest, amounting to one percentage point. This pattern follows from the pattern of variability of quarter to quarter rates of change of both money and expenditures during this six-quarter period. The annual rate of change of money varied from 4.2 to 11.3 percent to yield the 6.5 percent average rate of change for the period, whereas Federal expenditures varied between -3.4 and 24 percent, averaging 8.6 percent.

Error attributable to the steady rate assumption would not normally be expected to be this large, but it is a factor to consider when using this equation for a horizon as short as six quarters. It is not only the variability but also the pattern of the variability that leads to this type of error. For example, consider Chart IV, where two patterns of money growth are shown, both of which yield the same average for the period.

Because of the lags in the impact of monetary actions, the money growth pattern in Case B will be associated with a larger growth of total spending for the period than case A. If total spending growth were considered for a longer period of time, the pattern would be irrelevant. Furthermore, the error in total spending attributable to the steady rate assumption can be traced primarily to the pattern of variation in monetary growth, rather than Federal expenditures, because of the nature of the coefficients in the total spending equation.

Money growth in 1971 is a case in point. Assuming lags in the impact of monetary actions, as used in the St. Louis model, the steady rate equivalent is calculated as follows:

CHART IV

Alternative Patterns of Money Growth

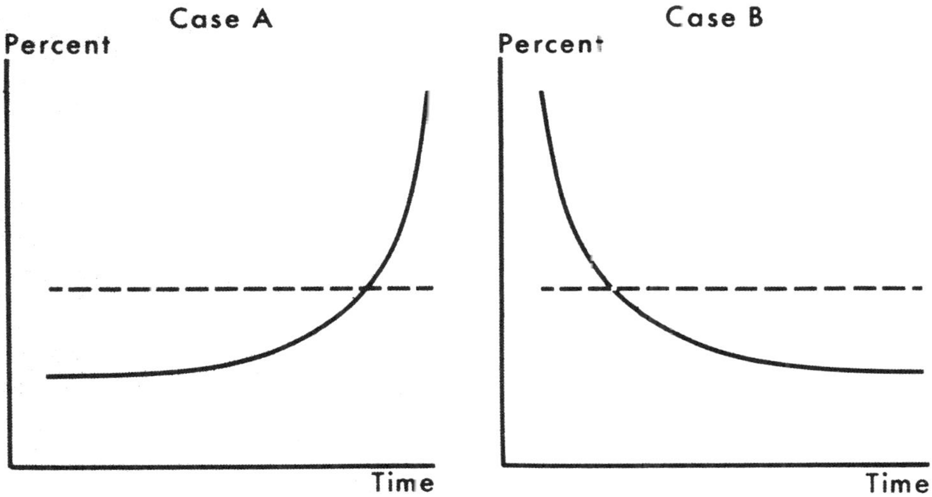

Source: Keith Carlson, Projecting with the St. Louis Model: A Progress Report", Federal Reserve Bank of St. Louis Review (February, 1972), p.25.

	Annual Rate of Change of Money	Weight	Weighted Annual Rate of Change
I/71	7.3	.375	2.74
II/71	11.3	.320	3.62
III/71	7.7	.214	1.65
IV/71	.4	.090	.04
			8.05

An unweighted average of the monetary growth rates would be 6.7 percent. The economic impact of monetary actions in 1971, though averaging a 6.7 percent growth, is the equivalent of an 8 percent steady rate in the St. Louis model.

Prices - the total error for price projections was 0.35 percentage points during the six-quarter simulation period. However, the unexplained error was negligible.

The major source of error in the price projections was associated with changing economic structure. Updating the price equation with observations from the six-quarter simulation period alters the coefficients significantly - in particular, increasing the coefficient on the weighted sum of past prices. The implications of this result are unclear, since our knowledge of the determinants of price level movements and price expectations and their interaction is so limited.

Error attributable to the steady state assumption was in a direction opposite that due to changing economic structure. In other words, the steady growth case (ex ante B) tended to predict faster inflation than when the actual course of the policy variables (ex ante A) was included in the ex ante simulations. Like total spending, the error for prices attributable to the steady rate assumption can be traced to the pattern of variation in monetary growth.

Real product - The projections of real product are dependent on those for total spending and prices because real product is calculated by subtracting from the change in total spending that portion which is associated with estimated price change. Over prediction of total spending along with underprediction of prices leads to an average overproduction of real product of 1.62 percentage points. Unexplained error is about the same as for total spending because such error is negligible for prices.

Changing economic structure accounts for a substantial portion of total error for real product, reflecting the underprediction of prices. Error due to the steady state assumption is also significant and of the same order of magnitude as for total spending projections, though it does receive some correction from such error in the price projections. The real product projections bear the brunt of two types of errors - that due to the steady state assumption in the total spending projections and that due to changing economic structure in the price expectations.

Unemployment rate - Projections of the unemployment rate can be expected to reflect the projection errors for real product. The total error associated with the unemployment rate averaged 0.43 percentage points. The total was equally divided among three categories of error.

It should be noted that the sources of error are difficult to identify for the unemployment rate because the errors are derived from full model simulations rather than the unemployment equation alone. All types of errors come into play, operating through total spending and prices, as well as the unemployment rate equation itself.

Corporate Aaa rate - Examination of the corporate Aaa rate projections indicate total error averaged 33 basis points.

Unexplained error averaged 13 basis points, but the changing economic structure is the key factor in the Aaa projections. This result is to be expected because price movements play an important role in the corporate Aaa equation. Because prices tended to be underpredicted in the ex ante A simulation, the Aaa rate is underpredicted also. There is a partial offset from the overprediction of real product growth, but clearly the price effect dominates.

Commercial paper rate - Commercial paper rate projections exhibit an average total error of about the same absolute magnitude as the corporate Aaa projection, but, in contrast, it is overpredicted. Surprisingly, both unexplained error and that due to changing economic structure are small during the simulation period. The reason is that the overprediction of real product and the underprediction of prices tend to offset each other. The price effect does not dominate the short-rate projections like it does the long-term rate.

Error attributable to the steady state assumption accounts for most of the total error in the commercial rate projections. One of the reasons is that the direct effect of money tends to be larger in the short-rate equation than for the long rate. In addition, over predictions of both real product and prices, as associated with the steady assumption effect, reinforce each other in the commercial paper rate projections.

Carlson concludes by saying that policymakers and private forecasters may find that the St. Louis model is inadequate for many of their purposes - for example, quarter by quarter forecasts or detailed forecasts of the components of GNP. Nevertheless, it is hoped that this identification of strengths and weaknesses of the model will provide further understanding on its use and interpretation.

TABLE XI

The Record of Prediction

		St. Louis[1]	Consensus[2]	Actual
1969	GNP (Billions)[3]	$957.2	$940.0	$948.0
	Prices[4]	4.1%	3.5% (6.0)[4]	5.1%
	Unemployment[5]	3.5%	4.1%	3.6%
1970	GNP	$997.2	$1007.0	$988.4
	Prices	4.6%	4.0% (5.6)	5.7%
	Unemployment	5.4%	4.6%	5.9%
1971	GNP	$1076.9	$1066.0	$1072.9
	Prices	4.0%	4.0% (3.3)	3.4%
	Unemployment	5.7%	5.6%	5.9%

[1]St. Louis predictions were made in "A Monetarist Model," this *Review* (April 1970), pp. 18-19. These predictions are based on the assumption of 6 percent money growth.

[2]Consensus predictions are from J. A. Livingston, *American Banker*, December 30, 1968, December 29, 1969 and December 28, 1970.

[3]GNP predictions and actual figures are for the fourth quarter of the year.

[4]Rate of change of prices for St. Louis predictions is the change in the GNP deflator from fourth quarter to fourth quarter, and the "actual" figure is GNP deflator. Consensus' price predictions are for the consumer price index from December to December. Actual consumer price index changes are in parentheses.

[5]The St. Louis predictions and the actual rate are for the fourth quarter, while the consensus prediction is for December.

Source: Darryl Francis "Has Monetarism Failed? The Record Examined", Federal Reserve Bank of St. Louis Review (March, 1972), p.35.

Another look at the predictive powers of the St. Louis model at this time is provided by President Francis in his speech of February 23, 1972. As one can appreciate, the difficulty which faces all models which look at the effects of monetary policy, is to forecast accurately the rate at which the Federal Reserve is going to expand or contract the money stock. Simulations were therefore done for three alternative rates:

1. A '**no-change**' case reflecting the situation in the second half of 1969.

2. A '**three percent case**' corresponding to the trend rate of increase in money from 1961 to 1965.

3. A '**six per cent case**' representing monetary actions similar to those of 1967 and 1968.

The growth of Government expenditures was based on those as projected in the fiscal 1971 budget.

In the event, the 'six per cent case' proved to be closer to the actual rate of expansion of the money stock than either of the other two cases. How did the Model do?

President Francis gives us the answer in his speech and it is illustrated in Table XI.[58] One must stress that the calculations in this table were based on the assumption of 6 percent money growth over the period as set out in the AC article of April 1970 and use of the projected 1971 federal budget to fix the high-employment expenditures for the period 1969 - 1971. The interesting feature of these figures is their comparison with the Concensus estimates found in the American Banker of December 30, 1968, December 29, 1969 and December 28, 1970 and which were made annually.

As Francis notes, the St. Louis predictions, while doing well when compared with the Consensus predictions, tended to overshoot the actual results. Thus the St. Louis figures surpassed actual GNP figures by $9 billion (.95%) in 1969, $9 billion (.91%) in 1970, and $4 billion (.38%) in 1971. However, this overshooting is understandable in the years 1969 and 1970, when the money stock (M1) increased at rates of only 3.2% and 5.1% respectively. But in the year 1971, the overshooting would have increased slightly because MI actually rose by 6.5%.

Moreover, as AC have indicated, with the money stock increasing at the end of the period, rather than at the beginning, one would expect undershooting in the first two years and overshooting in the third year. These errors would tend to offset each other.

The over-all results of the St. Louis model, for the purposes for which it was conceived, were excellent. But soon a statistical problem was to rear its ugly head.

REFERENCES

1 In conversation with the author on May 3, 1983.

2 Darryl R. Francis, "Has Monetarism Failed? Record Examined," The Federal Reserve Bank of St. Louis Review (March, 1972), p.32.

3 As related by Homer Jones in a conversation with the author.

4 Milton Friedman, Homer Jones, George Stigler, and Allen Wallis, eds., The Ethics of Competition (New York: Harper Brothers, 1935).

5 In an interview with the author, May 2, 1983.

6 Quoted from John Kenneth Galbraith, Money, Whence it Came, Where it Went (Boston: Houghton, Mifflin Company, 1975), p.216

7 Milton Friedman, "Homer Jones, A Personal Reminiscence," Journal of Monetary Economics 2 (1976), pp. 435-436.

8 A. James Meigs, "Campaigning for Monetary Reform: The Federal Reserve Bank of St. Louis in 1959 and 1960," Journal of Monetary Economics 2 (1976), p.443 (footnote).

9 The three articles were:

1. "Monetary Policy, Balance of Payments and Business Cycles: The Foreign Experience," Federal Reserve Bank of St. Louis Review, November, 1967.

2. "Monetary and Fiscal Influences on Economic Activity: The Historical Evidence," Federal Reserve Bank of St. Louis Review, November, 1969.

3. "Monetary and Fiscal Influences on Economic Activity, The Foreign Experience," Federal Reserve Bank of St. Louis Review, February, 1970.

10 Quoted in Thomas Mayer, The Structure of Monetarism (New York: W.W. Norton, 1978), p. 7 (footnote).

11 Leonall Andersen and Jerry Jordan, "Money in a Modern Quantity Framework," Federal Reserve Reserve Bank of St. Louis Review, December, 1967. p.5.

12 Ibid.

13 Federal Reserve Bulletin (September, 1967), p. 1552.

14 Darryl R. Francis, "An Approach to Monetary and Fiscal Management", Federal Reserve Bank of St. Louis Review, (November, 1968) p.7

15 Sherman Maisel, Managing the Dollar (New York: W.W. Norton, Inc. p. 168.

16 Leonall Andersen and Jerry Jordan, "Monetary and Fiscal Actions: A Test of Their Relative Importance in Economic Stabilization," Federal Reserve Bank of St. Louis Review, (November, 1968), p.11.

17 Ibid., p. 16.

18 Economic Report of the President, 1979, p.221.

19 Leonall Andersen and Jerry Jordan "Monetary and Fiscal Actions" Op. Cit. p.12.

20 James L. Pierce, "Open Market Policies and Operating Procedures - Staff Studies" (Washington, D.C.: Board of Governors of the Federal Reserve System, 1971) p. 97.

21 Milton Friedman, A Program for Monetary Stability (New York: Fordham University Press, 1960), p.87.

22 Leonall Andersen and Jerry Jordan, "Monetary and Fiscal Actions" Op. Cit. p.20.

23 Ibid., quoted in a footnote to p. 18.

24 Ibid., p. 17.

25 Alan S. Blinder and Robert M. Solow, "Analytical Foundations of Fiscal Policy," in The Economics of Public Finance, (Washington, D.C.: Brookings Institution, 1974), pp.66-67.

26 See for example:

1. Frank de Leeuw and John Kalchenbrenner, "Monetary and Fiscal Actions: A Test of Their Relative Importance in Economic Stabilization - Comment," Federal Reserve Bank of St. Louis Review (April, 1969), pp. 6-11.

2. Richard Davis, "How Much Does Money Matter? A Look at Some Recent Evidence," Federal Reserve Bank of New York Monthly Review (June, 1969), pp. 119-131.

3. E. Gerald Corrigan, "The Measurement and Importance of Fiscal Policy Changes," Federal Reserve Bank of New York Monthly Review (June,1970), pp. 133-45.

4. Edward Gramlich, "The Usefulness of Monetary and Fiscal Policy as Discretionary Stabilization Tools," Journal of Money, Credit and Banking (May, 1971), pp. 506-32.

5. Franco Modigliani and Albert Ando, "Impacts of Fiscal Actions on Aggregate Income and the Monetarist Controversy: Theory and Evidence," in Jerome Stein, ed., Monetarism (New York: New Holland Publishing Company, 1976), pp. 17-42.

27 See Equation 1.4, Exhibit B.

28 Leonall Andersen, "Additional Evidence on the Reverse - Causation Argument", Federal Reserve Bank of St. Louis Review, August, 1969.

29 P. Schmidt and R.N. Waud, "The Almon Lag Technique and the Monetary versus Fiscal Policy Debate, Journal of The American Statistical Association, (March, 1973), p. 11-19.

30 Leonall Anderson and Jerry Jordan, "Monetary and Fiscal Actions,: Op. Cit., p. 14.

31 In a conversation with the author, May 5, 1983.

32 Darryl R. Francis, "The Usefulness of Applied Econometrics to the Policymaker", Federal Reserve Bank of St. Louis Review (November, 1968) p.7.

33 Leonall Anderson and Keith Carlson, "A Monetarist Model for Economic Stabilization", Federal Serve Bank of St. Louis Review, (April, 1970) p.10.

34 W.E. Gibson and G.C. Kaufman, "The Relative Impact of Money and Income on Interest Rates, An Empirical Investigation" (Washington, D.C.: Board of Governors of the Federal Reserve System, Staff Economic Studies, 1966).

35 L.R. Klein "Comments on Modigliano and Ando", in Monetarism, J.L. Stein ed. (Amsterdam: New Holland, 1976) p. 55.

36 Milton Friedman "Comments on Tobin and Buiter", in Monetarism, J.L. Stein ed., (Amsterdam, New Holland, 1976) p. 315.

37 Keith M. Carlson, "Inflation, Unemployment and Money, Comparing the Evidence from Two Simple Models", Federal Reserve Bank of St. Louis Review (September, 1978), p.3.

38 Leonall Andersen and Keith Carlson "A Monetarist Model for Economic Stabilization" Op. Cit., p. 11.

39 Milton Friedman, "A Theoretical Framework for Monetary Analysis: in R. Gordon, ed., Milton Friedman's Monetary Framework (Chicago: University of Chicago Press 1974). p.9.

40 Alan S. Blinder and Robert M. Solow, "Analytical Foundations of Fiscal Policy," in The Economics of Public Finance, (Washington, D.C.: Brookings Institution, 1974), p.88.

41 Leonall Andersen and Keith Carlson "A Monetarist Model for Economic Stabilization" Op. Cit., p. 11.

42 Franco Modigliani and Albert Ando, 'Impacts of Fiscal Actions on Aggregate Income and The Monetarist Controversy: Theory and Evidence", in Monetarism, J.L. Stein, ed. (Amsterdam, New Holland, 1976)m p. 17-42.

43 R.J. Gordon, "Comments on Modglianai and Ando" - Monetarism J.L. Stein, ed. (Amsterdam, New Holland, 1976), pp. 60-65.

44 Ibid. p. 63.

45 John Maynard Keynes, The General Theory of Employment, Interest and Money (London,: The Macmillan Press, Ltd., 1936), p. 296.

46 Laurence Meyer and Chris Varvares, "A Comparison of the St. Louis Model and Two Variations: Predictive Performance and Policy Implications", Federal Reserve Bank of St. Louis Review (December, 1981), p. 15.

47 In a personal letter to the author.

48 Otto Eckstein, The Great Recession with a Postscript on Stagflation (Amsterdam: North Holland, 1978), p. 163.

49 Milton Friedman, The Counter-Revolution in Monetary Theory, Institute for Economic Affairs, 1970, p. 23.

50 Peter Kenyon "Pricing" in A Guide to Post Keynesian Economics (White Plains, N.Y.: M.S. Sharpe 1970) p.34.

CHAPTER FIVE

THE CHANGING FACE OF THE ST. LOUIS MODEL - 1970-1983

> There cannot, in short, be intrinsically a more insignificant thing in the economy of society, than money; except in the character of a contrivance for sparing time and labour. It is a machine for doing quickly and commodiously, what would be done, though less quickly and commodiously, without it; and like many other kinds of machinery, it only exerts a distinct and independent influence of its own when it gets out of order.
>
> John Stuart Mill[1]
> 1848

John Stuart Mill tells us that money can get out of order, and the St. Louis Fed during the decade of the 1970's was to learn that its model could also get out of order, not only statistically but also through such exogenous influences as Federal wage and price controls and the OPEC oil cartel.

Generally the model is updated each quarter but sometimes a "fluke" quarter will enter into the decision, and a sample period is used that ends elsewhere. This is where judgment enters into the process; inspection is done informally in light of considerations of parameter stability.[2]

Thus by February 1972, it was clear that the St. Louis Model could not forecast short-run price changes because of the wage-price controls which were instituted in August, 1971. So the price equation was temporarily put in drydock. As an alternative, Andersen and Carlson suggested to another investigator that he employ a price equation using changes in the supply of money

TABLE XII

Estimated Equations of the St. Louis Model*

I. Total Spending Equation

A. Sample period: I/1953 – IV/1968 — $R^2 = .632$

$\Delta Y_t = 2.30 + 5.35\,\Delta M_{t-i} + .05\,\Delta E_{t-i}$ — S.E. = 3.948

(2.69) (6.69) (.15) — D-W = 1.741

B. Sample period: I/1953 – II/1973 — $R^2 = .683$

$\Delta Y_t = 1.52 + 5.30\,\Delta M_{t-i} + .54\,\Delta E_{t-i}$ — S.E. = 5.169

(1.59) (8.10) (1.36) — D-W = 1.894

II. Price Equation

A. Sample period: I/1955 – IV/1968 — $R^2 = .788$

$\Delta P_t = 2.95 + .09\,D_{t-i} + .73\,\Delta P_t^A$ — S.E. = 1.072

(6.60) (9.18) (5.01) — D.E. = 1.415

B. Sample period: I/1955 – II/1973 — $R^2 = .748$

$\Delta P_t = 2.46 + .09\,D_{t-i} + .96\,\Delta P_t^A$ — S.E. = 2.350

(5.03) (6.00) (12.92) — D-W = 1.408

III. Unemployment Rate Equation

A. Sample period: I/1955 – IV/1968 — $R^2 = .915$

$U_t = 3.94 + .06\,G_t + .26\,G_{t-i}$ — S.E. = .307

(67.42) (1.33) (6.15) — D.W. = .596

B. Sample period: I/1955 – II/1973 — $R^2 = .918$

$U_t = 3.90 + .04\,G_t + .29\,G_{t-i}$ — S.E. = .293

(77.00) (1.00) (8.20) — D-W = .647

IV. Long-Term Interest Rate

* Constraints and lag structures correspond to those set forth in the original article discussing the St. Louis model. See Andersen and Carlson, [4]. Coefficient values on lagged variables (subscripted "$t-i$") are sums of the coefficients for current and lagged quarters. Figures enclosed by parentheses under the coefficients are "t" statistics.

Source: Leonall Andersen and Keith Carlson, "St. Louis Model Revisited", *International Economic Review*, (June, 1974) pp. 325-326.

A. Sample period: I/1955 — IV/1968 $R^2 =$ .854

$$R_t^L = 1.28 - .05\dot{M}_t + 1.39\,Z_t + .20\dot{X}_{t-i} + .97\,\dot{P}/(U/4)_{t-i} \quad \text{S.E.} = .306$$
$$(4.63)(-2.40)(8.22)\quad(2.55)\quad(11.96) \qquad \text{D-W} = .564$$

B. Sample period: I/1955 — II/1973 $R^2 =$ .954

$$R_t^L = 1.44 - .04\dot{M}_t + 1.50\,Z_t + .12\dot{X}_{t-i} + .99\,\dot{P}/(U/4)_{t-i} \quad \text{S.E.} = .320$$
$$(5.46)(-2.11)(12.03)\quad(1.67)\quad(21.81) \qquad \text{D-W} = .652$$

V. Short-Term Interest Rate Equation

A. Sample period: I/1955 — IV/1968 $R^2 =$ .839

$$R_t^S = -.84 - .11\dot{M}_t + .50\,Z_t + .75\dot{X}_{t-i} + 1.06\dot{P}/(U/4)_{t-i} \quad \text{S.E.} = .443$$
$$(-2.43)(-3.72)(2.78)\quad(9.28)\quad(12.24) \qquad \text{D-W} = .593$$

B. Sample period: I/1955 — II/1973 $R^2 =$ .827

$$R_t^S = -.44 - .12\dot{M}_t + .89\,Z_t + .54\dot{X}_{t-i} + 1.16\dot{P}/(U/4)_{t-i} \quad \text{S.E.} = .679$$
$$(-1.02)(-3.23)(3.66)\quad(5.18)\quad(13.23) \qquad \text{D-W} = .495$$

Symbols are defined as:

ΔY = dollar change in total spending (GNP in current prices)
ΔM = dollar change in money stock
ΔE = dollar change in high-employment federal expenditures
ΔP = dollar change in total spending (GNP in current prices) due to price change
$D = Y - (X^F - X)$
X^F = potential output
X = output (GNP in 1958 prices)
ΔP^A = anticipated price change (scaled in dollar units)
U = unemployment as a percent of labor force
$G = ((X^F - X)/X^F) \cdot 100$
R^L = Moody's seasoned corporate AAA bond rate
$\dot{M}$ = annual rate of change in money stock
Z = dummy variable (0 for I/1955 — IV/1960) and (1 for I/1961 — end of regression period)
$\dot{X}$ = annual rate of change in output (GNP in 1958 prices)
$\dot{P}$ = annual rate of change in GNP price deflator (1958 = 100)
$U/4$ = index of unemployment as a percent of labor force (base = 4.0)
R^S = four- to six-month prime commercial paper rate.

instead of the price expectations variable in determining the change in the price level.[3]

ST. LOUIS MODEL REVISITED

By 1974 it was time to look at the St. Louis model and see how it had survived the previous four years. The results were published in a paper titled as is this section and it will draw heavily on that article.[4]

Leonall Andersen and Keith Carlson explain again:

> ...the model was not designed for exact quarter-to-quarter forecasting. Its purpose rather, was to indicate the general nature of the differential response of certain key economic variables to alternative course of monetary and fiscal action ...A reduced form approach is not without its dangers, but the results based on this approach represent an important addition to the results of existing models.[5]

In Table XII we see the changes in the coefficients which developed in the period from IV/1968 to II/1973. The points of interest that the authors make are as follows:

TOTAL SPENDING (GNP)

The projected annual rate of increase for GNP was understated by .4 of a percentage point, broken into two periods that tended to offset each other. The first subperiod IV/1968 to III/1971 saw an overestimate of 1.1 percent while the subsequent period from IV/1971to II/1973 saw an underestimate of 3.4 percent. AC state that the problem was one of capturing the changes in velocity during the period. This question will be looked at in detail in Chapter 8.

PRICES

In the period before price controls IV/1968 to II/1971 the model underestimated projected inflation at a 4.4 percent average annual rate whereas the actual increase was 5.3 percent. Interestingly the Nixon price controls did not affect the model's projections too greatly. From II/1971 to II/1973 the model projected a 4.6 percent average annual rate compared to the actual increase of 4.1 percent.

OUTPUT

The results were the same as they had been for total spending - but over the whole period, output was overestimated while total spending was underestimated.

UNEMPLOYMENT

Projections showed greater accuracy over short periods than for long periods. The estimates for unemployment reflect the learning characteristics of the price equation, since it determines how much real output is contained in nominal GNP - for it is real output which is the chief determinant of unemployment. The D-W rate is still very low, indicating autocorrelation.

INTEREST RATE

Projections of the long term corporate bond rate were surprisingly accurate, showing an error of only .3 of a percentage point for the full period. Again, the D-W rate is very low.

These St. Louis forecasts were relatively good considering that they could only be made on the basis of steady growth rates of money and no revisions in the data. Since these ingredients are rarely, if ever, attained - the model can never be expected to forecast with absolute accuracy.

A HARBINGER OF A STATISTICAL PROBLEM

A review of the equations shows that one coefficient had dramatically altered during the previous four and one-half years. Namely the multiplier of high-employment government expenditures in the total spending equation. Whereas for the sample period I/1953 - IV 1968, the equation was:

A $$Y_t = \underset{(2.69)}{2.30} + \underset{(6.69)}{5.35}\,M_{t-i} + \underset{(.15)}{.05}\,E_{t-i} \qquad R^2 = .632,\ S.E. = 3.948,\ DW = 1.741$$

for sample period I/1953 - II/1973, the equation was:

B $$Y_t = \underset{(1.59)}{1.52} + \underset{(8.10)}{5.30}\,M_{t-i} + \underset{(1.36)}{.54}\,E_{t-i} \qquad R2 = .683,\ S.E. = 5.169,\ DW = 1.894$$

The effect of high employment government expenditures has increased by ten times from .05 to .54 - certainly enough to make such expenditures important factors in total GNP.

Now for each \$1.00 increase in government spending, GNP rose not by .05¢, but rather .54¢ over the course of five quarters. Moreover, the equation was to become even more Keynesian. In 1977, Benjamin M. Friedman, using data running into 1976 came up with the following results.[6]

C Sample period I/1953 - II/1976

$$Y_t = \underset{(0.40)}{0.55} + \underset{(6.30)}{4.94}\,M_{t-i} + \underset{(4.30)}{1.42}\,E_{t-i} \qquad R^2 = .70,\ S.E. = 7.55,\ DW = 1.93$$

TABLE XIII

EFFECT OF UPDATING ST. LOUIS EQUATION

$$\Delta Y_t = \text{constant} + \sum_{i=0}^{4} m_i \Delta M_{t-i} - \sum_{i=0}^{4} e_i \Delta E_{t-i}$$

	Sample Period: I/1953—IV/1969		Sample Period: I/1953—IV/1976	
m_0	1.37	(2.96)	2.24	(4.04)
m_1	1.92	(7.62)	1.55	(4.39)
m_2	1.58	(3.96)	.43	(.88)
m_3	.63	(2.59)	.07	(.21)
m_4	−.24	(−.52)	.40	(.70)
Σm_i	5.26	(8.01)	4.48	(5.98)
e_0	.48	(2.32)	.34	(1.83)
e_1	.52	(4.07)	.25	(1.80)
e_2	.15	(.81)	.21	(1.34)
e_3	−.40	(−3.07)	.36	(2.65)
e_4	−.67	(−3.22)	.48	(2.47)
Σe_i	.07	(.21)	1.64	(4.50)
Constant	2.32	(2.82)	.45	(.35)
R^2	.69		.70	
S.E.	3.97		7.55	
D.W.	1.93		1.77	

Source: K.M. Carlson "Does the St. Louis Equation Now Believe in Fiscal Policy"? Federal Reserve Bank of St. Louis Review, (February, 1978) p. 15.

Now a \$1 increase in government spending in a quarter would increase nominal income by \$1.42 over five quarters and this result was statistically significant. Thus, Friedman concluded, "this was not very dissimilar to the values reported in familiar non-monetarist models." Monetary policy was still the dominant force but he concluded his article by remarking "Even the St. Louis Model now believes in fiscal policy."[7]

In February 1978, Keith Carlson answered Friedman's charge in an article entitled "Does the St. Louis Equation Now Believe in Fiscal Policy"? The sample period had been extended to IV/1976 and seemingly served to confirm and strengthen Friedman's results.

D Sample period I/1953 - IV/1976

$$Y_t = \underset{(.35)}{0.45} + \underset{(5.93)}{4.48}\, M_{t-i} + \underset{(4.50)}{1.64}\, E_{t-i} \qquad \begin{array}{lcl} R^2 & = & .70 \\ S.E. & = & 7.55 \\ DW & = & 1.77 \end{array}$$

In the comparison shown in Table XIII, the increase of the S.E. from 3.97 to 7.55 is particularly large in statistical terms.

Tests were done to see if revised data could be the source of such a large fiscal multiplier. However, data through February 1978 gave results virtually identical to the original 1970 total spending equation.

E Sample period I/1953 - February 1978

$$Y_t = \underset{(2.82)}{2.32} + \underset{(8.01)}{5.26}\, M_{t-i} + \underset{(0.21)}{.07}\, E_{t-i}$$

To try and understand what had happened, the error pattern of the spending equation was examined in detail and the variance of the

ALTERNATIVE SPECIFICATION OF ST. LOUIS EQUATION

$$\dot{Y}_t = \text{constant} + \sum_{i=0}^{4} m_i \dot{M}_{t-i} + \sum_{i=0}^{4} e_i \dot{E}_{t-i}$$

	Sample Period: I/1953—IV/1969		Sample Period: I/1953—IV/1976	
m_0	.30	(2.06)	.40	(2.96)
m_1	.47	(5.90)	.41	(5.26)
m_2	.38	(3.01)	.25	(2.14)
m_3	.09	(1.19)	.06	(.71)
m_4	−.16	(−1.10)	−.05	(−.37)
Σm_i	1.08	(4.95)	1.06	(5.59)
e_0	.07	(1.77)	.08	(2.26)
e_1	.09	(3.63)	.06	(2.52)
e_2	.03	(.75)	.00	(.02)
e_3	−.09	(−3.68)	−.06	(−2.20)
e_4	−.16	(−4.07)	−.07	(−1.83)
Σe_i	−.06	(−.88)	.03	(.40)
Constant	3.22	(4.04)	2.69	(3.23)
R^2	.53		.40	
S.E.	3.25		3.75	
D.W.	1.85		1.78	

Source: K.M. Carlson "Does the St. Louis Equation Now Believe in Fiscal Policy"? Federal Reserve Bank of St. Louis Review, (February, 1978) p. 17.

error term showed that for the sample period I/1953 -IV/1976, the equation was plagued by heteroscadisity. In the circumstances it was decided to rework the equation using the rate of change method, mentioned but not demonstrated in the original 1968 Andersen-Jordan article. This is a standard statistical approach to eliminate the problem and it did so.

Using rate of change in place of first differences, the results are seen in Table XIV. Quantitatively, the new spending equation for the sample period I/1953 - IV/1976 was:

$$\dot{Y}_t = \underset{(3.23)}{2.69} + \underset{(5.59)}{1.06}\,\dot{M}_{t-i} + \underset{(.40)}{.03}\,\dot{E}_{t-i} \qquad \begin{array}{l} R^2 = .40 \\ S.E. = 3.75 \\ D\text{-}W = 1.78 \end{array}$$

and the coefficients did not differ greatly from those obtained for the sample period I/1953 - IV/1969. Therefore, Carlson concluded, "The evidence does not support the contention that the St. Louis equation now 'believes in' fiscal policy".

It is interesting to note that the R^2 statistic for the original AC spending equation was .53 whereas in the new equation it has dipped to .40 - implying that the variances in M and E are responsible for only 40% of the variance in Y.

Carlson tells us that Andersen and Jordan "opted for the first difference form because it gave direct estimates of multipliers which, at the time, were more commonly used than elasticities in summarizing the economic impact of changes in policy variables."[8] They had also stated that "Test regressions of relative changes were run and they did not alter the conclusions of this article,"[9] but did not publish their results.

It is interesting to test the two methods with respect to E. To do so we note that Government expenditures in 1967 were approximately $242 billion and were equivalent to high-employment expenditures since unemployment was then 3.9%. A one percent increase in this sum would amount to $2.42 billion. Nominal GNP was approximately $800 billion. Assuming a one percent increase in high- employment government expenditures in the first quarter of 1968, one could have expected that nominal GNP would increase over that quarter and the following four quarters, as set out below:

TABLE XV. Comparison of Results

Quarter	Rate of Change Equation Using Coefficients in Sample Period I/1953 - IV.1969 (See Table XIV)	First Difference Equation Using Coefficients in Sample Period I/1953 - IV/1969 (See Table XIII)
t_o	$2.42 b.x .07 = $ .17 b.	$2.42 b. x .48 = $1.16 b.
t_1	2.42 x .09 = .22 b.	$2.42 x .52 = 1.26
t_2	2.42 x .03 = .08 b.	$2.42 x .15 = .36
t_3	2.42 x-.09 = - .22 b.	$2.42 x-.40 = - .97
t_4	2.42 x-.16 = - .39 b.	$2.42 x-.67 = -1.62
Total Additon to Nominal GNP	2.42 x-.06 = $-.15 b.	2.42 x .07 = $ .17 b.

In each equation the aggregate results of a one percent increase ($2.42 billion) in government spending in one quarter are so small (-$0.15 billion and $0.17 billion) and so contrary to what one would expect that one seeks theoretical reasons for these results.

Blinder and Solow suggest that if greater government expenditures are paid for by additional taxes, then these taxes are immediately incorporated into business costs and passed on to customers in the form of higher prices. These greater prices then decrease total spending by virtually the same amount that government expenditures increase it.[10] - i.e. total 'crowding out' occurs.

Milton Friedman gives an example of this kind of tax offset:

> Suppose the government had imposed a special excise tax on automobiles and had used the proceeds to pay for antipollution equipment on automobiles that it now requires each of us to pay separately. That would have been economically equivalent to the present requirement, yet it would have shown up in the national income accounts as government rather than private spending...[11]

If greater government expenditures are financed by issues of federal securities then Milton Friedman also hypothesized that there is complete 'crowding out':

> ...in connection with a deficit financed by borrowing...evidences of government debt are largely issued in place of evidences of private debt - people hold Treasury bills instead of bills issued by, for example, U.S. Steel.[12]

Moreover, as we see in Table XIV, monetary policy is shown to be most powerful in the short-term, since fully 92 percent of its influence is felt in the first three quarters and by the fifth quarter it has turned negative. No explanation is given for this last feature and one can only assume that an inflation premium is being built into interest rates at this time and as interest rates rise they choke off spending.

As noted, the new 1978 Spending equation can now be expressed as:

$$\dot{Y}_t = \underset{(3.23)}{2.69} + \underset{(5.59)}{1.06}\,\dot{M}_{t-i} + \underset{(.40)}{.03}\,\dot{E}_{t-i} \qquad \begin{array}{ll} R^2 & = .40 \\ S.E. & = 3.75 \\ DW & = 1.78 \end{array}$$

The dots above each variable symbolize rates of change in percentages.

In January 1982, St. Louis staff economist R.W. Hafer reviewed the role of fiscal policy in this spending equation from a statistical point of view and came to the following conclusions:

The fiscal policy $\dot{E}$ measures:

1. do not significantly increase the explanatory power or forecasting ability of an equation that already incorporates money growth.

2. do not exhibit stable statistical relationships with GNP growth.

3. are not exogenous with respect to GNP growth.

He goes on to say:

> The evidence suggests that fiscal actions are ineffective for stabilization purposes. Moreover the results add increasing stature to the use of monetary policy as a tool in stabilizing fluctuations in economic activity.[13]

In the body of his article he put the extreme Monetarist position thusly, "One could just as well, on average, use only money growth to predict future GNP growth."[14] As has been noted, Milton Friedman agrees wholeheartedly with Hafer.

However, Keith Carlson, as "Keeper of the Model" was not so certain and in May 1982, the Model, re-estimated for the sample period I/1960 - IV/1980 still contained a high-employment government spending variable.

From appendix "C", we note that the 1982 spending equation is equivalent to :

$$\dot{Y} = 2.44 + 1.06\,\dot{M1} + .05\,\dot{E} \qquad \begin{array}{lcl} R^2 & = & 0.39 \\ S.E. & = & 3.50 \\ DW & = & 2.02 \end{array}$$

Most monetarists agree with Hafer that money growth 'alone' determines nominal GNP growth. This is an extreme statement - it implies obtaining R^2 values of unity. Yet over the 1970 - 1982 period we see that the R^2 statistic has decreased from 0.66 to 0.39.

These R^2 statistics indicate the existence of systematic influences other than money growth on nominal GNP growth. However, Monetarism requires only that the relationship between the money growth and nominal GNP growth be one on one. This is demonstrated in the 1982 equation where a 1 percent increase in M1 will increase Y by 1.06 percent of the change in M1 - whereas a 1 percent increase in E will only increase Y by .05 percent of the changes in E.

THE SPENDING CONSTANT = VELOCITY.

An interesting facet of the shift in the equation to rates of change means that the constant now represents only the change in velocity. The spending equation can be written:

$$\dot{Y} = a_o + a_1\dot{M} + a_2\dot{E} + e.$$

the a coefficients are constants and e is a random error term. Statistical estimation of this equation generally has supported the long-run propositions that

$$a_1 = 1 \text{ and } a_2 = 0.$$

Placing these steady-state restrictions in the spending equation yields the steady-state result that

$$\dot{Y} = a_o + \dot{M} \quad \text{or} \quad \dot{Y} - \dot{M} = a_o$$

Rearranging the income Quantity Theory of Money ($\dot{Y} = \dot{M} + \dot{V}$) we see that

$$\dot{Y} - \dot{M} = \dot{V} = a_o$$

In the long-run, the St. Louis equation suggests that velocity, (i.e. the demand for money) fluctuates randomly around a fixed value which is estimated in the 1982 equation to be a 2.44 percent increase per year. All other exogenous factors such as changes in taste, consumption, investment, weather, etc., are then contained in the error term e, which is assumed to be a random variable that fluctuates about zero - changes in one factor are offset by changes in another.

THE COMPARISON - 1970 SPENDING EQUATION vs. 1982 SPENDING EQUATION

A comparison between the algebraic form of the spending equation in 1970 and that of 1982 shows little variation in its form, except as previously noted, the new equation uses rates of change rather than first differences and an error term is added for mathematical completeness. Thus:

$$1970 \quad \Delta Y_t = 2.67 + \sum_{1=0}^{4} n_i M_{t-i} + \sum_{1=0}^{4} e_i \, \Delta E_{t-i} \qquad \begin{array}{ll} R^2 & = 0.66 \\ S.E. & = 3.84 \\ DW & = 1.75 \end{array}$$

$$1982 \quad \dot{Y}_t = 2.44 + \sum_{1=0}^{4} CM_i \dot{M}_{t-i} + \sum_{1=0}^{4} CE_i \dot{E}_{t-i} + el_t \qquad \begin{array}{ll} R^2 & = .39 \\ S.E. & =3.50 \\ DW & =2.02 \end{array}$$

where $CM_i \equiv m_i$ and $CE_i \equiv e_i$.

As previously explained the 1970 demand pressure equation was:

$$D_t = y_t - (X_t^F - X_{t-i})$$

This specific was replaced in the 1982 price equation by:

$$D_t = CD_i(\dot{X}_{t-i} - \dot{X}F^*_{t-i})$$

OPEC and Potential Output

The new Potential Output variable is XF* - the Rasche-Tatom measure of potential full capacity which takes into account labour measured in man hours, the effective flow of capital services and the flow of energy resources. Thus Rasche and Tatom hold that "Higher prices of energy resources relative to the prices of labour and capital resources, resulted in a loss of economic capacity and higher output prices."[15]

In fact, they estimated that:

> ...four to five percentage points of both the higher price level and reduction in national output in 1974 were due to the increased scarcity of energy resources entailed by the quadrupling of OPEC petroleum prices.[16]

As a result, the St. Louis Fed now makes available estimates of the potential output of the United States based on these premises to economists and other interested parties as part of their service to the public. And it is the difference between this measurement of potential real output and the actual output which quantifies the "slack" in the economy - and thus the demand pressure.

However OPEC was to play havoc with the economy and affect other equations in the model. The theoretical question was whether dramatic increases in the price of crude oil could affect potential output and/or the GNP deflator. Another problem of the early 1970's was the Nixon administration's Price and Wage Controls. To what extent, if any, did they affect the price equation?

THE CHANGING PRICE EQUATION

It is in the price equation that the St. Louis Model has felt the brunt of changing world events and economic theory. Thus:

$$1970\ \Delta P_t = 2.70 + \sum_{1=0}^{5} d_i D_{t-i} + .86\ PA_t \qquad \begin{array}{ll} R^2 & = 0.87 \\ S.E. & = 1.07 \\ DW & = 1.41 \end{array}$$

$$1982\ \dot{P}_t = 0.96 + \sum_{1=0}^{5} CD_i (\dot{X}_{t-i} - \dot{XF^*}_{t-i}) + CPA\ (\dot{PA}_t)$$

$$+ \sum_{i=1}^{4} CPE_i\ (\dot{PE}_{t-1-i}) + CDUM1\ (DUM\ 1) + CDUM2\ (DUM\ 2) + e_{2t}$$

$$\begin{array}{ll} R^2 & = .80 \\ S.E. & = 1.28 \\ DW & = 1.97 \\ \hat{p} & = 0.12 \end{array}$$

Where:

$CD_1 \equiv d_i$
P = GNP deflator (1972 = 100)
PE = relative price of energy
PA = anticipated price
X = output in 1972 dollars
XF* = potential output (Rasche/Tatom)

DUM1 control dummy (III/1971 - I/1973 = 1; 0 elsewhere)
DUM2 post control dummy (I/1973 - I/1975 = 1; 0 elsewhere)

D = demand pressure equation
e = error term.

OPEC and the Price Level

It is also noticeable that the new Price equation includes a variable PE - the relative price of energy which reflects the problem with a small model of the economy - namely - that there are few ways of dealing with special factors like energy and food supply crises. With energy problems so pervasive after the OPEC cartel quadrupled prices of crude oil between 1972 and 1974, the price equation had to be modified to capture the effects of rising energy prices. Originally this was done by adding an excise tax variable to the price equation.[17] Later it was altered to use the producer price index for fuels, related products and power, lagged for four quarters.

Wage and Price Controls

In their 1974 article "St. Louis Model Revisited," Andersen and Carlson set out four shortcomings of the model to that date. One of these shortcomings was: "The St. Louis model was in no way able to predict the actions of the Cost of Living Council during the period of controls beginning in the third quarter 1971."[18]

To overcome the effects of these controls, the dummy variables DUM1 and DUM2 are introduced for the periods in which they were in effect.

PRICE EXPECTATIONS EQUATION

Originally, this equation was rather cumbersome. By 1982, it had become much less complicated.

$$1970 \qquad \Delta PA_t = Y_{t-2}\left(\left[\left(\sum_{i=1}^{17} P_i \frac{P_{t-1}}{U_{t-i/4}}\right) .01 + 1\right]^{\frac{1}{4}} - 1\right)$$

$$1982 \qquad \dot{P}A_t = \sum_{i=1}^{21} CPRL_i \,(\dot{P}_{t-i})$$

$R2 = 0.80$
$S.E. = 1.28$
$DW = 1.97$
$\hat{p} = 0.12$

Anticipated price changes is a weighted sum of past price changes with the weight obtained by estimating the coefficient $CPRL_i$ which comes from the long-term corporate interest rate and which is presumed to embody past Fisherian price anticipations and thus is used as proxy for them.

In correspondence with Keith Carlson about this particular equation, it was suggested that the change was made to PA_t to bring it into conformity with the spending equation which, as we have seen, was converted to rate of change in 1978. His answer gives an insight into how these variations come about.

> I clung to the ΔP version for a long time simply because the model simulated better than with $\dot{P}$ specification. There was a desire to have a $\dot{P}$ form for quite some time, but it wasn't until Scott Hein (another economist on the staff of the St. Louis Fed) started experimenting with specifications that a satisfactory one was obtained. The original ΔP was also deemed unnecessarily complicated.[19]

THE UNEMPLOYMENT RATE

While the unemployment rate no longer plays a role in the price expectations equation, it is interesting to see how it has changed:

$$1970 \quad U_t = \underset{(72.50)}{3.90} + \underset{(1.10)}{.04}\, G_t + \underset{(6.80)}{.28}\, G_{t-1} \qquad \begin{array}{lcr} R^2 & = & 0.92 \\ S.E. & = & .30 \\ DW & = & .60 \end{array}$$

Where:

U_t = unemployment as a percent of labour force in quarter t
G_t = XF_t - X_t .100
F_t = potential output in quarter t
X_t = output (GNP in 1958 prices) in quarter t
the constant 3.90 = the rate of unemployment which represented 'full employment.'

$$1982 \quad U_t - UF_t = \underset{(11.89)}{0.28}\,(GAP_t) + \underset{(6.31)}{0.14}\,(GAP_{t-1}) \qquad \begin{array}{lcr} R^2 & = & 0.63 \\ S.E. & = & 0.17 \\ DW & = & 1.95 \\ \hat{p}_1 & = & 1.43 \\ \hat{p}_2 & = & 0.52 \end{array}$$

U_t = unemployment as a percent of labour force in quarter t
UF = unemployment rate at full employment as determined by Peter Clark.[20]
GAP_t = $(XF_t^* - X_t)/XF_t^*) \cdot 100$
X = output in 1972 dollars
XF^* = potential output (Rasche-Tatom)

The 1982 unemployment equation no longer has a constant to represent the 'natural' rate of employment. Moreover the gap in quarter t has become very much more important than the gap in quarter t-i. While the R^2 statistic shows a reduction from 0.92 to 0.63, the DW statistic is very good at 1.95. The value of $\hat{p}_1$ and $\hat{p}_2$ represent statistical measures taken to overcome the autocorrelation which affected the 1970 equation.

THE LONG-TERM CORPORATE Aaa BOND RATE

Theoretically interest rates remain as they were in 1970, primarily an end result of the process rather than a Keynesian link in the transmission mechanism and provide part of the information necessary to measure price anticipations.

$$1970 \quad RL_t = \underset{(5.20)}{1.28} - \underset{(-3.53)}{.06}\,\dot{M}_t + \underset{(11.01)}{1.42}\,Z_t + \sum_{i=0}^{16} X_i \dot{X}_{t-i} + \sum_{i=0}^{16} P_i \left(\frac{\dot{P}_{t-i}}{U_{t} - i/4} \right) \qquad \begin{array}{l} R^2 = .92 \\ SE = .30 \\ D\text{-}W = .69 \end{array}$$

where:

RL_t = Moody's seasoned corporate Aaa bond rate in quarter t

M_t = annual rate of change in money stock in quarter t

$Xt-i$ = annual rate of change in output (GNP in 1958 prices)

Z_t = dummy variable in quarter t (0 for I/1955 - IV/1960) and 1 for I/1961 - IV/1969

P_{t-i} = annual change in GNP deflator (1958 - 199) quarter t-i

$U_{t-i/4}$ = index of unemployment as a percent of labour force (base - 4.0) in quarter t-i.

Updating the estimates of RL indicated that the coefficients on M and X were no longer significant - and its complicated form required simplification. Thus

$$1982 \quad RL_t = 2.97 + 0.96 \sum_{1=0}^{20} \dot{P}_{t-i} \qquad \begin{array}{l} R^2 = 0.32 \\ S.E. = 0.33 \\ D\text{-}W = 1.76 \\ \hat{p} = 0.94 \end{array}$$

$\dot{P}_{t-i}$ = annual change in GNP deflator (1972 = 100) in quarter t-i.

The real rate of interest is considered to be invariant at 2.97 percent and it is altered by the current and lagged changes of the GNP deflator over the last five years. The $CPRL_i$ of the Price Expectations Equation is now represented by the coefficient 0.96 demonstrated in the 1982 equation.

By 1983, it was recognised that the real rate of interest could no longer be considered invariant and the new specification is shown in Exhibit "D".[21]

$$RL_t = \underset{(3.50)}{0.87} \sum_{i=0}^{20} \dot{P}_{t-i} \qquad R^2 = 0.12 \quad S.E. = 0.32 \quad DW = 1.76 \quad \hat{p} = 1.00$$

The long term or Aaa bond rate is now estimated as a function of past inflation.

SHORT TERM INTEREST RATE EQUATION

As indicated previously Andersen and Carlson did prepare a short-term interest rate equation in 1970. It is not further mentioned in the Review and is not part of the May 1982 Revised Form of the model. However a new version is estimated in the 1983 form of the model (see Exhibit "D") as:

$$RS_t = 0.05 \sum_{i=1}^{2} \dot{PE}_{t-i} - \underset{(2.84)}{0.08}\dot{M}_t + \underset{(3.22)}{0.77} \sum_{i=0}^{16} \dot{X}_{t-i} + \underset{(5.62)}{0.97} \sum_{i=0}^{16} \dot{P}_{t-i} \qquad \bar{R}^2 = 0.32 \quad SE = 0.90 \quad DW = 1.83 \quad \hat{p} = 0.89$$

The short term or 4 month commercial paper rate is a function of contemporaneous M1 growth and current and lagged values of changes in the relative price of energy, output and prices.

One would think that the 4 month commercial paper rate would reflect what is expected to happen to the price level in the next 120 days. It is difficult to understand how the data with respect to the price level and real output lagged over a 4 year period can effect the short term interest rate.

THE MODEL'S PREDICTIVE ABILITY

Whether econometric models are useful, or course, depends on the accuracy of their predictions. As we have noted, one way to test that accuracy is to use the model to look at the immediate past and see how it would have predicted if the actual changes in the variables had been known to the operators. This Carlson and

TABLE XVI

Out-of-Sample Simulations of the Level of Output
(I/1978-IV/1980)

		Actual X_t	Dynamic Forecast of X_t	Static Forecast of X_t
1978	1	1402.30	1407.68	1407.68
1978	2	1432.8	1423.59	1418.29
1978	3	1446.7	1442.6	1450.46
1978	4	1465.8	1464.28	1466.83
1979	1	1479.9	1481.99	1480.68
1979	2	1473.4	1499.23	1493.79
1979	3	1488.2	1519.56	1489.86
1979	4	1490.6	1536.64	1502.
1980	1	1501.9	1549.85	1501.36
1980	2	1463.3	1549.62	1500.24
1980	3	1471.9	1550.79	1463.44
1980	4	1485.6	1564.83	1485.55

Out-of-Sample Simulations of Output Growth
(I/1978-IV/1980)

		Actual $\dot{X}_t$	Dynamic Forecast of $\dot{X}_t$	Static Forecast of $\dot{X}_t$
1978	1	3.14064	4.73242	4.73242
1978	2	8.98771	4.59776	4.6382
1978	3	3.93696	5.44789	5.02195
1978	4	5.38597	6.14986	5.68066
1979	1	3.90329	4.92496	4.12331
1979	2	-1.74535	4.73394	3.80707
1979	3	4.07839	5.53722	4.54416
1979	4	0.6464	4.56991	3.76167
1980	1	3.06644	3.48377	2.91739
1980	2	-9.89072	-0.059622	-0.442017
1980	3	2.37131	0.301933	0.03891
1980	4	3.77483	3.67012	3.76043

Source: Keith Carlson and Scott Hein "An Analysis of a Modified St. Louis Model", Spring conference, Washington University (St. Louis, Mo.) April 20, 1982.

TABLE XVII

Out-of-Sample Simulations of the Price Level
(I/1978-IV/1980)

		Actual P_t	Dynamic Forecast of P_t	Static Forecast of P_t
1978	1	144.93	145.004	145.004
1978	2	148.63	147.194	147.108
1978	3	151.42	149.369	150.982
1978	4	154.99	151.458	153.702
1979	1	158.16	153.542	157.428
1979	2	161.17	155.597	160.632
1979	3	164.23	157.975	164.015
1979	4	167.46	160.834	167.529
1980	1	171.23	163.959	170.958
1980	2	175.28	167.099	174.676
1980	3	179.18	170.666	179.135
1980	4	183.81	173.877	182.508

Out-of-Sample Simulation of Inflation
(I/1978-IV/1980)

		Actual $\dot{P}_t$	Dynamic Forecast of $\dot{P}_t$	Static Forecast of $\dot{P}_t$
1978	1	5.77459	5.99012	5.990112
1978	2	10.6091	6.17876	6.1471
1978	3	7.72238	6.04353	6.48022
1978	4	9.76925	5.71346	6.16474
1979	1	8.43525	5.61714	6.44064
1979	2	7.83215	5.46103	6.44068
1979	3	7.81307	6.25477	7.25002
1979	4	8.12759	7.4379	8.28056
1980	1	9.28736	8.00095	8.59385
1980	2	9.80167	7.8826	8.29668
1980	3	9.20105	8.81596	9.09033
1980	4	10.20105	8.81596	7.63969

Source: Keith Carlson and Scott Hein "An Analysis of a Modified St. Louis Model", Spring conference, Washington University (St. Louis, Mo.) April 20, 1982.

Hein have done for the 1982 version of the Model for X_t, $\dot{X}_t$, P_t and $\dot{P}_t$.

The empirical results were set out in a paper prepared by Keith Carlson and Scott Hein entitled "An Analysis of a Modified St. Louis Model," and given at the Spring Conference on Comparing the Predictive Performance of Macroeconomic Models at Washington University in St. Louis (April 20, 1982) and are outlined in Tables XVI and XVII.

Both the Dynamic and Static forecasts are ex-post results. The difference is that the dynamic forecast takes as given at the commencement of 1978 the potential output and as well, past and anticipated changes in the price level. The money stock and high-employment expenditures are altered each quarter to correspond with actual figures, and the equations are then worked out. For the static forecast, the actual figures for each quarter are used in each of the model's equations.

How close should the results conform to reality? Sherman Maisel tells us that the Council of Economic Advisors and many others use a range of plus and minus one percent as a measure of the irreducable level of uncertainty in all forecasts.[22] It is to be noted that this level is exceeded in most quarters - however, it must be remembered that crude oil prices doubled during the 1978- 1980 period with all the difficult consequences which such actions produce for estimating prices and real output.

VARIATIONS OF THE MODEL

While Keith Carlson is known as the "Keeper of the Model" - and certainly all versions have come out under his authorship, nevertheless two others are mentioned in the Review as will be detailed later.

John Tatom has formulated a reduced form equation relating GNP not only to money stock and high-employment federal expenditure variables, but it also includes variables for strikes and lagged values of the rate of change in the relative price of energy.[23]

He also has a slightly different price equation, which regresses the price variable on values of the money stock lagged over twenty quarters and enables him to conclude that "the stage of the business cycle does not affect the inflation rate." Thus he concludes, "slack" does not influence the rate of inflation independently of the course of monetary growth.[24]

Dallas Batten and R.W. Hafer have also looked at a modified version of the St. Louis spending equation. Initially they say:

> Because the equation is formulated solely to test the relative efficacy of monetary and fiscal actions, it is not intended to incorporate all of the exogenous forces that affect nominal GNP. Conceptually therefore the equation is misspecified. This conceptual misspecification poses a statistical problem, however <u>only</u> if the omitted exogenous variables are correlated with the policy measures used in the equation. If, as assumed generally the 'missing' exogenous variables are neither policy variables nor closely correlated with the variables representing monetary and fiscal actions, their omission does not pose a serious statistical problem.[25] (Emphasis in original)

TABLE XVIII

TWO ST. LOUIS TYPE EQUATIONS

Reduced-form equations for nominal GNP - compound growth rates, percent per annum
(standard errors in parentheses).

Estimation period: 1953I–68IV

$$\underset{}{\%\Delta GNP} = \underset{(0.85)}{1.99} + \sum_{i=0}^{3} \underset{(0.25)}{1.07}\ \%\Delta M1_{t-i} + \sum_{i=0}^{2} \underset{(0.39)}{0.72}(\Delta G/GNP_{-4})_{t-i}$$

$$- \sum_{i=0}^{7} \underset{(1.00)}{2.61}\ (\Delta T/GNP_{-4})_{t-i} - \underset{(4.03)}{10.35}\Delta S,$$

$\bar{R}^2 = 0.43, \quad SEE = 3.49, \quad DW = 1.46.$

$$\%\Delta GNP = \underset{(1.11)}{1.36} + \sum_{i=0}^{3} \underset{(0.23)}{0.78}\ \%\Delta M2_{t-i} + \sum_{i=0}^{2} \underset{(0.46)}{0.50}(\Delta G/GNP_{-4})_{t-i}$$

$$- \sum_{i=0}^{7} \underset{(1.11)}{2.40}\ (\Delta T/GNP_{-4})_{t-i} - \underset{(4.24)}{8.63}\Delta S,$$

$\bar{R}^2 = 0.36, \quad SEE = 3.70, \quad DW = 1.43.$

Estimation period: 1953I–76II

$$\%\Delta GNP = \underset{(0.76)}{2.19} + \sum_{i=0}^{3} \underset{(0.17)}{1.04}\ \%\Delta M1_{t-i} + \sum_{i=0}^{2} \underset{(0.32)}{0.44}\ (\Delta G/GNP_{-4})_{t-i}$$

$$- \sum_{i=0}^{7} \underset{(0.72)}{1.96}\ (\Delta T/GNP_{-4})_{t-i} - \underset{(3.15)}{10.76}\Delta S,$$

$\bar{R}^2 = 0.44, \quad SEE = 3.51, \quad DW = 1.58.$

$$\%\Delta GNP = \underset{(0.97)}{1.86} + \sum_{i=0}^{3} \underset{(0.16)}{0.71}\ \%\Delta M2_{t-i} + \sum_{i=0}^{2} \underset{(0.38)}{0.42}(\Delta G/GNP_{-4})_{t-i}$$

$$- \sum_{i=0}^{7} \underset{(0.82)}{1.93}\ (\Delta T/GNP_{-4})_{t-i} - \underset{(3.66)}{8.56}\Delta S,$$

$\bar{R}^2 = 0.35, \quad SEE = 3.79, \quad DW = 1.50.$

Source: M.J. Hamburger, "Behaviour of the Money Stock: Is There a Puzzle"? Journal of Monetary Economics (1977-83), p. 286.

They go on to say that in response both to past criticism of the St. Louis equation and the likely interrelations of domestic and external influences on GNP in other countries; they use a spending equation which allows for the lagged effects of exports. However they find that none of the individual coefficients are large in comparison with those of M or G, and most are statistically insignificant. And they conclude "the cumulative effect of export growth on GNP is not statistically significant at any conventional level.[26]

M1 OR M2?

In 1975 a sharp rise in the velocity of the money stock, uncharacteristic of a recession year, persuaded some economists to argue that the Federal Reserve should reduce the importance which it attached to the money aggregates M1 and M2.

To see if these monetary aggregates had deteriorated in significance, M.J. Hamburger designed two St. Louis type spending equations, using M1 for the money aggregate in one equation and M2 in the other. Moreover, he employed an 'initial stimulus' estimate $\Delta G/GNP$ for Federal government expenditures and $\Delta T/GNP$ for tax receipts - explaining that these variables eliminate the inflation bias which is included, for example, in Andersen-Jordan's spending equation 1.2 (see Exhibit "B:). He also added a variable S, "to measure industrial man hours lost due to strikes to allow for disturbances emmanating from the labour market."

Hamburger tested each equation over two periods, 1953/I -1968/IV and 1953/I - 1976/II and found the relationships, illustrated in Table XVIII, between the aggregates and the economy to be remarkably stable over both periods, and therefore concluded

TABLE XIX

Ordinary Least Squares Estimates of the St. Louis-Type Equation

		Sample Period		
		II/1962–III/1982	II/1962–IV/1982	II/1962–I/1983
M1 EQUATION				
Summed Coefficients	Lags			
$\dot{M}$	10	1.150* (4.52)	1 096* (3.92)	0.952* (3.43)
$\dot{G}$	9	−0.042 (0.31)	−0 090 (0.61)	−0.047 (0.31)
Summary Statistics				
$\bar{R}^2$		0.48	0.38	0.34
SE		3.16	3.48	3.56
DW		2.12	1.97	1.89
M2 EQUATION				
Summed Coefficients				
$\dot{M}$	11	1.310* (4.64)	1.291* (4.35)	1.281* (4.38)
$\dot{G}$	2	0.066 (0.76)	0.042 (0.46)	0.041 (0.46)
Summary Statistics				
$\bar{R}^2$		0.26	0.19	0.19
SE		3.77	3.97	3.94
DW		1.91	1.79	1.85

Note: Absolute values of t-statistics in parentheses.

*Statistically significant at the 5 percent level.

Source: Dallas Batten and Daniel Thornton, "M1 or M2, Which is the Better Money Target?" Federal Reserve Bank of St. Louis Review (June/July, 1983), p. 39.

that the M1 and M2 aggregates "have not outlived their usefulness as policy guides."[27]

Of particular interest is the fact that the R^2s of each M1 equation are higher than their counterparts in the M2 equations, suggesting that M1 explains the variance of nominal GNP better than does M2.

Changes in the velocity of the money stock continued to plague the St. Louis spending equation and spurred the Research department to examine their preference for M1 anew. In 1981, R.W. Hafer did so in an article entitled "Much ado about M2".[28] He shows how the creation of money commences with an increase in bank reserves and then expands through the money multiplier to M1 and M2. Since M2 is the second link in the chain, he concluded that M1, as the first link, is the better target. Furthermore, he found evidence that the relationship between the growth of M1 and nominal GNP growth had been more stable historically.

The early 1980's saw many financial innovations (e.g. money market deposit accounts) and, in 1983, Dallas Batten and Daniel Thornton set out to test whether the variations in the way individuals held their stock of money had caused the relationship between M1 and nominal GNP to deteriorate relative to the relationship between M2 and nominal GNP. They estimated the St. Louis spending equation over three periods 1962/II - 1982/III, 1962/II - 1982/IV and 1962/II - 1983/I, using both M1 and M2 for the money stock and their results are illustrated in Table XIX.

Batten and Thornton conclude that M1 explains more of the variation of nominal GNP growth (R^2 = 0.48, 0.38 and 0.34) as compared with the M2 equation (R^2 = 0.26, 0.19 and 0.19). However, they note that these rates deteriorate substantially when the last two quarters of data are added - undoubtedly because there was more substitution between M1 and M2 balances and non-M1 or M2 financial assets - though the M1 equation retains more explanatory power. Nevertheless, they did not feel that there was enough evidence to conclude that M1 should be de-emphasized as an empirical target of monetary policy.[29]

ESTIMATING TECHNIQUE

In their original article Andersen-Jordan stated that "the structure of lags present in the regressions was estimated with the use of the Almon technique". Andersen and Carlson expand on this saying "Lag structures, with one exception, are estimated by the Almon technique. The reported relationships reflect considerable experimentation with the number of lags and the degree of the polynominal."

In the spending equation, the coefficients of each lagged variable were constrained to lie on a fourth degree polynomial with both endpoint coefficients for each variable constrained to equal zero.

Smith and Waud were the first (in 1973) to investigate the lag lengths of Andersen-Jordan's spending equation 1.2 (Exhibit "B") in an article entitled "The Almon Lag Technique and the Monetary versus Fiscal Policy Date". They show that freeing the estimates from an arbitrary lag of four quarters and removing the endpoint restrictions reduced the money multiplier to 4 and reduced the relative superiority of monetary policy.[30]

However, it was not until 1983 that the St. Louis Fed reported directly on this estimating technique. Dallas Batten and Daniel Thornton reviewed the criticisms that had been made about this procedure. They then tested statistically Carlson's respecified spending equation which used annual rates of change in place of the original first differences of the variables. They concluded:

> Our results indicate that the important policy conclusions of the St. Louis equation are insensitive to the lag length specified and the polynomial restrictions imposed. ...there is no evidence that the conclusions of the St. Louis equation can be traced to these types of econometric misspecification.[31]

REFERENCES

1 John Stuart Mill. Principles of Political Economy, Book III, Ashley ed., New York, 1929, p. 488.

2 As stated in a private letter to the author from Keith Carlson, March 30, 1983.

3 Dan M. Bechter, "Money and Inflation," Federal Reserve Bank of Kansas City Monthly Review (July-August, 1973), p. 5.

4 Leonall Andersen and Keith Carlson, "St. Louis Model Revisited," International Economic Review (June, 1974), pp. 305-327.

5 Ibid., p. 307.

6 Benjamin M. Friedman, "Even the St. Louis Model Now Believes in Fiscal Policy," Journal of Money, Credit and Banking (May, 1977), pp.365-367.

7 Ibid., p. 367.

8 Keith Carlson, "Does the St. Louis Equation Now Believe in Fiscal Policy?" Federal Reserve Bank of St. Louis Review (February, 1978), p. 14.

9 Leonall Andersen and Jerry Jordan, "Monetary and Fiscal Actions: A Test of Their Relative Importance in Economic Stabilization," Federal Reserve Bank of St. Louis Review (November, 1968), footnote to p.16.

10 Alan S. Blinder and Robert M. Solow, "Analytical Foundations of Fiscal Policy," in The Economics of Public Finance (Washington, D.C.: The Brookings Institution, 1974), p. 98.

11 Milton Friedman, "Comments on Tobin and Buiter," in Jerome Stein, ed., Monetarism (New York: New Holland Publishing Company, 1976), p. 315.

12 Ibid., p. 313.

13 R.W. Hafer, "The Role of Fiscal Policy in the St. Louis Equation," Federal Reserve Bank of St. Louis Review (January, 1982), p. 22.

14 Ibid.

15 Robert Rasche and John Tatom, "Energy Resources and Potential GNP,"Federal Reserve Bank of St. Louis Review (June, 1974), pp. 10-24.

16 Robert Rasche and John Tatom, "The Effects of the New Energy Regime on Economic Capacity Production and Prices," Federal Reserve Bank of St. Louis Review (May, 1977), pp. 2-12.

17 Keith Carlson, "The 1975 National Economic Program: Another Exercise in Fiscal Activism, "Federal Reserve Bank of St. Louis _Review_ (March, 1975), p. 10.

18 Leonall Andersen and Keith Carlson, "St. Louis Model Revisited," _International Economic Review_ (June, 1974), p. 309.

19 In a personal letter to the author.

20 Peter Clark, "Potential GNP in the United States, 1948-1980," _U.S. Productivity Capacity, Measuring the Utilization Gap_ (St. Louis: Washington University, Center for the Study of American Business, 1977), pp. 21-66.

21 Keith Carlson and Scott Hein, "Four Econometric Models and Monetary Policy: Longer Run View," The Federal Reserve Bank of St. Louis _Review_ (January, 1983), p. 24.

22 Sherman Maisel, _Managing the Dollar_ (New York: W.W. Norton, 1968), p. 190.

23 John Tatom, "Energy Prices and Short-Run Economic Performance," Federal Reserve Bank of St. Louis _Review_ (January, 1981), pp. 3-17.

24 John Tatom, "Does the State of the Business Cycle Affect the Inflation Rate," Federal Reserve Bank of St. Louis _Review_ (September, 1978), pp.7-15.

25 Dallas S. Batten and R.W. Hafer, "The Relative Impact of Monetary and Fiscal Actions on Economic Activity: A Cross-Country Comparison," Federal Reserve Bank of St. Louis _Review_ (January, 1983), p. 6.

26 Ibid.

27 M.J. Hamburger, "Behaviour of the Money Stock - Is There a Puzzle?" _Journal of Monetary Economics_ (1977) pp.254-288.

28 R.W. Hafer "Much Ado about M2" Federal Reserve Bank of St. Louis _Review_ (October 1981) pp. 13-18.

29 Dallas Batten and Daniel Thornton, "M1 or M2, Which is the Better Money Target?" Federal Reserve Bank of St. Louis _Review_ (June/July 1983) pp. 36-42.

30 Peter Schmidt and Roger Waud, "The Almon/Lag Technique and The Monetary versus Fiscal Policy Debate" _Journal of The American Statistical Association_ (March 1973).

31 Dallas Batten and Daniel Thornton "Polynomial Distributed Lag and The Estimation of The St. Louis Equation", Federal Reserve Bank of St. Louis _Review_, (April 1983) pp. 13-25.

CHAPTER SIX

THE PROBLEM IS MONEY

> Money opens the Pandora's box of expectation and uncertainty, the limitless field of imagination is brought into view and determinancy must evaporate.
>
> G.L.S. Shackle [1]
> 1972

Writing in 1974 Andersen and Carlson discussed the 'successes' and 'failures' of the St. Louis Model. The first failure that they mention is:

> Failed to educate policymakers on the long-run effects of their short run decisions...The recent experience of the U.S. experience of the U.S. economy with recession, inflation and experiences with price controls serves as ample evidence indicating that the model has failed in this objective.[2]

If the St. Louis Fed felt that it had failed with Congress and the Federal Reserve Board, they had made their point with prominent Keynesian economists, as can be seen in the reaction of Professors Milton Friedman and Arthur Okun (Chairman of the Council of Economic Advisors in 1968) to the 1964 tax cut. In 1969 Friedman states:

> As far as I see, there has been no empirical demonstration that the tax cut had any effect on the total flow of income in the U.S. There has been no demonstration that if the monetary policies had remained unchanged...the tax cut would have been really expansionary on nominal income. What Arthur Okun did was to assume away the whole problem because he looked only at the effect of fiscal policy without asking what role monetary policy played during that period.[3]

Mr. Okun replied:

> Both preceding and following the enactment of the tax cut, monetary strategy was geared to provide the reserves needed to stabilize interest rates and the availability of credit...Perhaps this analogy will help. During the sixties, the Federal Reserve took the position of a ticket seller ready to sell tickets at a fixed price to anyone in line. Given this policy, sales of tickets were determined by the number of people who got in line. One cannot explain adequately why more people saw a show by saying that the ticket seller sold more tickets (at a given price).
>
> It doesn't make any more sense to say that the economic stimulus in 1964-65 came from a change in monetary policy. The tax cut does explain why more people got in line given the willingness of the ticket seller to expand his sales, activity increased. I was concerned with estimating the magnitude of that expansion, and hence, had no reason to ask what

> would have happened if the ticket seller had refused to sell more tickets.
>
> ...There are a number of other empirical judgments in comparable hypothetical situations on which "new economists" and "monetarists" can agree. For one thing, I believe that the success of the fiscal strategy depended on the monetary response. If, when the tax cut was enacted, our ticket seller had been reluctant to issue more tickets, interest rates would have risen rather than remaining stable, and credit availability would have been restricted; GNP would then have moved along a lower path than the one that actually resulted. Surely the Fed could have imposed a sufficiently restrictive monetary policy to nullify entirely the expansionary effects of the tax cut.
>
> Moreover, I have no reasons to doubt that, in principle, there existed a monetary route to high employment, as an alternative to the fiscal route that was traveled. As much additional demand as resulted from the tax cut could have been generated without fiscal support, by a sufficiently aggressive Federal Reserve policy to increase liquidity and reduce interest rates.[4]

The important paragraph is the last one. Okun is admitting that no longer is monetary policy "a string which can be pulled but not pushed," but rather that it is powerful enough in its own right to bring about full employment.

Later, Alan Blinder and Robert Solow expressed the Keynesian view in discussing the lessons of the 1968 Federal surtax which had been intended to deflate the rising tide of inflation, concluding that the size of the surtax was inadequate for four reasons:

> 1. There was concurrent exogenous strengthening of consumer demand.
>
> 2. It was not recognized that the temporary form of the surtax would reduce its effectiveness.
>
> 3. Federal expenditures for the Vietnam War were underestimated, as were state and local outlays.
>
> 4. There was hangover of expansionary monetary policy dating back to the reversal of monetary policy after the credit crunch (of 1966) and not reversed by any tightening in 1968. Fiscal restraint probably did not allow adequately for the need to offset the lagged effects of this monetary expansion.[5]

The fourth section echoes what the St. Louis Fed was saying in 1967 before the surtax was passed and is a signal recognition by two eminent Keynesian economists of the power of monetary actions.

Andersen and Carlson's econometric equations explained why changes in the money supply should be the primary target of monetary policy, and such a policy continued to be called for by Darryl Francis and other monetarists as well as by a Concurrent Resolution passed by Congress in 1975. Their views were seemingly adopted in that year when the FOMC began setting and announcing publicly each quarter its target ranges for the growth of M1, M2 and M3 for the succeeding twelve-month period. At the same time, the Fed selected a Federal Funds interest rate which it felt was consistent with these targets.

But success is fleeting for the evidence shows that the Fed was paying more attention to the Federal Funds rate than to the money aggregates. Thus in the forty-seven months after the adoption of this policy, the Federal Funds interest rate had fallen outside of its target ranges only five times whereas the growth of M1 had fallen outside its ranges twenty-three times - or virtually fifty percent of the time.[6] One can only infer that the FOMC was using the Federal Funds interest rate as its standard for monetary policy.

If Monetarists were making progress among academic economists and Congress, why were they not able to persuade the Board of Governors of the Federal Reserve System to adopt their views? Governor Maisel was not unsympathetic to the monetarist cause, particularly when they advocated the use of monetary aggregates as measures of monetary policy. Nevertheless, he writes:

> The primary reason for their rejection, I believe, is that the Fed saw the monetarists' prescriptions as too simplistic...There is no agreement as to what is meant by the money supply. The velocity of money is held to be predictable; but it is hard to find a period when this was true. A variety of lags are acknowledged, possibly long ones. The data on

> money are subject to large errors and revisions...But a probably more important element than any of these reasons...is the belief that, because our economic system is complex, it cannot be realistically analyzed without complex theories.[7]

This belief has proven difficult for the St. Louis Fed to change!

WHY DID THE MONEY STOCK CHANGE?

If the Board of Governors of the Federal Reserve felt that changes in the money stock were brought about for many complex reasons, the St. Louis Fed emphasized only one--the Fed was monetizing the deficit in proportion to the size of that deficit.

This proposition is set out in an address given by President Francis at the University of Southern Mississippi in 1974. The title is interesting, namely: "How and Why do Fiscal Actions Matter to a Monetarist?" On the basis of the St. Louis spending equation, one would anticipate that the answer would be none at all! However, as Francis expressed it - fiscal actions taken by Congress could mean that Federal budget expenditures would exceed Federal tax receipts. This would bring about Federal budget deficits and then:

> The experience has been that larger deficits have tended to be accompanied by more than proportional debt acquisition by the Federal Reserve Banks. During periods when deficits are large, upward pressure on market interest rates - downward pressure on security prices - occurs at the time Treasury financings take place. In the past the Federal Reserve often

> has "even keeled" the money markets - that is, provided reserves through open market operations to "lean against" the tendency for interest rates to rise in the short run.
>
> In theory, the Federal Reserve would "unwind" after the even-keel operation by reducing its portfolio of securities. In practice, the desire to resist upward pressure on market interest rates, especially during periods of a strengthening economy and rising demands for credit has militated against behaving according to this ideal. Also, during past fiscal years of very large budget deficits, the Treasury has been involved in some sort of financing the majority of the time which has left the monetary authorities little opportunity to "unwind".
>
> I would submit that the correlation between big Government deficits and rapid increased in the money stock in recent years, as was true during the second World War are high enough to impress the most casual of observers.[8]

On the basis of Mr. Francis' conclusion, what should we expect to find if we look at the empirical evidence? First, in the years when the federal debt increased as compared to those of the previous years, the Federal Reserve System not only bought more of the Federal debt - but proportionately more. Table XX sets out the data for the period 1960-1980.

Looking back from 1974, we can see that in seven of the previous thirteen years, the amount of the Federal debt and the amount

TABLE XX

Amount of Federal Debt Held by the Board of Governors (1960-1980)

Year	Total Federal Debt	Amount held by U.S. Agencies and Trusts	Net Debt	Amount held by Federal Reserve	Increase in Net Debt	Increase in amount held by Federal Reserve	Percent bought by Federal Reserve	Percent of net debt held by Federal Reserve	GNP Deflator
1960	290.4	55.1	235.3	27.4				11.6	1.4
1961	296.5	54.5	242.0	28.9	6.7	1.5	22.3	11.9	2.0
1962*	304.0	55.6	248.4	30.8	6.4	1.9	29.7	12.3	1.8
1963*	310.1	58.0	252.1	33.6	4.3	2.8	65.1	13.3	1.5
1964	318.8	60.6	258.2	37.0	6.1	3.4	55.7	14.3	1.5
1965*	320.9	59.7	261.2	40.8	3.0	3.8	126.7	15.6	2.2
1966*	329.3	65.9	263.4	44.3	1.8	3.5	194.4	16.8	3.2
1967	344.7	73.1	271.6	49.1	8.2	4.8	58.5	18.1	3.0
1968*	358.0	76.6	281.4	52.9	9.8	3.8	38.7	18.1	4.4
1969*	368.2	89.0	279.2	57.2	7.8	6.3	80.8	18.8	5.1
1970	389.2	97.1	292.1	62.1	6.9	4.9	71.0	21.3	5.4
1971	424.1	106.0	318.1	70.2	26.0	8.1	31.1	22.1	5.0
1972	449.3	116.9	332.4	69.9	14.3	-0.3	-2.0	21.0	4.2
1973*	469.9	129.6	340.3	78.5	7.9	8.6	108.9	23.1	5.7
1974*	492.7	138.2	354.5	80.5	14.2	2.0	14.1	22.7	8.7
1975	576.6	139.1	437.5	89.8	83.0	9.3	11.2	20.5	9.3
1976	653.5	147.1	506.4	97.0	69.1	7.2	10.4	19.1	5.2
1977	718.9	154.8	564.1	102.8	57.7	5.8	10.0	18.2	5.8
1978*	789.2	170.0	619.2	109.6	54.9	6.8	12.4	17.7	7.3
1979*	845.1	187.1	658.0	117.5	38.8	7.9	20.4	17.9	8.5
1980*	930.2	192.5	737.7	121.3	79.7	3.8	4.8	16.4	9.0

*Years in which the amount of debt and the amount acquired by the Federal Reserve System went in different directions--as compared to the previous year.

Source: Various issues of the Federal Reserve Bulletin and Economic Reports of the President.

acquired by the Federal Reserve System moved in opposite directions as compared to the previous year.

For example, in 1961, the Federal debt increased by $6.7 billion and the Federal Reserve System purchased $1.5 billion. In 1962 the Federal debt increased by a lesser amount - $6.4 billion - but the Federal Reserve purchased $1.9 billion.

On the other hand, between 1973 and 1974 the increase of the Federal debt was reduced from $14.3 billion to $7.9 billion, whereas the Federal Reserve System increased its purchases from $0.03 billion to $8.6 billion.

However, from 1960 to 1973 the Fed was purchasing a higher percentage of the Federal debt than it had originally held in 1960 (11.6%) and thus the percentage of the Federal debt which it held, rose. Just as surely, it fell, as the Fed bought smaller percentages of the greatly increased deficits of the late 1970s. (see Chart V)

The data was studied by professional economists with the following conclusions:

> **1.** Niskanen (1978)...my conclusions are that federal deficits have significantly increased the level of federal spending but have had no apparent effect on the rate of inflation.[9]
>
> **2.** Dwyer (1981) - No evidence is found that larger government deficits increase spending, interest rates or the money stock. Neither is there any evidence found that the Federal Reserve acquires more debt when deficits are larger.[10]

CHART V

Influence of Federal Government Debt on Monetary Expansion

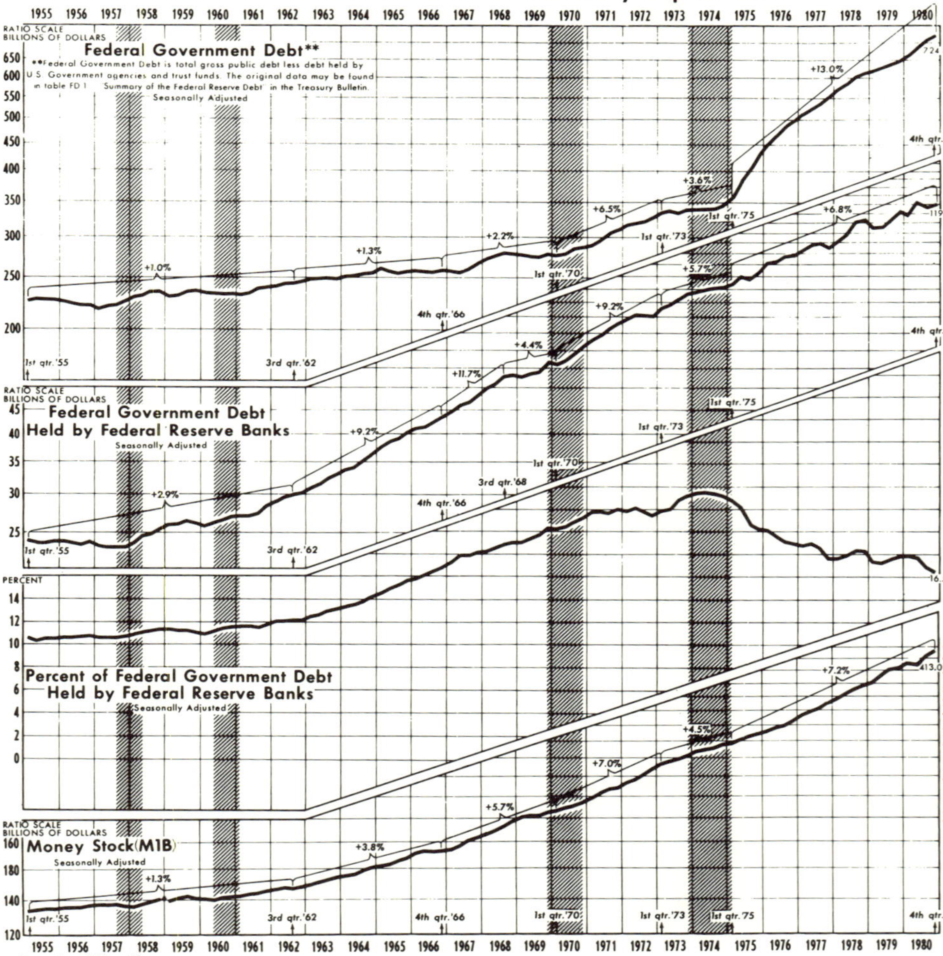

*Data prior to 1959 are M1.
Shaded areas represent periods of business recessions.
Percentages are annual rates of change for periods indicated.
Latest data plotted: 4th quarter

Source: Scott E. Hein "Deficits and Inflation" Federal Reserve Bank of St. Louis Review (March, 1981), p. 8.

3. Hamburger and Zwick (1981) - Monetary policy is strongly influenced by the Federal government's fiscal policy actions, measured either by expenditures or budget deficits for the period 1961-1974.[11]

4. McMillin and Beard (1982) - Unlike Hamburger-Zwick, we do not find any strong evidence of a positive Federal budget - money growth relationship over the period 1961 - 1974. When the estimation period is extended to 1976 and then to 1978, the results suggest no relationship between deficits and money growth.[12]

5. Hamburger and Zwick (1982) - For the longer period (1961-1981) it is clear that it is deficits and not Federal expenditures that are the important linkage between monetary policy and fiscal policy.[13]

Perhaps with this mixed bag of conclusions, we should turn to the St. Louis Fed for the final word. In March 1981, Scott Hein published an article in the Review entitled "Deficits and Inflation". After reviewing the data illustrated in Chart V, he states that "the evidence is not consistent with the view that increases in the federal debt (i.e. deficits) cause inflation. (Emphasis in the original). It is interesting that one of the reasons that he gives for this conclusion is "because recent deficits have not put undue pressure on market rates."[14]

Of course, if deficits were the cause of increases in the money stock, monetary policy would no longer be under the control of the Federal Reserve System. Instead, responsibility would have been transferred to the Administration and Congress and would be governed by the size of the deficit or surplus which they decreed.

The question then arises - on what basis does the FOMC increase the money supply? Does it do so as some sort of a random walk - or is there method behind its madness?

COST-PUSH?

Governor Maisel, in his book Managing the Dollar, published in 1973, commented on the original St. Louis spending equation as follows:

> It is well recognised that past correlations are no indication of causality. This was obvious to me as a Federal Reserve policy maker. For the entire period on which the (St. Louis) correlations were based, the Fed allowed changes in spending to be the critical influence on the growth of money. As a result, a definite correlation does exist. As GNP grew, so did money.[15]

But we know that spending or GNP is equivalent to $\dot{P} + \dot{X}$, where P is the GNP price deflator and X is real output. Can cost-push pressures raise prices P and thereby force the FOMC to validate the increase by increasing M proportionately in order that:

$$\dot{GNP} = \dot{P} + \bar{X} = \dot{M} + \bar{V}$$

and thereby avoid more unemployment?

Professor G. L. Bach, in a book published in 1973 and entitled, The New Inflation, states that:

> ...a half century ago...most economists saw inflation as basically the result of excessive spending...generally based on an excessive creation of money...More recently...these beliefs have been challenged. Certain economists see a new inflation - one caused by big unions pushing up costs and big businesses (and one should add OPEC) pushing up prices, with or without an excess of total spending.[16]

Dallas Batten, a St. Louis Fed economist, reviews this proposition in a 1981 Review article, and the title, "Inflation, the Cost-Push Myth" tells us where he stands on the issue. He defines inflation as:

> a continuous rise in the average price level - and therefore a one-time increase caused by some random shock (e.g. a drought or reduction in the quantity of oil supplied by OPEC) is not considered inflation...but simply a transitory deviation of inflation from its trend.[17]

Nor he says, can private firms or labor unions be blamed because even if they had monopoly power and charge higher prices for their products and services, since "this does not imply constantly rising prices". Batten concludes that inflation is the result of a persistent excess supply of money and the culprit is the Federal Reserve System since the money supply is under its control. But he gives no explanation why the Federal Reserve persists in such an unsatisfactory policy.

Nor does Batten mention the point emphasized by modern cost-pushers, namely, if one assumes a zero monetary growth and 'sticky' (downwardly inflexible) prices, then particular price increases will tend to generate compensating reductions, not of other prices, but rather output and employment. Since the American government is required to 'maximize' employment, such an outcome cannot be permitted to occur unless the rate of inflation is considered dangerous to the economy as it was in 1966 and 1981. Instead, specific price increases must necessarily be accommodated by whatever monetary expansion is required to maintain output and employment at high levels. Thus individual price increases are translated into general inflationary pressures.

However, there are hints in a number of articles in the Review that the power of unions to obtain wage increases not related to productivity cannot be overlooked in the money supply process. One such is by Roger W. Spencer, published in May 1975 and entitled "Inflation, Unemployment and Hayek." Here Spencer writes:

> Elsewhere in the 'Constitution of Liberty', Hayek specifically singled out labor unions for their part in fostering inflation and unemployment. It is his contention that by permitting unions to force up wages, the government is put into the position of validating the wage-price pressure through money supply increases or facing general unemployment by failing to validate the union action.[18]

Four years later, Lawrence K. Roos, then President of the Federal Reserve Bank of St. Louis, put the situation this way:

> A third frequently directed argument against a constant rate of money increase is that if labor

> unions demand wage increases or businesses set prices in excess of the rate of growth of productivity, unemployment would result. This, I think, emphasizes the critical importance of central bank credibility. If it becomes clear that monetary authorities are going to adhere to their announced money growth targets, I doubt that business or unions would risk the loss of sales or employment that would accompany exorbitant wage or price demands.[19]

The problem is set out succinctly by Charles L. Schultze in an article in the Wall Street Journal of March 20, 1981:

> In the mid-1960's hourly employment costs (wages and fringe benefits) in the major auto companies were about 20% above the average for manufacturing industries. Every three years since, the labour contract negotiated between the industry and the union has widened the gap. By 1978 wages and fringes at the major auto companies had risen to almost 50% above the all-manufacturing average. Those extra costs were passed on in higher prices.
>
> Finally, in 1979 - faced with mounting interest rates, an incipient recession, sharply higher gasoline prices, growing resistance to large American cars and increased imports from Japan - what did the industry do? It negotiated a contract that by 1980 put auto wages and fringes about 60% above the manufacturing average.[20]

Undoubtedly this is why Milton Friedman has said "Full employment is, however, a modern invention for producing inflation."[21]

What this implies for the St. Louis Fed's GNP equation is set out in a footnote of Dennis Karnosky's to a June 1976 article:

> It is irrelevant that labor might act on the supposition that the monetary authorities will validate wage increases in excess of productivity gains, hoping thereby to avoid the increase in unemployment. That is a policy decision, reflected in the relative weight given to unemployment in the policy deliberations of the monetary authorities. Even though the money supply would then appear to be <u>endogenous</u>, relative to the wage rate, the fact remains that the monetarist position holds that in the absence of the increased rate of money growth, the rate of change in the general price level will not be affected in a permanent way by the increase in factor prices. (Emphasis added)[22]

We know that if real output exceeds the trend growth rate of velocity of M1, then the money supply must be increased in order to avoid unemployment as industries reduce output and employment rather than prices. Thus when ex-Governor Maisel says "As GNP grew, so did money" it makes sense to ask questions such as - How much inflation will the country put up with before demanding that it be reduced and thereby cause greater unemployment? - and - How much unemployment will the country put up with before demanding that action be taken to produce jobs - even if inflation be the result?

One can appreciate that the money stock can be considered to be exogenous because it is controlled by the Fed - as the 1966 and 1969 credit crunches proved vividly. Major monetary stock increases or decreases in the immediated past have depended on whether inflation or unemployment was seen to be the greatest problem facing the country. But there are many other influences, as set out below, all or part of which may be influential at any one time.

1. The strength or weakness of the American dollar and other important currencies.[23]

2. The American political situation - are Presidential elections in the offing?[24]

3. The needs of the Treasury as previously explained.[25]

4. The economic philosophies of the members of the Board of Governors of the Federal Reserve System and the Presidents of the Reserve Banks.

5. The general feeling of optimism or pessimism in the business community, in other words - 'the touch and feel' of the market.

6. Cost-push factors.

MONEY - EXOGENOUS OR ENDOGENOUS?

To the economist who builds formal mathematical models, applying the term exogeneity to a variable means that the variable is used in an explanatory equation to account partially for variatons in the dependent or endogenous variable. Thus, it must be independent of the disturbance term of the equation. If it cannot meet this test of independence, it will bias the results which purport to show its impact on the endogenous variable.

On the other hand, exogenous has also been used to describe those variables which can be directly controlled by policymakers.

There can be a conflict. In our present case, if the FOMC passively expands or contracts the money supply depending on the needs of trade or of the financial requirements of the Treasury, many econometricians and economists would call the resulting money supply an endogenous variable.

The St. Louis Fed sees exogeneity in terms of control. The money supply is considered to be exogenous, since the FOMC has the power to alter the monetary base and thereby exercise control over the money stock - whether or not it chooses to do so. From their point of view, causality and control ability go hand and hand. This was one of the reasons that DeLeeuw and Kalchbrenner objected to the 1968 Andersen-Jordan equations [26] and it has been a matter of continuing controversy.[27]

Nevertheless, as Professor Thomas Mayer has written, "If M is endogenous, then M1 might still 'predict' Y well, in the sense that if you know M1, you also know Y."[28]

REFERENCES

1 G.L.S. Shackle, "The Harvest, "History of Political Economy (1972), p. 601.

2 Leonall Andersen and Keith Carlson, 'St. Louis Model Revisited, "International Economic Review (June, 1974), p. 323-324.

3 Milton Friedman and Walter W. Heller, Monetary vs. Fiscal Policy (New York: W.W. Norton, 1969), p. 55.

4 Arthur Okun, The Political Economy of Prosperity (Washington, D.C.: Brookings Institution, 1970), pp. 55-56.

5 Alan S. Blinder and Robert M. Solow, "Analytical Foundations of Fiscal Policy," in the Economics of Public Finance (Washington, D.C.: Brookings Institution, 1974), pp. 114-115.

6 Lawrence K. Roos, "Monetary Targets - Their Contribution to Policy Formation, "Federal Reserve Bank of St. Louis Review (May, 1979), p. 13.

7 Sherman Maisel, Managing the Dollar (New York: W.W. Norton, 1973), pp. 259-260.

8 Darryl Francis, "How and Why Do Fiscal Actions Matter to a Monetarist? "Federal Reserve Bank of St. Louis Review (May, 1974), pp. 2-7.

9 William A. Niskanen, "Deficits, Government Spending and Inflation, "Journal of Monetary Economics (1978), pp. 591-602.

10 Gerald P. Dwyer, Jr., "Inflation and Government Deficits, "Economic Inquiry (1981), pp. 316-329.

11 M.J. Hamburger and Barton Zwick, "Deficits, Money and Inflation." Journal of Monetary Economics, 1981, p. 149.

12 W.D. McMillin and T.R. Beard, "Deficits, Money and Inflation: Comment." Journal of Monetary Economics, 1982, p. 273.

13 M.J. Hamburger and Barton Zwick, "Deficits, Money and Inflation: Reply." Journal of Monetary Economics, 1983, p. 282.

14 Scott E. Hein, "Deficits and Inflation," Federal Reserve Bank of St. Louis *Review* (March, 1981), p. 9.

15 Sherman Maisel, *Managing the Dollar*, Op. Cit., p. 274.

16 G.L. Bach, *The New Inflation* (Providence: Brown University Press, 1973), p. 7.

17 Dallas S. Batten, "Inflation: The Cost-Push Myth," Federal Reserve Bank of St. Louis *Review* (June-July, 1981), pp. 20-24.

18 Roger W. Spencer, "Inflation, Unemployment and Hayek", Federal Reserve Bank of St. Louis *Review* (May, 1975), P. 7.

19 Lawrence K. Roos, "Monetary Targets - Their Contribution to Policy Formation," Federal Reserve Bank of St. Louis *Review* (May, 1979), p.15

20 Charles L. Schultze, "Against Auto Import Protection" *Wall Street Journal*, March 20, 1981.

21 Milton Friedman, *Dollars and Deficits* (Englewood Cliffs, New Jersey: Prentice-Hall, 1968), p.30.

22 Dennis Karnosky, "The Link Between Money and Prices," Federal Reserve Bank of St. Louis *Review* (June, 1976), p. 19.

23 See for example, Sherman Maisel, *Managing the Dollar*, Op. Cit., pp. 211-227.

24 Robert E. Weintraub, "Congressional Supervision of Monetary Policy," *Journal of Monetary Economics* 4 (1978), pp. 341-362.

25 See for example, Darryl Francis, "How and Why Fiscal Actions Matter to a Monetarist," Op. Cit., pp. 2-7.

26 Frank DeLeeuw and John Kalchenbrenner, "Monetary and Fiscal Actions: A Test of Their Relative Importance in Economic Stabilization - Comment," Federal Reserve Bank of St. Louis *Review* (April, 1969), pp. 6-11.

27 See Chapter Four, Reference 26.

28 Professor Thomas Mayer - in a personal letter to the author.

CHAPTER SEVEN

IS THE ST. LOUIS FED TRULY MONETARIST?

> I came to the Council (of Economic Advisors) with the determination to be a monetarist if anybody provided me with the flimsiest of evidence, and Willie (Fellner) provided it.
>
> Herbert Stein [1]
> 1975

Unlike Herbert Stein, the St. Louis Fed was monetarist long before the term was created and had provided the data and charted the relationships which allowed it to take that position. However Professor Thomas Mayer has defined twelve propositions which characterize monetarists and distinguish them from Keynesians. It will be obvious from the preceding material that the St. Louis Fed qualifies without question as monetarist. Nevertheless, there are some interesting positions which the St. Louis Fed has taken which can be conveniently discussed within Mayer's framework.

His distinguishing characteristics are:

1. The quantity theory of money, in the sense of the predominance of the impact of monetary factors on nominal income.
2. The monetarist model of the transmission process.
3. Belief in the inherent stability of the private sector.
4. Irrelevance of allocative detail for the explanation of short-run changes in money income, and belief in a fluid capital market.
5. Focus on the price level rather than on individual prices.
6. Reliance on small rather than large econometric models.

7. Use of the reserve base or similar measure as the indicator of monetary policy.
8. Use of the money stock as the proper target of monetary policy.
9. Acceptance of a monetary growth rule.
10. Rejection of an unemployment-inflation trade-off in favor of a real Phillips curve.
11. A relatively greater concern about inflation than about unemployment compared to other economists.
12. Dislike of government intervention.[2]

Martin Bronfenbrenner would add a 13th proposition as follows:

13. The Federal Reserve has the power, and accordingly the responsibility to regulate the money supply.[3]

And Keith Carlson of the St. Louis Fed has added:

14. A belief in crowding out.[4]

1. The quantity theory of money, in the sense of the predominance of monetary factors on nominal income. This goes without saying as the preceding material has set out. One need only set down again the 1982 spending equation to see that mathematically, the influence of one additional dollar in the money stock is twenty times that of one more dollar of high-employment government expenditures.

$$Y_t = 2.44 + 1.06\,\dot{M}_{t-i} + .05\,\dot{E}_{t-i}$$

2. The monetarist model of the transmission process. This relates to the manner by which changes in the money stock affect income. Mayer argues that to classify an economist as 'Monetarist' because he or she believes that changes in the money stock affect income directly, while Keynesians hold that such changes affect income indirectly through the rate of interest, is spurious. [5] The reason that he says this is because modern monetarists acknowledge that interest rate effects are always present. They view the direct mechanism merely as an empirical proxy for the indirect mechanism in which many specific interest rates cannot be captured statistically, either because they are implicit and hence unobservable or because they are too weak and too brief to be measured.

Nevertheless, for most economists this is one of the significant differences between the two schools of thought and certainly the St. Louis Fed has adopted the 'straight' monetarist hypothesis.

3. Belief in the inherent stability of the private sector. In the issue of the New Republic of February 20, 1935, Keynes addressed this question in an article entitled "A Self-Adjusting System." In this article he explained that there were two schools of thought amongst economists.

On the one side were those who believed that the existing economic system is, in the long run, self-adjusting though with creaks and groans and jerks, and interrupted by time-lags, outside interferences and mistakes.

Those on the other side of the gulf, however, rejected the idea that the existing system is in any significant sense, self-adjusting. In the General Theory, he set out his own position, writing:

> We oscillate, avoiding the gravest extremes of
> fluctuation in employment and prices in both

> directions, round an intermediate position appreciably below full employment and appreciably above the minimum employment a decline below which would endanger life.[6]

This was the main theme underlying the General Theory. It shocked the economics profession of the day and gave notice that something new was being said.

Andersen and Carlson differ, stating:

> The St. Louis model does not provide evidence of the proposition that the economy is inherently stable...However, simulations of the St. Louis model demonstrate properties which are consistent with a corollary to the inherent stability proposition, that monetary and fiscal actions are a source of instability. When the model is shocked by changing any one of the three exogenous variables (change in money stock, change in high-employment Federal expenditures and potential output), simulations indicate an initial period of oscillation, followed by a return to a steady long-run growth path.[7]

St. Louis Fed President Francis puts this position in more familiar terms:

> We should not seek policies designed to close the gap between what we are producing now and what could be interpreted as being real potential before the energy crisis, the environmental laws, the agricultural short-

> falls, and so on. That is simply unobtainable. Instead we are forced to be satisfied to see a resumption of the growth rate of real output consistent with long-term growth trends in population, technology and so forth - in other words, around three to four percent. But let me quickly add that this would occur without any overt actions by government policy makers. As long as we do not suffer any further adverse shocks to the economy, I believe that the inherent stabilizing properties and resiliency of the market system will return us to our potential growth path.[8]

But Fed Chairman Arthur Burns did not agree with the St. Louis Fed as he writes to Senator Proxmire:

> It seems self-evident that adherence to a rigid growth rate rule (for the money supply), or even one that is changed infrequently, would practically prevent monetary policy from playing an active role in economic stabilization. Monetarists recognise this. They believe that most economic disturbances are self-correcting, and they therefore argue that a constant or nearly constant rate of growth of the money supply would result in reasonably satisfactory economic performance.
>
> But neither historical evidence, nor the thrust of explorations in business-cycle theory over a long century, give support to the notion that our economy is inherently stable. On the contrary, experience has demonstrated

> repeatedly that blind reliance on the self-correcting properties of our economic system can lead to serious trouble. Discretionary economic policy, while at times it has led to mistakes, has more often proved reasonably successful.[9]

There are two problems endemic to the St. Louis Fed's position:

> a. Every country is continually subject to economic shocks of one kind or another.
>
> b. The idea of a stable growth path has a great deal of theoretical appeal - the difficulty is to put it into practice. The most serious problem results from two facts:
>
> i. Monetary and governmental policies have impacts which extend over several periods of time, and
>
> ii. It is impossible to choose a starting point without allowing for the residual effects of earlier policies.

4. Irrelevance of allocative detail for the explanation of short-run changes in money income, and belief in a fluid money market. A Keynesian economist focuses on what happens in the consumption (C), investment (I), government (G) and foreign trade (X-M) sectors of the economy. Thus fluctuations in interest rates are held to have greater effects on the residential sector than on the industrial sector. But the Monetarist disregards this allocative detail (except for the financial sector) from his belief in the strength of money supply changes in explaining the variance in income. The St. Louis spending equation has no place for changes in C, I, G or (X-M).

As previously described, the model has the property that the money stock effects spending directly through a kind of "black box". This helps to preserve the independence of long-term growth from changes in the rate of such expenditures as consumption, investment, and, for example, state and local government expenditures.

5. Focus on the price level rather than on individual prices. Mayer writes:

> One way of determining whether someone is a Keynesian or a monetarist is to ask him for a quick and intuitive answer to the following question: Suppose the price of petroleum rises. What will this do to the average of other prices?[10]

A Keynesian would answer without hesitation: Since the petroleum industry has an inelastic demand, the increase of its prices will reduce the aggregate demand for all other goods and services. If their prices are relatively inflexible to that change in demand (and Keynesians hold that this is the case) then the remaining industries will respond, not by cutting prices, but by reducing output and employment. Thus the general price level is raised - not just the relative price of the petroleum industry's output.

However, Milton Friedman would have none of such an argument. Thus, in commenting on the alleged source of the double-digit inflation of 1973-1974, he writes:

> What of (the rise in the prices) of oil and food...? Are they not the obvious immediate

> cause of the price explosion? Not at all. It is essential to distinguish changes in relative prices from changes in absolute prices. The special conditions that drove up the prices of oil and food required purchasers to spend more on them leaving less to spend on other items. Did that not force other prices to go down or to rise less rapidly than otherwise? Why should the average level of all prices be affected significantly by changes in the prices of some things relative to others? Thanks to delays in adjustment, the rapid rises in oil and food prices may have temporarily raised the rate of inflation somewhat. In the main, however, they have been convenient excuses for besieged government officials and harried journalists rather than reasons for the price explosion.[11]

The basic source of inflation, Friedman states, "is the faster growth in the quantity of money than in output".[12]

The St. Louis Fed echoes this position as President Francis says:

> In my view the successive upward ratcheting in the average growth rate of the money stock has been the primary cause of the acceleration in the average rate of inflation. I do not accept the analyses which point to the food price increases, to other special factors, as causes of the underlying trend. Certainly these factors influenced the timing and possible the magnitude of the sharp increases in the price indexes, but a rise in the price of any single commodity does not cause inflation any more

> than a fall in the price of a single commodity causes deflation.[13]

The early St. Louis Model uses the aggregative approach to the price level. Changes in the quantity of money determines the changes in aggregate demand which are then allocated between changes in prices and changes in output - without trying to define changes in the prices of any particular industry. But as we have seen, this was to change as OPEC quadrupled the price of crude oil in late 1973 and then doubled that price in 1979.

Francis had said "A rise in the price of any single commodity does not cause inflation." But now we have a quantum leap in the price of crude oil which affects so much of industrial production. If one then charts the relationship between long-term increase in the stock of money and the increase of prices (as in Chart VI), one can see real problems during the period 1973-1975 and 1979-80. How does the St. Louis Fed explain these aberrations?

In an article published in June 1976 entitled "The Link between Money and Prices - 1971 - 1976", Denis Karnosky indicates how cost-push factors influence the price level through their effect on productive capacity and subsequently the demand for money. His analysis is:[14]

> 1. Any unexpected increase in factor cost causes a decrease in the productive capacity of the economy. In this case it is the price of crude oil, but it could be just as easily be an autonomous increase of wage rates (e.g., by a strong union) above that justified by increased productivity. This interesting suggestion is not followed up in any subsequent issues of the <u>Review</u>.

CHART VI

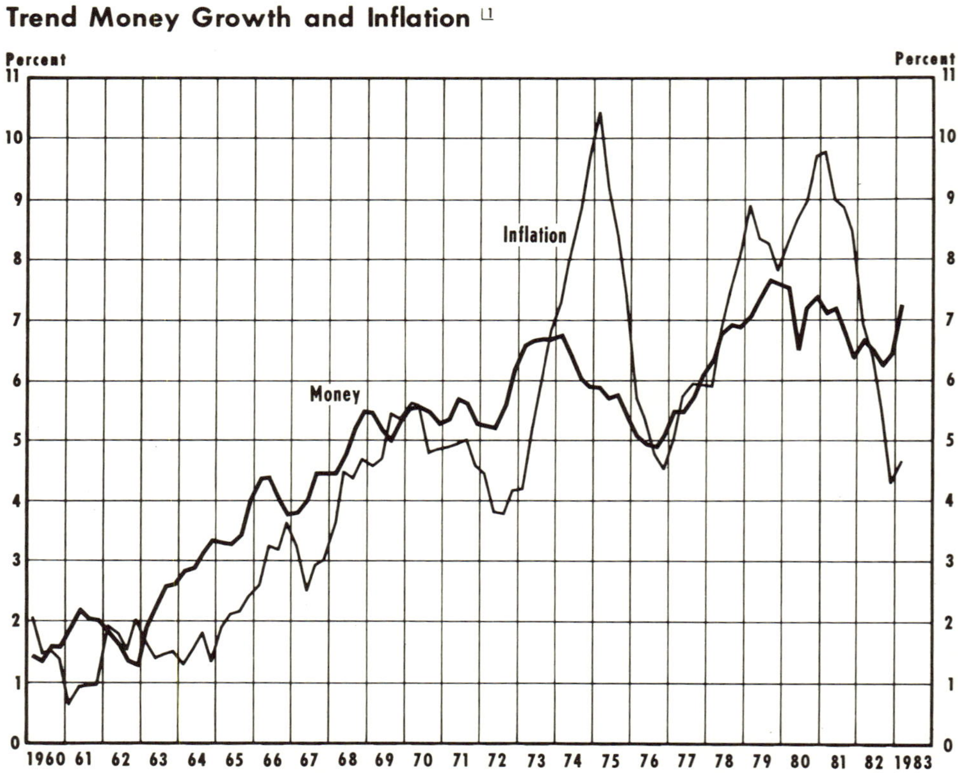

[1] Trend money growth is measured as a 13-quarter moving average of money growth. Inflation is a 4-quarter growth rate of the GNP deflator.

Source: R.W. Hafer, "Inflation: Assessing its Recent Behaviour and Future Prospects". Federal Reserve Bank of St. Louis Review (August/September, 1983), p. 36.

2. As a result of the higher energy cost, processes put in place in expectation of lower absolute and relative energy prices are rendered obsolescent.

3. No change in the money stock is required to accommodate the increase in energy prices, because real output declines sufficiently to offset the increasing price. In the equation $\dot{M} + \dot{V} = \dot{P} + \dot{X}$, if P increases by the same percentage that X decreases, there is no reason to alter the money stock. Thus Karnosky states: "The autonomous 4.5 percent increase in the price level in 1974 suggests an approximately equal decrease in productive capacity."[15] - and presumably - production!

4. Equilibrium in the demand for money is retained by a one shot increase in the general price level. This takes some time - in the OPEC case approximately two years - and then the rate of change of prices returns to the fundamental inflation rate consistent with the rate of monetary expansion.

5. Nothing happens to the productive capacity in an engineering sense, but the economically efficient rate of production is slashed.

The real life problems that result from this situation are two:

> 1. Decreased real output means increased short-term structural unemployment and thus pressure on the Federal government to stimulate employment with fiscal actions (viz. the 1975 tax cut).
>
> 2. Labour will act to resist absorbing their share of the national income lost to the OPEC nations and other oil-producing countries, as well as American oil corporations - to the extent that price and profit regulation allow these corporations to gain extraordinary profits.

But there may be no necessity for labour to resist higher prices. Many of the strongest unions (e.g., the automobile and steel workers) had three year contracts with built-in COLA clauses though these usually only give partial protection from rising prices. Thus in the recession year of 1975, the rate of wage increase for non-unionized workers dropped below 7%, while the unionized workers benefitted from a further increase to near 9%. The insensitivity of highly unionized industries to unemployment is not surprising. Wage determination in these industries is not a market solution but a bilateral negotiation. It is no wonder that Mr. Karnosky suggests:..."the problem requires structural changes in the form of easing restrictions on the operation of markets, and not more money."[16]

On December 6, 1974, just some six months after his earlier statement, President Francis recanted, adopting Karnosky's hypothesis:

> A temporary bulge in the rate of inflation, while the economy is adjusting to a new higher

> equilibrium price level, is not necessarily associated with a marked acceleration in the rate of growth of the money supply. On the contrary, it can be associated with a steady, continuing growth of the money supply and aggregate demand for goods and services, while at the same time there is a sudden drop in the economy's real economic capacity.[17]

John Tatom confirmed this view in 1981, using variations of the St. Louis spending, price and unemployment equations to explain and assess the effects of the 1978 energy price increases in quantitave terms. The sample period is I/1955 - III/1980 and the basic GNP equation is expressed in the form:

$$\dot{GNP} = a_o + \beta 1 \sum_{i=0}^{M} m_i \dot{M}_{t-i} + \beta 2 \sum_{j=0}^{N} e_j \dot{E}_{t-j} + \beta 3 \sum_{k=0}^{Q} p_k \dot{P}^e_{t-k} + S_t + e_t .$$

where $\dot{M}$ is the growth of money, $\dot{E}$ is the growth of high employment Federal expenditures, $\dot{P}$ is the change in the relative price of energy and S is a variable entered to capture the effect of major strikes on GNP. Quantified, this equation becomes:

$$\dot{GNP}_t = \underset{(-3.31)}{2.708} + \underset{(-8.05)}{1.165} \sum_{1=0}^{4} m_i \dot{M}_{t-i} - \underset{(-0.03)}{0.002} \sum_{j=0}^{4} e_j \dot{E}_{t-j} - \underset{(-3.71)}{0.453} S_t$$

$$- \underset{-(1.93)}{0.062} \dot{P}^e_t - \underset{(-0.77)}{0.032} \dot{P}^e_{t-1} - \underset{(-0.08)}{0.003} \dot{P}^e_{t-2} - \underset{(-1.08)}{0.032} \dot{P}^e_{t-3}$$

$$\underset{(-0.76)}{-0.032} \dot{P}^e_{t-4} + \underset{(0.24)}{0.10} \dot{P}^e_{t-5} + \underset{(2.93)}{.099} \dot{P}^e_{t-6}$$

$\bar{R}^2 = 0.54$ S.E. $= 2.96$ D.W. $= 1.99$

The sum of the coefficients of the rate of increase in energy prices indicates the effect on the growth of nominal GNP for a 1 percentage point increase in the annual rate of energy price increases. The pattern of these coefficients indicates that a current-quarter rise in the relative price of energy tends to reduce nominal GNP for six quarters and then increase it.

In 1979-80, GNP growth is estimated to have been 0.8 percentage points lower in 1979 and 2.0 percentage points lower in 1980 - all of which were offset by faster GNP growth in 1981.

Tatom's basic price equation for the same period, - without an energy price variable is:

$$\dot{P} = \underset{(27.57)}{1.020} \sum_{i=0}^{20} w_{t-i} \dot{M}_{t-i} - \underset{(-3.99)}{2.045} D1 + \underset{(5.30)}{2.625} D2$$

$$\bar{R}^2 = 0.75 \quad S.E. = 1.21 \quad D.W. = 1.66$$

where $\dot{M}$ is the growth of money and D1 and D2 are dummy variables included to account for the effects of President Nixon's price controls.

Tatom then adds a variable for energy prices and from the econometric results he concludes that, while a rise in the price of energy reduces potential output immediately, the price level effect occurs over the subsequent year. He indicates that in 1979 - 1980, energy prices temporarily added 2.1 percentage points to measured inflation rates.

Tatom also develops a basic employment equation with an energy price variable and finds that the pattern of the unemployment rate matches that for GNP. He estimates that the increase in energy prices increased unemployment by 0.5% in late 1980 and early 1981 - and this impact is considered to have been eliminated by the end of 1981.[18]

6. Reliance on small rather than large econometric models. Monetarists hold that monetary changes affect the economy in so many ways that it is impossible to quantify them all. Theoretically this means that a reduced form model is likely to be more reliable than a large structural model. Moreover, this view rules out any reverse causation feedbacks running from income to money. President Francis puts this situation in a human way:

> My personal preference is for small models rather than large models. This stems partly from my view that the Federal Reserve should be concerned with the aggregate effects of policy and should leave the allocative effects to the operation of the market place. Also, not being a practicing econometrican, I am willing to trade some so-called 'structural richness' much of which refers to matters I do not consider to be the proper concern of monetary policy makers for an ability to understand the process by which the model arrives at its results.[19]

Keynesians, on the other hand, remind one of Von Neuman's claim that the weather could be perfectly predicted - given a large enough organization and a big enough computer - since all the weather is somewhere and all we need to know is how the various parts of the weather system interact. Analgously, all of the world's economic weather is somewhere, and if one had enough knowledge to specify the relationships of the various sectors to each other and a big enough computer to resolve all the equations that would be involved, one could predict the consequences of any economic act.

But that is still to come. At the moment, our knowledge of the weather and the consequences of economic actions are still faulty and incomplete. Which, of course, may be fortunate for the economics profession.

7. Use of the reserve base or similar measure as the indicator of monetary policy. The St. Louis Fed produces U.S. Financial data weekly and the adjusted monetary base (currency and commercial bank reserves) is a part of that data. Thus President Francis says:

> The approach our staff uses to analyze the factors influencing the growth of the nation's money stock, demand deposits plus currency in the hands of the public - holds that the monetary base is the major determinant of changes in the rate of growth of the money stock.[20]

Moreover, Anatol Balbach holds that "The Federal Reserve can control the monetary base even on a weekly base if it so desires. There is, of course, no question that it can do so over time."[21]

But monetary policy maker's control of the monetary base does not guarantee a controlled supply of M1. Short run money multiplier movements must be taken into account if a stable growth of M1 is to be achieved. Hafer, Hein and Kool reported on the stability of the money multiplier in the October 1983 _Review_, and concluded:

> Monetary policy actions which utilize a constant base growth will not achieve a short

CHART VII

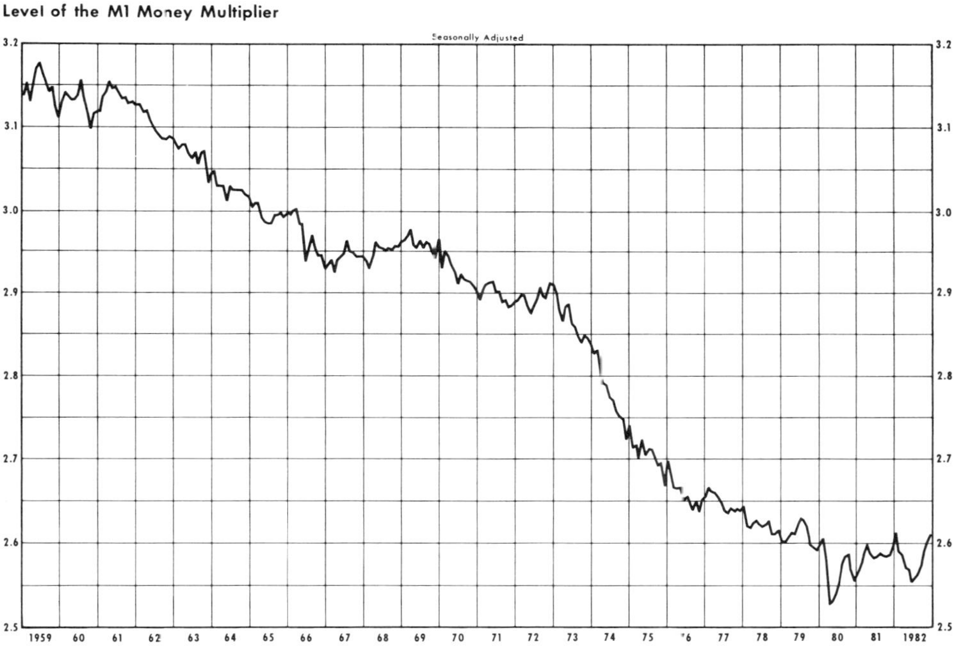

Source: R.W. Hafer, Scott Hein and Clemens Kool "Forecasting the Money Multiplier: Implications for Money Stock Control and Economic Activity", Reserve Bank of St. Louis Review, (October, 1983) p.27.

> run money growth. A post mortem of 1982 money growth indicates that much of the volatility in money growth last year was attributable to money multiplier fluctuations - not erratic monetary level growth. Consequently the growth of M1 must anticipate and react to multiplier movements.[22] (see Chart VII)

8. Use of the money stock as the proper target of monetary policy. As previously indicated, despite the qualifications mentioned above, the St. Louis Fed was continually advocating the use of the money stock as the target of monetary policy, while Keynesians were concerned with long-term interest rates, which they hold to be determinants of investment.

The problem with an interest rate target is that should interest rates increase, the Fed does not know whether it is the demand for money as an asset which has changed (liquidity preference) or the demand for credit as the economy expands. All the Fed sees is a rise in the interest rate. If it is caused by a slowdown in $\dot{V}$ the Fed should increase the stock of money to maintain $\dot{P} + \dot{X}$ in the equation $\dot{M} + \dot{V} = \dot{P} + \dot{X}$. Since P and X are stable, the money stock does not change. If it had been the target, the Fed would do nothing and the rising interest rates would bring about a decrease in X - real output and employment.

On the other hand, an autonomous increase in investment could unexpectedly increase the demand for credit and cause interest rates to rise. If the Fed had an interest rate target it would increase the money stock, further increasing expenditures and the probability of inflation. Here a money stock target would be preferable.

On this issue, the St. Louis Fed prefers an M1 target on the basis that V (the liquidity preference function) is more stable than the autonomous expenditure multiplier - that is net private domestic investment, plus government expenditures and exports minus imports - as found by Friedman and Meiselman.[23]

9. Acceptance of monetary growth rule

As Thomas Mayer says:

> The constant money growth rule is closely related to the quantity theory. If the demand for money is indeed constant when adjusted for trend, then a constant growth rate of the supply of money would result in income too growing at a constant rate.[24]

President Francis agrees:

> Since I hold the view that in the longer run a higher level of employment is consistent with relatively stable prices, I continue to advocate achieving a stable rate of monetary growth consistent with that objective.[25]

However, by 1979, the St. Louis Fed. was not so certain. World events had indicated that there could be a place for changing the rate of growth of the money stock. Thus President Roos:

> In the very few instances when sudden changes in money demand have occurred, such as the one induced by institutional changes, they have been of temporary duration and were readily recognizable. Should exogenous changes occur, the rate of money growth can be

> temporarily changed to meet specific situations, and such changes should be announced publicly and the rationale behind them explained.[26]

Keynesians say:

> In the Treatise (1930), Keynes insisted that money "comes into existence along with debts" - in other words, that the supply of money is related to production contracts and any debts which they necessitate ...(it is) the historical fact that the purpose of central banks has been to accommodate the stock of money to changes in the needs for trade.[27]

10. Rejection of an unemployment-inflation trade-off in favour of a real Phillips curve.

Professor Mayer writes that this proposition is based on a statement by Leonall Andersen, in the Review of September, 1973. There Andersen holds that "monetarists, as well as other economists" reject the argument that an economy must accept a high unemployment rate in order to have a low rate of inflation. However, the original and new price equations on the St. Louis Model contain demand pressure arguments - in effect saying that the difference between current output and potential output reflect current unemployment and thereby prices. Surely past and present experience tells us that this does happen in the real world.

In a conversation with the author, Keith Carlson indicated that there is a short-run trade-off but over the long run, - which he feels would be some 10-15 years - a steady growth of the money stock would bring unemployment and inflation under control with real output increasing at its potential 3 to 4 percent per annum. However, Anatol Balback, then Senior Vice President in charge of Research, was more optimistic, saying that if political factors did not intervene, this happy prospect could be brought about within five years.

11. A relatively greater concern about inflation than about unemployment compared to other economists

Sir Roy Harrod has observed that economists are born either little inflationists or little deflationists, and go through their lives fearing the onset of inflation or deflation respectively.[28] There is no doubt that the St. Louis Fed belongs in the first category. Thus President Francis speaks on March 29, 1973, saying:

> You will note that I have been talking about a "high employment" economy rather than one of "full employment." The reason is that "full employment" is often taken to refer to some specific rate of unemployment, such as the 4 percent level. I believe that attempts to achieve numerical targets of this sort have probably led to as many problems as they have solved. The single-minded pursuit of virtually any goal often results in undesireable side effects. In this case, zealous pursuit of a target rate of unemployment, without recognition of the lags in effect of monetary policy, has often been followed by inflationary pressures.[29]

This sentiment is echoed by President Roos in May 1980, in his address to the graduating class of Westminster College, Fulton Missouri when he says:

> No challenge facing this class of 1980 is more compelling than that of breaking the momentum of chronic inflation. Unless this is accomplished, there is no hope of restoring to this nation the economic growth and stability necessary for its continued prosperity and security.[30]

12. Dislike of government intervention

This often comes up in the speeches given by President Francis. His speech of April 3, 1975 entitled "Public Policy in a Free Economy" contains this excerpt which is characteristic of his views:

> I subscribe to the widely-held doctrine that the promotion of economic freedom is consistent with the attainment of the maximum possible standard of living for society. According to this view, state regulation should be viewed with suspicion as a potential enemy of society's material well-being.[31]

13. The Federal Reserve has the power, and accordingly the responsibility to regulate the money supply.

Federal Reserve Chairman Burns:

> I do not think that we have the power to achieve this or that rate of growth of the money supply ...within a period of three months, or even six months.[32]

And as has been noted - in the 47 months after 1975 - M1 was only in its targeted range approximately 50 percent of the time.

But St. Louis Fed President Roos says:

> Critics continue to assert that money stock growth cannot be measured with precision and thus cannot be controlled. My response to that argument is that a policy of explicitly controlling the growth of money has not been given a fair chance in the United States; in other economies that have made the effort, it has worked well.[33]

14. A belief in 'crowding out'

The quarrel that Monetarist have had with Keynesians with respect to fiscal policy, is not that an increase in federal expenditures cannot increase nominal GNP in the quarter in which they are made, but rather that Keynesians do not look beyond the initial spending in order to appreciate the over-all effects on the economy which depend on the way in which the increased expenditures are financed.

This is particularly true when the Federal government borrows the funds to cover those outlays. At full employment, of course - it is understandable that if the government spends more, it is merely re-allocating resources from the private to the public sector. There is only so much labour and industrial capacity available in a country.

However, at anything less than full employment, the concept of 'crowding out' is less clear. Why cannot the governmental authorities borrow and employ under-utilized human and real capital and thereby contribute to real GNP?

Every economist would agree that this could be done without harm if the extra governmental spending is paid for by funds created by the Fed. But in such a case, as we have seen in the Friedman-Okun dialogue, Monetarists hold that the greater GNP is brought about solely by the increases in money stock. Moreover, the St. Louis GNP equation gives empirical backing to that position.

But if one assumes no concurrent increase in the money supply, why does 'crowding out' occur? The IS/LM framework explains this development by illustrating how an increase in government expenditure financed by the sale of new government bonds causes interest rates to increase, and this increase reduces private spending for housing, consumer durables and other interest-sensitive components of private demand.

Keynes himself, pointed out how government spending financed by deficit borrowing could diminish entrepreneurial confidence.

> With the confused psychology which often prevails, the Government programme may, through its effect on 'confidence,' increase liquidity preference or diminish the marginal efficiency of capital, which, again, may retard other investment unless measures are taken to offset it,[34]

Keith Carlson illustrates this aspect in the IS/LM framework, demonstrating that: (See Chart VIII)

> An induced increase in liquidity preference, subsequent to an increase in Government spending from G_0 to G_1, is depicted in the IS/LM framework by a leftward shift of the LM curve and a diminished marginal efficiency of

CHART VIII

KEYNES CASE

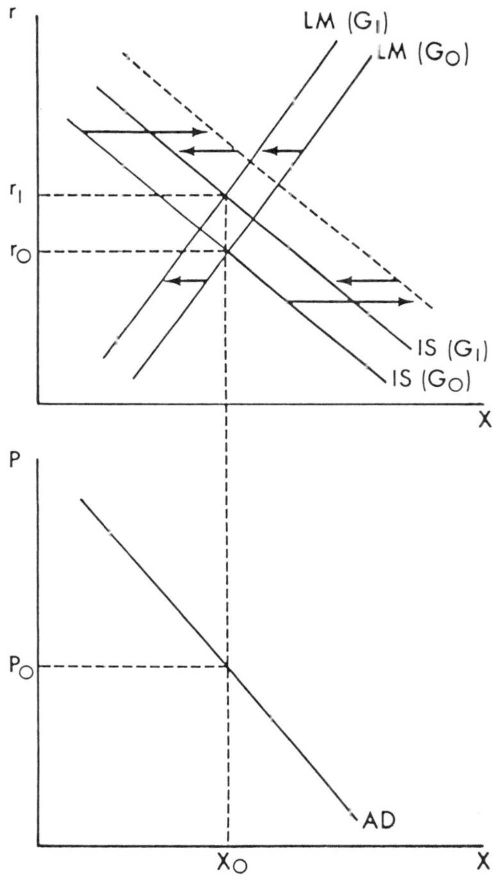

Source: K.M. Carlson and R.W. Spencer, "Crowding out and its Critics". Federal Reserve Bank of St. Louis Review (December, 1976), p. 6.

CHART IX

ALTERNATIVE KEYNES CASE

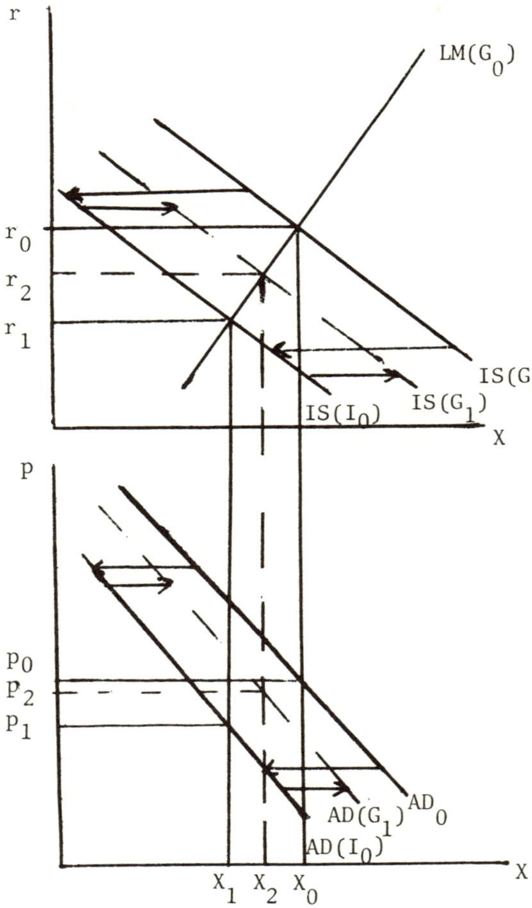

> investment schedule is reflected by the subsequent backward shift of the IS curve to the position denoted by IS(G_1). If these shifts in the IS and LM curves represent no change in aggregate demand at the given price level P_o, both nominal and real crowding out will occur. However the actual shift in aggregate demand could be positive, negative or negligible, depending on the relative shifts of the IS and LM curves.[35]

The 'text-book' analysis of the IS/LM paradigm starts from equilibrium and then shifts the IS curve to the right with increasing amounts of Consumption (C) Investment (I) or Government Expenditures (G).

However if we vary this picture and assume that with the economy is equilibrium, an exogenous shock, such as the quadrupling of crude oil prices by OPEC will also cause a loss of entrepreneurial confidence then - as illustrated in Chart IX - as investment falters, the IS curve will shift from IS(G_o) to IS(I_o) with a consequence reduction in interest rate from r_o rates to r_1. If we assume then that in order to overcome this declining IS curve, the government increases its expenditures for goods and services and/or transfer payments, the IS curve might readily shift to IS(G_1). Though interest rates would be higher at Y_2 than they would otherwise be, nevertheless they would be lower than they had formerly been at r_o. While prices are higher at P_2 than at P_1, real output has increased from X_1 to X_2. Can we not consider this 'crowding in'?

Moreover this result did occur during 1975 and 1976 as the U.S. came out of the 1974 OPEC induced recession stimulated by government expenditures which increased by $115 billion as compared to an increase of $81 billion for the previous two years. But even as Federal deficits reached record amounts, many economists were surprised to see interest rates fall continuously. However, some economists had foreseen this eventuality.

Thus Arthur Okun was saying:

> We face a huge federal debt because private saving is out-running private investment by a wide margin. And that generates a superfluity of credit supplies which will absorb short-term Treasury Securiters very happily.[36]

In January, 1977, the Review published an article by Richard W. Lang entitled "The 1975-76 Federal Deficits and the Credit Market," in which he referred to a similar prediction by James L. Pierce in 1975.[37]

In that article Lang provided Table XXI, to illustrate that U.S. Government spending was replacing private investment. However, as Okun and Pierce had predicted, these borrowings did not cause interest rates to rise.

The empirical evidence in Table XXII demonstrates how all interest rate were declining at the same time as the Treasury was selling greater and greater amounts of securities.

TABLE XXI

Funds Raised by Nonfinancial Sectors*

(Billions of Dollars)

Fiscal Year	Total**	U.S. Government	All Other Nonfinancial
1965	$ 71.2	$ 3.8	$ 67.5
1966	76.0	1.6	74.4
1967	60.8	1.8	59.1
1968	97.0	20.7	76.3
1969	96.7	−0.4	97.1
1970	93.6	3.8	89.8
1971	124.4	19.5	105.0
1972	161.5	19.4	142.1
1973	202.1	19.5	182.6
1974	191.5	3.3	188.1
1975	183.3	50.7	132.6
1976	241.0	82.8	158.2

*Based on the sum of unadjusted quarterly flows for each fiscal year, series updated as of November 1976.

**Columns may not sum to total due to rounding.

Source: Richard W. Lang "The 1975 Federal Deficits and the Credit Market", Federal Reserve Bank of St. Louis Review, (January, 1977) p.11.

TABLE XXII. Various Interest Rates I/1974 - IV/1976

	1974				1975				1976			
	I	II	III	IV	I	II	III	IV	I	II	III	IV
Prime Comm Paper 4-6 MOS.	8.4	10.9	11.2	8.9	6.0	5.7	6.8	5.9	5.3	5.9	5.4	4.7
Corporate Bonds Aaa	8.0	8.4	9.2	9.5	9.3	9.2	9.6	8.7	8.5	8.6	8.3	7.9
Fed Funds Rate	9.3	11.5	11.3	8.5	5.5	5.5	6.2	5.2	4.8	5.4	5.2	4.6
3 Month Treasury Bills	7.9	8.1	8.3	7.1	5.5	5.1	6.3	5.5	5.0	5.4	5.0	4.3

Source: Various Federal Reserve Bulletins.

And who was purchasing the new Treasury securities? The Federal Reserve System certainly, but through 1975 and 1976 their purchases were exceeded by each of individuals, corporations, and commercial banks - the very entities that one would expect to be liquidating their holdings to meet a credit crunch if the Treasury was in fact 'crowding out' the private sector demand for funds - (see Table XXIII). Surely this merely reflects a crisis of confidence in the private sector.

TABLE XXIII. Holdings of Federal Reserve Debt 1973-1976

Year	Total Fed. Debt	Fed Reserve	Indiv.	Frgn.	Comm. Banks	Mutual Banks & Ins Co.	Other Corps	State and Local	Misc. & U.S.Gov. Agencies
1973	469.9	78.5	77.2	55.6	60.3	9.3	10.9	29.2	148.9
1974	492.7	80.5	84.9	58.8	55.6	8.7	11.0	29.2	170.0
1975	576.6	89.8	91.3	66.5	85.1	14.0	20.2	34.2	177.1
1976	653.5	97.0	100.8	78.1	103.8	18.6	27.7	41.6	186.0

Source: Various Federal Reserve Bulletins.

THE ST. LOUIS FED CHANGES ITS VIEW ABOUT CROWDING OUT

Keith M. Carlson had been one of the authors of the article in 1970 which set out the original St. Louis GNP Equation. In October, 1976 he would have been aware of the way interest rates were falling as deficits rose. To explain this situation he published an article entitled, "Large Federal Budget Deficits: Perspectives and Prospects."[38]

In the article Mr. Carlson addressed the following questions:

1. Was the Federal deficit instrumental in promoting economic recovery, or did the recovery occur despite the deficit?

2. Is there no longer any need to worry about a large federal deficit?

3. Will it cause rising interest rates and/or lead to dislocations in the economy?

To develop an answer Carlson looks at the Federal deficit in two parts.

(a) 'passive' deficits - generated by the negative effects of the recession;

(b) 'active' deficits - generated by positive fiscal actions.

Carlson says " ...it was not until late 1974 that the recession took on the appearance of an aggregate demand induced recession of the type experienced in past periods of U.S. history"[39]

Examples of the fall in aggregate demand are illustrated in two Review articles, one by James E. Turley entitled "Automobile Sales in Perspective" in June, 1976 and the other by John Tatom, "Inventory Investment in the Recent Recession and Recovery," in April, 1977. Charts X and XI indicate how those two elements of demand fluctuated at this time.

James E. Turley says:

> The trend growth of auto sales has been far from smooth or steady. In fact, automobile sales, like most durable goods, have been highly volatile in the short run. Among other factors, such volatility appears to be closely related to an individual's perception of near-term income and employment prospects.[40]

John Tatom commences his article by saying:

> The behaviour of inventory investment since the beginning of the 1973-1975 recession has been a dominant concern of economic analysts. Initially, this concern was motivated by a recognition that a relationship between inventory investment and changes in total output and employment has been one of the most pronounced regularities of the business cycle. This relationship appears to be such a dominating factor in previous postwar recessions that they have been referred to as "inventory recessions."[41]

If automobiles are not selling very well and inventories are declining, then it seems sensible to have such losses of

CHART X

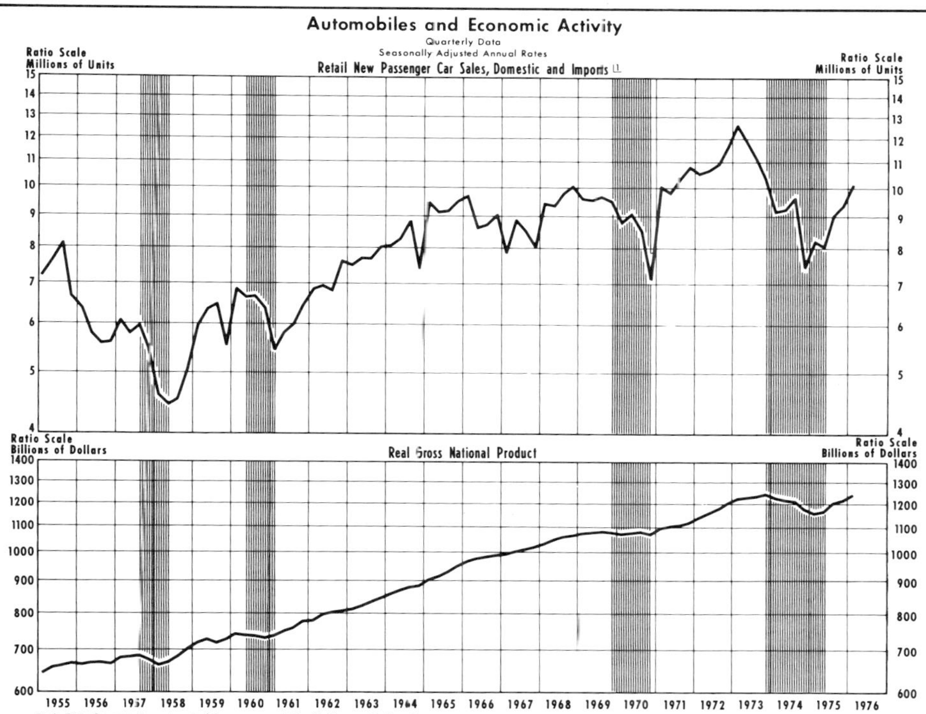

Basic Data Sources: Department of Commerce and Ward's Communication, Inc.

[1] Prior to 1958 sales data on imports are not available.

The first three shaded areas represent periods of business recessions as defined by the National Bureau of Economic Research. The fourth shaded area is tentative, and has been defined by the Federal Reserve Bank of St. Louis.

Latest data plotted: st quarter

Source: James E. Turley "Automobile Sales in Perspective", Federal Reserve Bank of St. Louis Review, (June, 1976) p.12.

CHART XI

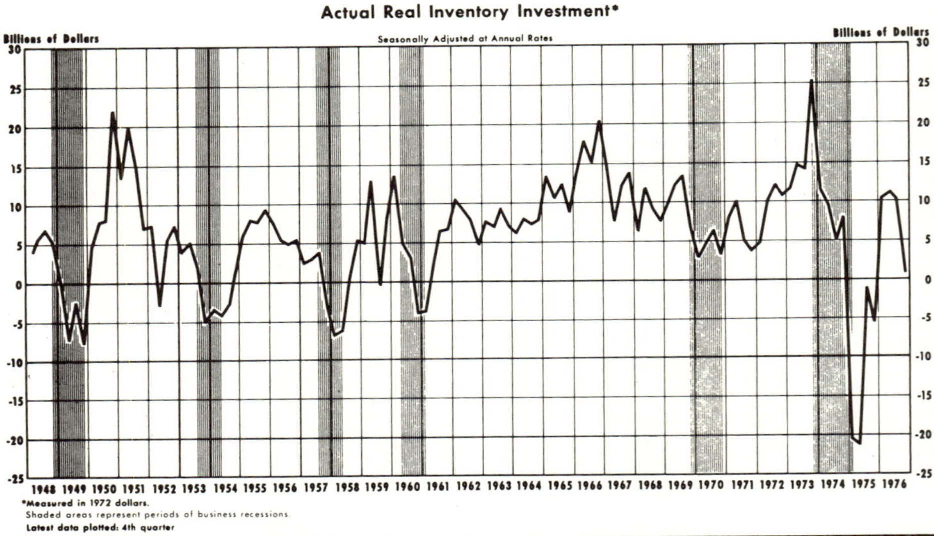

Source: John Tatom "Inventory Investment in the Recent Recession and Recovery" Reserve Bank of St. Louis Review, (April, 1977) p.4.

aggregate demand replaced by greater government transfer spending and additional funds should be allocated to specific sectors of the economy that have been badly hit. These conditions reflect a lack of confidence by the private sector, and political, if not moral, considerations will cause the Federal government to act.

Thus, Carlson concludes:

> ...a predominately active deficit incurred when the economy is strong provides an additional demand for funds over and above the already sizeable demands of the private sector... On the other hand a predominantly passive deficit resulting from a slowdown in economic activity generates little, if any, extra demands for funds because private sector borrowings are reduced during periods of declining or weak economic activity ...The Federal budget continues in deficit at an annual rate of near $60 billion. From the standpoint of economic stabilization, such a deficit has not caused great harm for either financial markets or the economy as a whole, because roughly two-thirds of it is attributable to relative weakness in economic activity.[42]

In budget terms, the deficit occurred because of a loss of taxes and an increase in stabilization payments such as unemployment insurance, food stamps and welfare. But these are the result of fiscal policy and were deliberately designed by Congress to offset any weakness in private demand.

One can make the argument that:

> Movements in the passive deficit are endogenous with respect to movements in real GNP, while active deficits are (exogenous). A rise in the passive deficit, when real GNP falls, may reduce the extent of the real GNP decline itself and the interest rate decline as well. Those adjustments, however, are endogenous because they are built-in to the structure of the economy.[43]

But surely one can add, "A rise in the active deficit, as long as GNP is falling, will also reduce the extent of the real GNP decline and the interest rate decline." Moreover, as the business cycle turns up, some added government spending will be required to "prime the pump" of private sector consumption and investment expenditures. Can these expenditures not be considered as 'crowding in' even if at some point near the top of the business cycle they will 'crowd out' private expenditures?

One can only agree with Carlson when, in 1976, he writes:

> The most obvious example of an active deficit causing trouble for the economy is the fiscal 1968 deficit of $25.2 billion. Relative to the size of the economy then, that deficit was little different from the present one. But the consequences were much different because it occurred when the economy was operating at a high level of resource utilization.[44]

The question is, of course, where is the line of demarcation between the two concepts?

Chart XII demonstrates how transfer payments have been rising while government expenditures for goods and services have been falling over the period 1950 - 1982 as a share of GNP. The total effect has brought about only a very gradual rise in Federal government expenditures as a share of GNP when measured from 1954. Surely this explains the apparent failure of high employment Federal expenditures to effect nominal GNP appreciably, - as set out in the St. Louis spending equation.

In December 1975, Keith Carlson has written:

> ...at the academic level 'crowding out' is at least one of the issues which helps to distinguish between followers the two major macroeconomic schools of thought - Keynesians and monetarists.[45]

May I suggest that in October, 1976, Mr. Carlson joined the ranks of Keynesians - at least during recessions!

By 1982, the impact of government spending was a feature of economic discussions, particularly in the news media, not so much for its direct effect on the economy, but rather because of the very large Federal budget deficits which were being incurred and their demands on the supply of loanable funds. In this connection Keith Carlson writes:

> The administrations' economic projections are of interest ...because of their impact on estimates of the budget deficit. The size of prospective deficits has become an issue

CHART XII

Federal Government Expenditures as a Share of GNP

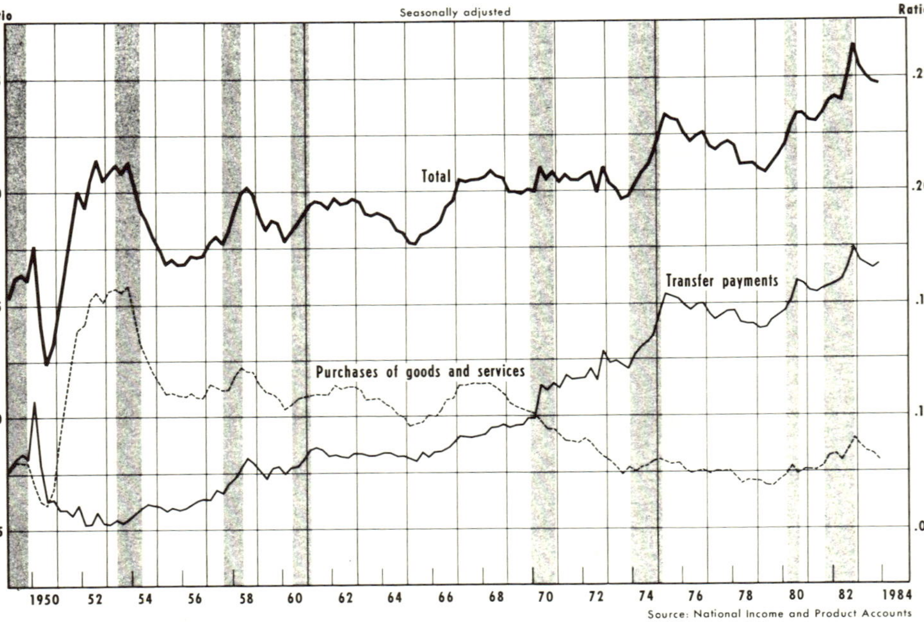

Shaded areas represent periods of business recessions.
Latest data plotted: 1st quarter

Source: John Tatom "A Perspective on The Federal Deficit Problem", Federal Reserve Bank of St. Louis Review, (June/July, 1984) p.8.

> amongst economic analysts, presumably because they consider it an indicator of the government's impact on credit markets and, thus, on long-term economic growth.[46]

Carlson points out:

> Such an effect is not in the St. Louis model, incorporation of this presumed relationship between the size of the deficit and the rate of economic growth would require specifying potential output as a function of either the size of the deficit or the size of government. The only role for federal deficits in the St. Louis model is their possible relationship to the rate of money growth.[47]

That these concerns have raised some doubts in his mind is reflected by the statement, "Although the effect of the budget on economic growth is <u>still an open issue</u>, there is no question that the budget is sensitive to the pace of economic activity".[48] The emphasis has been added to highlight the point which Carlson is making, namely: the jury is still out on the question of whether or not, "Money is all that matters", where nominal GNP is concerned.

REFERENCES

1 From remarks of the former Chairman of the Council of Economic Advisors in honour of retiring CEA member William Fellner, February, 1975. Quoted in Paul Wonnacott, Macroeconomics (Homewood, Illinois: Richard D. Irwin, Inc., 1978), p. 281.

2 Thomas Mayer, The Structure of Monetarism (New York: W.W. Norton, 1978), p.2.

3 Ibid., p. 51.

4 Keith Carlson, "Crowding Out and Its Critics", Federal Reserve Bank of St. Louis Review (December, 1975), p. 2.

5 Thomas Mayer, The Structure of Monetarism, Op. Cit., p. 8.

6 John Maynard Keynes, The General Theory of Employment, Interest and Money (London: The Macmillan Press, 1936), p. 254.

7 Leonall Andersen and Keith Carlson, "St. Louis Model Revisited", International Economic Review, (June, 1974) pp. 310 - 311.

8 Darryl Francis, "Unusual Factors Contributing to Economic TurMoil," Federal Reserve Bank of St. Louis Review (January, 1975), p. 13.

9 Arthur F. Burns "Letter on Monetary Policy to Senator William Proxmire" Federal Reserve Bank of St. Louis Review, (November, 1973), p. 16.

10 Thomas Mayer, The Structure of Monetarism, Op. Cit. p. 18.

11 Milton Friedman "Perspective on Inflation" Newsweek (June 14, 1974), p. 73.

12 Ibid.

13 Darryl Francis, "How and Why Fiscal Actions Matter to a Monetarist," Federal Reserve Bank of St. Louis Review (May, 1974), p.7.

14 Dennis Karnosky, "The Link Between Money and Prices - 1971-1976," Federal Reserve Bank of St. Louis Review (June, 1976), pp. 17-23.

15 Ibid., p. 22.

16 Ibid., p. 23.

17 Darryl Francis, "Unusual Factors Contributing to Economic Turnoil," Op. Cit. p. 9.

18 John Tatom "Energy Prices and Short Run Economic Performance" Federal Reserve Bank of St. Louis Review, (January, 1981), pp. 5-17.

19 Darryl Francis, "The Usefulness of Applied Econometrics to the Policymaker", Federal Reserve Bank of St. Louis Review (May, 1973), p. 9.

20 Darryl Francis, "How and Why Fiscal Actions Matter to a Monetarist," Op. Cit., p. 2.

21 Anatol B. Balbach, "How Controllable is Money Growth," Federal Reserve Bank of St. Louis Review (April, 1981) pp. 3-12.

22 R. W. Hafer, Scott Hein and Clements Kool, "The Wayward Money Supply: A Post-Morten of 1982" Federal Reserve Bank of St. Louis Review (March, 1983), p. 25.

23 Milton Friedman and David Meiselman, "The Relative Stability of Monetary Velocity and the Investment Multiplier in the United States," in the Commission on Money and Credit, Stabilization Policies (Englewood Cliffs, New Jersey: Prentice Hall, 1963), p. 187.

24 Thomas Mayer, The Structure of Monetarism, Op. Cit., p. 33.

25 Darryl Francis, "Problems of Interpreting Recent Monetary Developments," Federal Reserve Bank of St. Louis Review (July, 1973), p. 7.

26 Lawrence Roos, "Monetary Targets - Their Contribution to Policy Formation," Federal Reserve Bank of St. Louis Review (May, 1979), p. 3.

27 Basil J. Moore "Monetary Factors" A Guide to Post-Keynesian Economics (White Plains, N.Y.: M.E. Sharpe Inc. 1979), pp. 125, 126.

28 Robert Lekatchman, The Age of Keynes (New York, Random House, 1966), p. 165.

29 Darryl Francis, "The Problem of Re-Entry to a High-Employment Economy," Federal Reserve Bank of St. Louis Review (June, 1973), p. 12.

30 Lawrence Roos, "An Inflation Generation," Federal Reserve Bank of St. Louis Review (May, 1980), p. 3.

31 Darryl Francis, "Public Policy for a Free Economy," Federal Reserve Bank of St. Louis Review (May, 1975), p. 2.

32 U.S. Congress, Senate Committee on Banking, Housing and Urban Affairs, "Hearings on Senate Concurrent Resolution 18", (February 25 and 26 1974), p. 47.

33 Lawrence K. Roos, "Monetary Targets - Their Contribution to Policy Formation", Federal Reserve Bank of St. Louis Review (May, 1979), p. 15.

34 John Maynard Keynes, The General Theory of Employment, Interest and Money (London: Macmillan Press, 1936), p. 120.

35 Keith Carlson and Rogert W. Spencer, "Crowding-Out and Its Critics", Federal Reserve Bank of St. Louis Review (December, 1975), pp. 5-6.

36 Arthur Okun, "What's Wrong with the U.S. Economy? Diagnosis and Prescription," Quarterly Review of Economics and Business, Volume 15 (Summer, 1975), p. 30.

37 James L. Pierce, "Interest Rates and Their Prospect for Recovery," Brookings Papers on Economic Activity (I: 1975).

38 Keith Carlson, "Large Federal Budget Deficits: Perspectives and Prospects," Federal Reserve Bank of St. Louis Review (Actober, 1976), pp. 2-7.

39 Ibid., p. 3.

40 James E. Turley, "Automobile Sales in Perspective", Federal Reserve Bank of St. Louis Review (June, 1976), p. 14.

41 John Tatom, "Inventory Investment in the Recent Recession and Recovery," Federal Reserve Bank of St. Louis Review (April, 1977), p. 2.

42 Keith Carlson, "Large Federal Budget Deficits," Op. Cit., p. 5.

43 John Tatom, "A Perspective on The Federal Debt Problem", Federal Reserve Bank of St. Louis Review (June/July, 1984), p.6.

44 Keith Carlson, "Large Federal Budget Deficits", Op. Cit., p. 6.

45 Keith Carlson and Roger Spencer, "Crowding Out and Its Critics", Op. Cit., p.2.

46 Keith Carlson "A Monetary Analysis of the Administration's Budget and Economic Projections" Federal Reserve Bank of St. Louis Review (May, 1982), p. 10.

47 Ibid., p. 12.

48 Ibid.

CHAPTER EIGHT

THE ST. LOUIS MODEL - SUCCESSES AND FAILURES

> I want, so to speak, to raise a dust; because it is only out of the controversy that will arise that what I am saying will be understood.
>
> John Maynard Keynes
> 1935

While President Darryl Francis did not agree with Keynes' economic theories, he would certainly accept the sentiment expressed above, taken from a letter which Keynes wrote to his friend Roy Harrod.[1] Francis, himself, had said:

> In a nutshell, to engage in worthwhile research we must be willing to be wrong. This has been the underlying philosophy of our research efforts. We seek to pursue our theoretical formulation and empirical testing in a professional manner and then to present our results for all to examine. If subsequent events should prove us wrong, then we will accept it. In this manner economic knowledge is advanced.[2]

Certainly the St. Louis Model has been the centre of considerable controversy in the economic literature. As has been chronicled, the Monetarist creed has had considerable successes amongst professional economists and the Federal Government. As far as the St. Louis Model is concerned, Andersen and Carlson in a 1974 article gave a checklist of successes and failures of the Model as they saw them as of that date.[3] With ten more years of experience, let us see what has happened to that list.

SUCCESSES

1. Demonstrated short-run vs. long-run effects of stabilization policy. Using the original St. Louis model, Andersen and Carlson ran long-run simulations (thirty years) which confirmed Classical theories emanating from David Ricardo - monetary actions have no effect on real magnitudes, - growth of output, the real rate of interest, the unemployment rate, all of which move toward some equilibrium rate. Alternative rates of money expansion affect only nominal magnitudes: total spending, prices and market rates.

But policy makers are interested in short-run effects and the original St. Louis model successfully demonstrated empirically the differing response of nominal output, prices, interest rates and unemployment to various magnitudes of the growth of money and high employment spending. The 1982 model reiterates these responses. The hope was, of course, that the longer-run consequences of alternative monetary policies would be given consideration by policymakers in order to bring the U.S. economy into the stable equilibrium envisaged by Ricardo. The title of Andersen and Carlsen's original article was "A Monetarist Model for Economic Stabilization," and reflected this concern.

2. Demonstrated the importance of monetary actions in the determination of movements in economic activity. That the St. Louis Fed, in its own right and as part of the Monetarist school has persuaded the public of the importance of money to the well-being of the economy is seen in the importance given by the press following every announcement by the Fed of the most recent changes in the money stock. Moreover, such announcements receive detailed commentary not only in the business section, but frequently on the front pages as well.

The possible repercussions are bandied back and forth by the financial pundits and have strong influence on the stock and bond markets.

Here is a typical example from the Wall Street Journal of April 8, 1983:

> Nevertheless, many economists and investment bankers predict further declines in the money supply in coming months. "There is a growing perception that the economy is going to expand at a moderate and sustainable rate without the byproduct of higher inflation," said Jean J. Rousseau, director of the municipal securities division of Merrill Lynch Capital Markets Group, a unit of Merrill Lynch & Company. "Also, people clearly feel more comfortable about the money-supply's growth."
>
> The slowdown has come as a great relief to many traders, who previously worried that the money supply's explosive growth earlier this year would rekindle inflationary fears among investors and possibly encourage the Federal Reserve System to tighten its credit clamp.[4]

Unhappily, the slowdown in the money supply described above, caused Milton Friedman to make certain predictions which have led policymakers, as we shall describe in Chapter 10, to question monetarist policy recommendations. Late in 1983 he forecast a recession in the first half of 1984, based on the sharp slowdown of M1 growth in late 1983 and soaring inflation in the second half of 1984 as a result of the sharp growth in the money supply from mid 1982 to mid 1983. But as the Wall Street Journal observed,

"He was dead wrong: the economy boomed in the first half (of 1984) and there wasn't any major resurgence of inflation in the second half".[5]

3. **Demonstrated indirectly the role of costs of information in the stabilization analysis.** Search and information costs were a theoretical consideration which was implicit in the original St. Louis model, though not then explicitly recognised by model builders. Information about equilibrium prices takes time and is not costless to gather. Thus, economic units must search for such prices by sampling the market. As a result, lags develop while prices and output adjust to new levels in response to the change in pace of total spending.

The St. Louis model and the St. Louis Fed have been in the forefront in stimulating the idea of time in the economic process and the lags in the response of economic variables has been the subject of much econometric research.[6]

4. **Called attention to an alternative framework of analysis.** In 1970 there were a number of Keynesian type econometric models under development. Amongst them were the Federal Reserve MIT model, the Brookings Model and the Wharton Econometric Forecasting model. But as Andersen and Carlson then said, "Most econometric models have not assigned an important role to the stock of money or to any other monetary aggregate."[7]

But money was the St. Louis Fed's stock-in-trade and monetarism required its own model if it was to challenge the Keynesian doctrine being incorporated into the new large-scale models. That they have been successful in calling attention to their model goes without saying - if that were not the case, this book would not have been written!

Similar models have been developed by other economists, particularly those associated with other Reserve Banks. However they have not displaced the large structural MPS model used by the Federal Reserve in Washington nor the other large models used by prominent forecasting firms. This is probably due to the fact that the St. Louis model is not designed to provide information on the behaviour of individual sectors of the economy, information which is desired by the Federal Reserve in Washington and the clients of these firms.

5. **Demonstrated the usefulness of small models in capturing the aggregative impact of stabilization policies.** The record of the St. Louis Model is that it forecasts - over the short to mid-term (one to five years) - nominal and real GNP, unemployment and interest rates as well as the large structural models.[8] And of course, those are the variables that are of interest to the members of the FOMC. As President Francis has said:

> An economist must state his recommendations in a form that has empirical content. I am not primarily interested in statements that express relationships in abstract terms. I want to know what operations to direct the Desk to perform and how and when the performance of these operations will affect the prices people pay for goods and services and the number of people employed.[9]

Certainly the St. Louis Fed has been able to supply its president with that information.

FAILURES

1. Failed to educate policymakers on the long-run effects of their short-run decisions. Writing in 1974, Andersen and Carlson state:

> The recent experience of the U.S. economy with recession, inflation and experiments with price controls serves as ample evidence indicating that the model has failed in this objective.[10]

By those standards, the St. Louis model continues to fail as first prices and then unemployment has set new post World War II records during the 1970s and early 1980s. But what Andersen and Carson are really saying is that if there has been any failure of the St. Louis model, it is that its empirical results have not convinced policymakers to require that the Fed produce a steady growth of the money stock. If that were monetary policy, their simulations reveal that, over the long run, high employment and price stability are compatible.[11]

The St. Louis Fed agrees wholeheartedly with Fritz Machlup when he says:

> While we are on the distinction between the short run and the long, I may be allowed to comment on the famous dictum by Keynes to the effect that we always live in the short run and in the long run we'll all be dead. My counterdictum is that the short run is awfully short and before long we'll all be awfully sick. This does not mean that we should forget about the short run, but it does mean that serious

> economics should deal chiefly with the long run consequences of our public decisions.[12]

But for policymakers, that is easier said than done. The political process will not long allow them to appear to be doing nothing about the alarums and excursions of the real world, even when they might agree with Machlup that they should be concerned with the long run results of their actions.

2. Failed to capture short-run movements in velocity. Velocity in the income quantity theory of money $\dot{M} + \dot{V} = \dot{P} + \dot{X}$ is measured by $\dot{V} = \dot{P} + \dot{X} - \dot{M}$ - the total percentage change of P and X less the percentage change of M. Based on empirical observations, economists have differed on the predictability of the response of nominal income to a change in the money stock.

Thus Milton Friedman says:[13]

> It is a tautology, or identity, that Growth Rate of Nominal Income = Growth rate of Money plus Growth Rate of Velocity, provided that velocity is defined consistently with whatever concept of money is employed.
>
> If velocity...were a will-of-the-wisp that fluctuated all over the lot in an unpredictable fashion - as naive Keynesians initially asserted - this tautology would be of no use. However, velocity is not a will-of-the-wisp. It behaves in a consistent and fairly predictable way.

Friedman went on to analyse the velocities of M1 and M2 over the period 1962 - 1972 and concluded:

CHART XIII

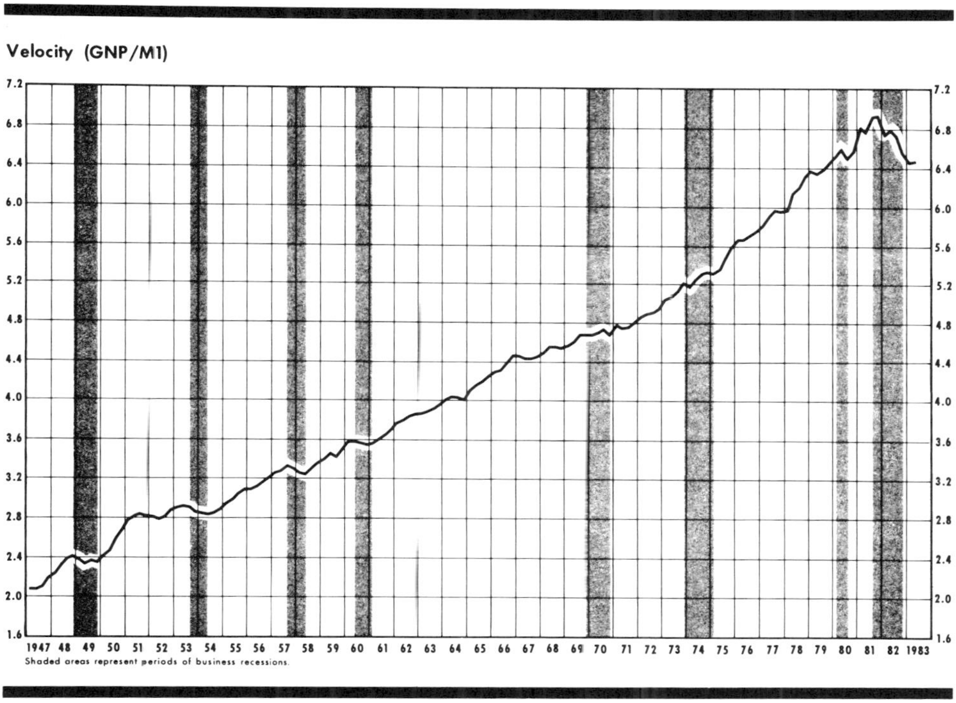

Source: John Tatom "Was the 1982 Velocity Decline Unusual", Federal Reserve Bank of St. Louis Review, (August/September, 1983) p.6.

> The greater stability (long-run) of the velocity of M2 than of the velocity of M1, suggests that it is safer to specify monetary objectives in terms of M2 than in terms of M1, since doing so requires no allowance for an uncertain secular trend in velocity.

Federal Reserve Chairman Arthur Burns, reviewing the movements of velocity following the recession of 1969 - 70, pointed out that they first appeared to offset and then to have re-inforced the influence of money on income and concluded:

> Occurrences such as this are very common because the willingness to use the existing stock of money, expressed in the rate of turnover, is a highly dynamic force in economic life.

He went on to say:

> In short, what growth rate of the money supply is appropriate at any given time cannot be determined simply by extrapolating past trends or by some preconceived arithmetical standard.[14]

which explains in large measure why the Board of Governors of the Federal Reserve System has never fully adopted the views of Monetarists.

The trend growth of the velocity of M1 is illustrated in Chart XIII. On average, M1 velocity increased by 3.4 percent in the 1956-1961 period, 3.8 percent in the 1962 - 1966 period, 1.8

percent in the 1967 - 1971 period and 3.6 percent in the 1972 - 1981 period.

By 1974, Andersen and Carlson recognised that for their spending equation to make reasonable forecasts of nominal GNP, the trend rate for velocity (i.e. the demand for money) had to be reasonably stable. At the same time, they were aware that velocity declined frequently and sharply relative to its trend rate, which their spending equation was unable to predict. As they said, "The problem with the total spending equation is one of capturing the changes in velocity during the period, though for the full period (1968/4 - 1973/2) the average increase in velocity was apparantly captured with a fair degree of accuracy".[15] Thus they called for more research in this area in order to increase the usefulness of the model's spending equation.

In 1950, Clark Warburton had explained that velocity declines relative to trend during a recession because of the same slowing of money growth that causes the recession.[16] The fear of unemployment or of falling demand for product, will be a strong incentive for individuals and corporations alike to maintain larger amounts of money in their checking accounts than they would normally.

However, in 1982, the velocity of M1 fell at a rate that was not only unpredicted but seemingly unpredictable.

In the 1982 St. Louis spending equation, the constant is 2.44, which is not significantly different from the average rate of the increase of velocity of 3.2 percent for the period 1959 - 1981, as illustrated in Chart XIII.

TABLE XXIV

Factors Accounting for Velocity Growth: III/1981–IV/1982[1]

Direct Contribution of:	
Constant	3.9%
Cycle	−4.9
Variations in money growth	−0.7
Inflation changes	−0.5
Interest rate changes	−0.3
High-employment federal expenditure growth	−0.3
Energy price shocks	−0.1
Strike activity	0.0
Unexplained residual	−1.3
TOTAL	−4.3%

[1]Based on table 4 coefficients and actual changes in the factors influencing velocity. The results are converted to compounded annual rates. Total does not add due to rounding.

Source: John Tatom "Was the 1982 Velocity Decline Unusual", Federal Reserve Bank of St. Louis Review, (August/September, 1983) p.12.

But as one can see, during 1982 the turnover velocity of M1 fell sharply, actually by 2.3 percent - making a total diminution from the previous average - 3.2 + 2.3 = 5.5 percent. No spending equation could have forecast a fall of this dimension, especially when one notes that in the 1973 - 1975 recession, velocity actually increased. It seemed that the changes in the rate of velocity had become indeterminate.

Some economists interpreted this development as the breakdown of monetarist theory. Thus in an article entitled " The Failure of Monetarism", published in Business Week, April 4, 1983, Robert J. Gordon stated that "Monetarism has been decimated by the collapse of velocity in 1982".

The St. Louis Fed could not allow such a statement to go unchallenged. Thus, the 1983 Reviews contain three articles dealing with the subject of velocity. The first by John Tatom is entitled "Was the 1982 Velocity Decline Unusual?", and it appeared in the August/September issue.

Tatom builds a model of GNP velocity growth and Table XXIV illustrates the factors which he states account for the change in the growth of velocity in the period III/1981 - IV/1982. He concludes that though the 1982 velocity decline appears to represent a major break from past experience, it was only a temporary fall as is typical of most recessions. The sizeable decline in the rate of monetary growth initially set off the recession and caused a decline in real output. Then the variations in real output and velocity were further enlarged temporarily by inventory adjustments.[17]

Tatom ends by saying: "Thus, the extent of the decline in velocity in the recent recession was not unusual, nor did it represent an atypical shift with important, but unknown, implications for policy making."[18]

The second article appeared in the October Review, the authors were Scott Hein and Paul Veugelers and it was entitled, "Predicting Velocity Growth, A Times Series Perspective". The article "examines the predictability of recent M1 velocity growth to assess claims that the relationship between M1 and nominal GNP has deteriorated".

In their paper, Hein and Veugelers evaluate four different time series techniques used to predict velocity growth over the period II/1975 - I/1983, which contained the last two full business cycles. Their results are "consistent with the notion that quarterly velocity growth fluctuates randomly about a fixed mean" and therefore "forecasting next quarter's velocity growth using average velocity growth over some extended period of time is as effective as any other more sophisticated techniques".[19]

Once can appreciate that in typical recessions, this means that the St. Louis spending equation will always overshoot the actual rate of GNP growth.

The third article on velocity was published in the December issue of the Review. Its author is Daniel Thornton and his title "Why Does Velocity Matter?" This paper sets forth the concept of income velocity in historical terms commencing with Irving Fisher's equation of exchange and proceeds to illustrate the "potential effects of a change in velocity for monetary policy."

Thornton concludes by saying:

> ...it appears that, even if a conservative estimate of the one-quarter ahead forecast

> standard deviation is used the forecast errors are large for policy purposes. Thus, while it might seem desirable for the monetary authority to respond to permanent changes in the level of the growth rate of velocity, it is difficult to predict such changes, or to verify them ex post."[20]

This is undoubtedly one of the reasons why Fed Chairman Paul Volker contends that it would be "exceedingly dangerous and in fact practically impossible to eliminate substantial elements of discretion in the conduct of Federal Reserve policy."[21]

Since velocity of M1 is, on occasion, a "will-of-the-wisp", then the St. Louis spending equation cannot expect to forecast nominal GNP with preciseness.

3. Failed to shed light on price developments during periods of governmental controls and worldwide inflation. Now, as then, the St. Louis model depends on the thrust of past monetary and fiscal actions. While dummy variables can take care of past price controls, they will not predict when Congress will adopt new ones. Similarly there are exogenous factors like the explosive leap in energy prices due to the activities of OPEC which will affect the model. An energy price variable can be added to the Price equation after the fact but the model can't forecast the need for such a variable. A similar leap in the price of food (assuming a world-wide drought) would be destabilizing until a food variable could be incorporated into the equations.

In any model, variations which are beyond historical experience can give rise to large errors in the short run.

4. Failed to cope successfully with large variations in government spending, in the money stock and to anticipate revisions in the money stock data. Such failures are endemic in the model and that is why - as Keith Carlson has said - judgment is necessary. However the St. Louis Fed may be judging itself too harshly - they can hardly be blamed for what Congress and the FOMC do.

The problem of revisions of the money stock data can be enormous. B.M. Friedman gives an example of the difficulties:[22]

> As of the end of May, 1974, for example, the best available data indicated that the narrowly defined money stock had grown during the three month period February-March-April by 11.2% per annum, well above the Open Committee's target; the revised data a year later indicated that the money stock actually grew during these three months by 8.7% per annum, only modestly above the target. This problem persisted throughout the spring of 1974. In retrospect it seems highly unlikely that the Open Market Committee would have adopted so restrictive a policy, driving short-term interest rates to record levels and halting monetary growth altogether in the summer of '74, had it accurately known at what rate the money stock was actually growing.

Again, we have another reason why the Board of Governors of the Federal Reserve System is reluctant to accept the monetarist prescription of a steadily growing money supply, because, as Friedman concludes: "Efforts to improve the available data, as well as research on how best to conduct monetary policy in the presence of whatever data errors will inevitably remain, are clearly in order."

REFERENCES

1 Quoted in Paul Wonnacott, Macroeconomics (Homewood, Illinois: Richard D. Irwin, Inc., 1978), p. 1.

2 Darryl Francis, "The Usefulness of Applied Econometrics to the Policymaker," Federal Reserve Bank of St. Louis Review (May, 1973), p.7.

3 Leonall Andersen and Keith Carlson, "The St. Louis Model Revisited," International Economic Review (June, 1974), p. 323.

4 The Wall Street Journal, April 28, 1983.

5 The Wall Street Journal, December 10, 1984.

6 See for example, Dallas S. Batten and Daniel Thornton. "Polynomial Distributed Lags and The Estimation of Equation, Federal Reserve Bank of St. Louis Review (April, 1983), pp. 13-25.

7 Leonell Andersen and Keith Carlson "A Monetarist Model for Economic Stabilzation: Federal Reserve Bank of St. Louis Review (April, 1970), p. 7.

8 See for example, Keith Carlson and Scott Hein, "Four Econometric Models and Monetary Policy: The Longer Run View" Federal Reserve Bank of St. Louis Review, (January, 1983), p. 13-23.

9 Darryl Francis, "The Usefulness of Applied Econometrics to the Policymaker," Op. Cit., p. 8.

10 Leonall Andersen and Keith Carlson, "St. Louis Model Revisited," Op. Cit., p. 324.

11 Leonall Andersen and Keith Carlson, "A Monetarist Model for Economic Stabilization" Op. Cit., pp. 8, 9.

12 Fritz Machlups, in Emil Classen and Pascal Salem, eds. Stabilization Policies in Interdependent Economics, (Proceedings of a Conference held at The University of Paris, Dauphine in March, 1972), p. 34.

13 Milton Friedman "How Much Monetary Growth" The Morgan Survey (February, 1973), pp. 5-10.

14 Arthur Burns "Letter on Monetary Policy", Federal Reserve Bank of St. Louis Review (November, 1973), pp. 17-18.

15 Leonall Andersen and Keith Carlson, "The St. Louis Model Revisited," Op. Cit., p. 315.

16 Clark Warburton, "The Theory of Turning Points in Business Fluctuations" Quarterly Journal of Economics (November, 1950), pp. 529-49.

17 John Tatom "Was the 1982 Velocity Decline Unusual?" Federal Reserve Bank of St. Louis Review (August/ September, 1983), p. 15.

18 Ibid.

19 Scott Hein and Paul Vengelers "Predicting Velocity Growth: A Time Series Perspective", Federal Reserve Bank of St. Louis Review (October, 1983), p. 43.

20 Daniel Thornton, "Why does Velocity Matter?" Federal Reserve Bank of St. Louis Review (December, 1983), p. 12.

21 Wall Street Journal, December 10, 1984, p. 16.

22 B.M. Friedman, "Empirical Issues in Monetary Policy", Journal of Monetary Economics, 1975, p. 99.

CHAPTER NINE

THE MAVERICKS

> I once teased William McChesney Martin, Jr., at a Federal Reserve meeting by referring to some critical remarks that his father had made at an open market meeting in 1930 or so when his father was Governor of the St. Louis Bank, remarking, "You see Bill, St. Louis was a maverick even then"
>
> Milton Friedman[1]
> 1976

The American Heritage Dictionary defines the word 'maverick' as follows: 'An independent minded person who refuses to abide by the dictates of or resists adherence to a group; a dissenter.' It is not hard to understand why the St. Louis Fed was considered to be a maverick, particularly by the Federal Reserve in Washington.

As the previous material has indicated, throughout the period 1958-1983, by its charts, mathematical procedures and articles, the St. Louis Fed developed a body of Monetarist doctrine which can be set out in four principles.

1. the Federal Reserve, through its purchase and sales of Treasury securities, controls and determines the monetary base.

2. Movements in the monetary base dominate changes in M1 (defined as private holdings of demand deposits and currency), because there is a strong relationship between them.

3. Accelerations and deceleration of M1 are directly followed by accelerations and decelerations in economic activity. Thus the St. Louis Fed agrees with the Friedman and Schwartz analysis that the errant behaviour of the Federal Reserve is the paramount cause of business cycles.

4. Since Federal fiscal policy has extremely little influence on the economy, the Federal Reserve should increase the stock of M1 at a steady rate rather than being influenced by 'money market conditions.' If this were done, the economy could be stabilized with high employment and little inflation within five to fifteen years.

This is a pretty strong indictment of Federal Reserve policies and began almost immediately after Homer Jones was appointed Vice-President in charge of Research in 1958. Delos C. Johns was President of the Bank at that time. He enjoyed controversy and was more than willing to take positions contrary to those espoused by the FOMC.

During the fourth quarter of 1958, M1 had grown at a rate of about six percent per annum. Johns, undoubtedly primed by Homer Jones, felt that this was not restrictive enough. The minutes of the first meeting of the FOMC in 1959 set out that he argued:[2]

> Accordingly, it was (Johns') view that the Committee's expressed decision had not been fulfilled. In making this statement, he did not intend nor did he wish to imply any criticism of the management of the Open Market Account, for in his view the fault lay with the Committee itself due to the kind and manner of instruction that had been given to the Manager of the Open Market Accounts.[3]

The St. Louis Fed wanted to improve the 'view to' provision of the instructions given by the FOMC to the Manager. In January 1959, he was instructed to conduct open market operations, "with a view to (a) to relating the supply of funds in the market to the needs of commerce and business, (b) to fostering conditions in the money market that would contribute best to the sustainability, without inflation of prospective economic expansion."[4]

In his daily open market operations, the Manager tried to keep free or net borrowed reserves (excess reserves minus member bank borrowings from Reserve Banks) at a level that he thought would satisfy the directive. However, he had to deduce the desired levels of these reserves from the remarks made by the members of the FOMC at their meetings - not from the directive itself.

At the February 10, 1959 meeting, Johns was on the attack again, suggesting:

> ...the Committee ought to begin now - in fact should have begun sooner - to pay more attention to what was happening to the money supply and less to what was happening day-by-day and week-by-week in terms of a reserve target of some particular figure.[5]

At that time, the size of the money stock was based on member bank deposits reported on the last Wednesday of each month. The Manager of the Open Market Account would be left in the dark for much of the month if Johns' suggestions were adopted. However, the St. Louis Fed's William Abbot and Marie Wahlig were developing a better money supply series based on daily-average member bank deposits. With modifications, it was adopted by the Board of Governors in 1960.

Still Johns and the few members of the FOMC who agreed with him, were unable to persuade Chairman Martin and the remainder of the Committee to adopt their suggestions. One is reminded of Sir Montague Norman, pre-World War II Governor of the Bank of England, who was once asked to state the reasons for a decision he had made. He replied, "Reasons, Mr. Chairman? I don't have reasons. I have instincts."[6]

However, that these proposals were bothering Chairman Martin is reflected in his statement of September 13, 1960:

> The System must not let itself be persuaded that if it had expanded the money supply exactly the right amount on a statistical basis, there would not have been any recession. This is what critics of the System have been arguing for many years. If it got to that point, the only thing necessary would be to keep the levers moving ad infinitum.[7]

Frustrated by his lack of success, President Johns continually pressed his Research staff for quantitative answers to the actions which could be taken by the FOMC. The staff were delighted to be brought into discussions of the FOMC, which had been hitherto kept secret from them and most other economists employed by the Federal Reserve Board and other Reserve Banks.

Moreover, Homer Jones was willing to allow his staff to develop new concepts and speak their minds - softly at first and then with increasing insistence - through their articles in the Review, even when their conclusions disagreed with views espoused by Washington and New York. As indicated previously, A. James Meigs was a junior employee of the Research Department at this time. He remembers that:

> This was immensely heartening in view of the Federal Reserve tradition in those days that economists at the outlying Banks were not to be seen or heard on the subjects of national and international monetary policies or the New York money market.[8]

Nevertheless an outlying Reserve Bank had to phrase its thoughts carefully. During 1958, the stock of money and its velocity had increased rapidly. In April, 1959 the Review commented:

> If the turnover of money should continue to rise, it may be found that the volume of money need not expand much more for a considerable period of time in order to support a rising level of activity.[9]

Of this innocuous statement, Meigs comments, "This was about as specific as a Reserve Bank dared to be when discussing future monetary policy in print."[10]

THE ST. LOUIS FED CHANGES ITS POSITION

During 1960, Homer Jones changed his outlook significantly. Earlier, Jones' recommendations had been based on the long-run effect of an increase of the money supply on prices - reflecting the Fisherian Quantity Theory. Now the St. Louis Fed recognised that short run changes in the money stock had lagged effects on real output and employment, as well as prices. During 1960 the money stock was contracting and on July 16th, Johns was saying:

> There is opinion to the effect that monetary action may act with a lag of varying and uncertain length. While this idea may not be

> so well established or precise enough to have great weight in our decisions, I think it needs to be borne in mind. Reserves and money have declined for a year. If there is anything to the lag idea, we may discover later that we have been more restrictive than we thought we were being or wanted to be.[11]

At the final meeting of the FOMC in December, 1960, the minutes report Johns as having said:

> He could only express the hope that when the history of the period was written, it would not be the conclusion of historians that the almost unprecedented contraction of the money supply which occurred from mid-1959 to mid-1960 had put to too severe a test the question of the relationship between the money supply and economic activity.[12]

Johns was to be proved correct when the National Bureau of Economic Research declared the interval III/1960 - I/1961 as a period of business recession in the United States.

Meigs believes that "their frustration at having their warnings go unheeded in 1959 and 1960 does much to explain why President Johns and Homer Jones undertook the extraordinary program of monetary research to which all of us are indebted today."[13]

When Delos Johns' term as President expired in 1962, the Board of Directors of the St. Louis Fed recommended to Washington that Darryl Francis be promoted from his position as First Vice President. However this recommendation was not accepted by the Board of Governors. Harry A. Shuford of the Dallas Bank was appointed President, and he was happier to go along with the majority of the FOMC. Francis feels that he was not given the opportunity at this time because of his close connection with Delos Johns.

However, Homer Jones was not deterred, and the work of research continued apace. When Shuford returned to a commercial bank in Dallas in 1966, the Board of Governors then accepted Darryl Francis as President. With Homer Jones, he was to lead the St. Louis Fed during its 'glory years.'

RELATIONS WITH THE BOARD OF GOVERNORS

Initially the 1968 findings of Andersen-Jordan were received with a bit of derision by the Board of Governors in Washington. This is evident in a speech given by Lyle Gramley to the Financial Conference of the National Industrial Conference Board in New York on February 21, 1969., entitled "Guidelines for Monetary Policy, - the Case against Simple Rules."

In his opening remarks, he says:

> ...there is much diversity of view within the Federal Reserve as elsewhere on the appropriate guidelines for monetary policy. You might already have guessed that from reading the November 1968 Review of a certain Midwestern Reserve Bank, whose brand of monetary policy is known around the Board as Brand X.[14]

Later on there is an implication that Chairman Martin found it advantageous to have at least one Reserve Bank take a 'maverick' outlook on monetary policy.

During an interview with Jerry Jordan, he was asked about the relationship between the St. Louis Fed and the Board of Governors of the Federal Reserve System and the reaction of Chairman Martin to it. His answer is enlightening.

> It is useful to have one dissenter in an organization like the System which is designed to represent diverse regional interests and different income sectors...The Fed had to always and still does have to be careful not to appear to be a captive of the big banking interest or any other interest. So having a Reserve Bank like St. Louis, it was somewhat of a maverick then, suited the purposes of William McChesney Martin.[15]

Jordan also suggested that because Martin's father had been the first president of the St. Louis Bank, it was allowed more freedom of expression than other Reserve Banks. Darryl Francis agrees that Chairman Martin used the 'maverickness' of the St. Louis Fed on occasion when giving evidence before Committees of Congress, in order to illustrate that the Federal Reserve System was not a monolithic organization dominated from the top. As for Martin's family relationship, Francis says, "It is true, he did have family connections, but I doubt if that had a helluva lot to do with his permissiveness as far as we were concerned."[16]

However, that members of the Board of Governors could be upset by the St. Louis Fed's criticism of their management of the money stock is illustrated in an anecdote told by Francis. He recalls being a speaker along with Governor George Mitchell at a seminar at the School of Banking of the University of Wisconsin. They had been good friends, but when Francis, in jest, suggested that the Board of Governors had allowed the money supply to run wild and that it needed to be brought under control, Mitchell was not amused. Moreover, for a few years, their relationship was much cooler.[17]

This kind of problem also arose between the staffs of the two organizations. It had been for many years a regulation that articles, no matter the source, appearing in Reserve Bank publications had to have prior approval by a staff economist in Washington. This led to differences of opinion between the two organizations. Karl Brunner was in close contact with the staff members of the St. Louis Fed during the late 1960's and he gives us a flavor of the give and take between the professional economists as he says:

> Intellectual disputes do not proceed within a political or institutional vacuum. They usually affect in various ways institutional positions and political interests. Questions and arguments developed as the St. Louis Fed increasingly clashed with well-established views of the Federal Reserve System and particularly with the notions inherited by the staff at the Board of Governors of the Federal Reserve System. The unique position of the St. Louis Fed in crucial matters pertaining to touchy issues of policy should therefore be recognized as a somewhat remarkable institutional event.[18]

Brunner goes on to say, "William McChesney Martin explicityly tolerated an articulate dissenter in the Federal Reserve System. His attitude contrasted remarkably with the staff's subtle and harassing pressures designed to stifle unorthodox questions and arguments."[19]

As Brunner has suggested, the remainder of the Federal Reserve System was not prepared to accept the St. Louis positions without argument. Four articles appeared, two in the Federal Reserve Bulletin and one each in the Monthly Reviews of the Federal Reserve Bank of New York and Kansas City during the period 1965-1968.[20] These articles comprised a countercritique and set out that:

1. Monetary impulses are neither properly measured nor actually transmitted by changes in the money stock.

2. Monetary impulses are not the chief factor determining variations in economic activity.

3. Cyclical fluctuations of monetary growth cannot be attributed to the behaviour of the Federal Reserve. These fluctuations were claimed to result primarily from the behaviour of commercial banks and the public.

Karl Brunner felt that this countercritique should be answered in the pages of the Review. However, since such an article would be critical of Federal Reserve work, it was decided that he would write a 'guest' article, but to indicate its importance, it would be introduced by an editorial. At this time, the Review had no specific editor - it was supervised by the Vice President, Research. Nevertheless, an editorial was written by Leonall Andersen and Jerry Jordan and to soften its impact, it asserted that Brunner's article:

> ...is presented in this Review with the anticipation that his examination of the issues involved in this (Monetarist) debate will bring forth further discussions by proponents of the

> various views. Such discussions are essential for development of the framework required for rational stabilization policy.[21]

The article, intitled "The Role of Money and Monetary Policy," was edited by Andersen, Jordan and Keith Carlson and appeared in the July 1968 issue of the Review. It is in this article that the term 'Monetarist' was used for the first time.

As one can appreciate, this procedure would have had to be approved by Homer Jones and Darryl Francis, and the article itself by a Washington staff economist. The importance of the article stems not only from its content, which vigorously supports the monetarist position, but also because it exemplifies the greater freedom given to the St. Louis Fed to express monetarist views.

When Arthur Burns became Chairman of the Board of Governors in January 1970, his concern was that the officials of the St. Louis Fed should not make public statements which had not been cleared with Washington. When Darryl Francis was subpoenaed to give evidence before a Committee of Congress, he did so, but as he says:

> The next time I was at an Open Market Committee meeting, Mr. Burns invited me into his office and in a very pious manner, he looked at me and said "I wouldn't believe that anybody in the Federal Reserve would accept an invitation to testify before a Congressional committee without talking to me first."[22]

Similarly, Francis was invited to Paris to speak to a monetary meeting. Shortly after having done so, a regulation was put into effect requiring all foreign trips by Federal Reserve personnel to be approved by Washington. In a world where pronouncements seeming to flow from the Federal Reserve System can be broadcast worldwide in a few moments with unknown repercussions on money markets and international relations, one can sympathize with the Chairman's need to know the subject matter of such speeches. Every Chief Executive is required to be able to comment quickly and precisely on the public statements made by his officials. To do so, he must have prior knowledge of what will be said. The St. Louis Fed, proud of its independence, was somewhat unhappy to have to give up any part of it.

At present, relations are much better. Articles are occasionally held up for some period if they appear to be taking a different position than that being advocated by the Washington Fed. However, by and large, monetarism has become 'old hat.' In recent years the emphasis has switched to 'supply-side' economics and 'Reaganomics'. Many Reserve Banks have their own reduced form Models based on premises which they believe to be important. As an example, the Federal Reserve Bank of Minneapolis has adopted 'rational expectations' as the basis for its theories. Twenty-five years have passed since Homer Jones set out to prove that money does matter. The old passions have died down. The only argument now is, "How much does money matter?"

REFERENCES

1 Milton Friedman, "Homer Jones, a Personal Reminiscence," Journal of Monetary Economics, 2 (1976), p. 435.

2 This section relies heavily on A. James Meigs, "Campaigning for Monetary Reform, Federal Reserve Bank of St. Louis in 1959 and 1960," Journal of Monetary Economics, 2 (1976), p. 439.

3 Ibid., p. 439.

4 Ibid., p. 440.

5 Ibid., p. 442.

6 Quoted in Andrew Boyle, Montague Norman (London: Cassell, 1967), P. 327.

7 A. James Meigs, "Campaigning for Monetary Reform" Op. Cit., p. 448.

8 Ibid., p. 441.

9 Ibid., p. 442.

10 Ibid.

11 Ibid., p. 448.

12 Ibid.

13 Ibid., p. 440.

14 Lyle Gramley, " Guidelines for Monetary Policy - The Case against Simple Rules," in R.L. Teigen, ed., Readings in Money, National Income and Stabilization Policy 4th ed., (Homewood, Ill., Richard D. Irwin Inc. 1978) p. 374.

15 In an interview with the author, May 2, 1983.

16 In an interview with the author, May 3, 1983.

17 Ibid.

18 Karl Brunner, "Contributions in Honor of Homer Jones: Forward," Journal of Monetary Economics, Op., Cit., p. 432.

19 Ibid.

20 1. Lyle Gramley and Samuel Chase, "Time Deposits in Monetary Analysis," Federal Reserve Bulletin (October, 1965).

2. John H. Karenken, "Commercial Banks and The supply of Money," Federal Reserve Bulletin (October, 1967).

3. J.A. Cacy, "Alternative Approaches to the Analysis of the Financial Structure," Monthly Review, Federal Reserve Bank of Kansas City (March, 1968).

4. Richard G. Davis, "The Role of the Money Supply in Business Cycles," Monthly Review, Federal Reserve Bank of New York (April, 1968).

21 Editor's Note to "The Role of Money and Monetary Policy," Federal Reserve Bank of St. Louis Review (July, 1968), p. 8.

22 In an interview with the author, May 3, 1983.

CHAPTER TEN

SUMMARY AND CONCLUSIONS

> None of us really understands what's going on with all these numbers.
>
> David Stockman[1]
> Atlantic Monthly, December, 1981

In the introductory chapter four questions were posed.

1. How did the St. Louis Fed come to adopt Monetarism as its basic philosophy?

2. How has the St. Louis Model changed over the period 1970 - 1983?

3. Is the St. Louis Fed truly monetarist?

4. What contributions has the St. Louis Fed made to monetary theory and policy?

The answer to Question one can be best given in terms of percentages. One asks, what weight should be assigned to the influence of Homer Jones as head of the Research Department from 1958 - 1971 and to Darryl Francis, President of the Bank from 1966 - 1976? I would assign 35 percent of a total of 100 percent to each man. The remaining 30 percent is distributed equally among three other sources.

Homer Jones was the catalyst who guided and motivated not only Darryl Francis, but the staff economists in their search for better economic theory and better quality of empirical data with which to test their hypotheses. President Francis deserves equal billing with Homer Jones. Every college professor is aware of the extent to which his or her Department reflects the preferences and energy of the Department head. This was particularly true at the St. Louis Fed where its theories and policy recommendations were often contrary to those held by the majority of the Board of Governors and the members of the FOMC.

In this situation, it took a bold, convinced and dedicated man to continue to assert the positions held by the St. Louis Fed. In stating his views however, Darryl Francis was fortified by the fact that the predictions of the Research Department on the basis of its early charts and empirical data, proved to be accurate.

The recession of 1960 - 1961, the mini-recession of 1967 and the failure of the 1968 surtax, were forecast from charts which graphed the relationships between the money base, the money stock, nominal and real income. These charts demonstrated that year in and year out, autonomous changes in the money supply led to similar changes in aggregate demand. But it wasn't enough to illustrate that money was the causal force in the fluctuations of the economy. To convince others, analytically rigorous monetarist theory and methodologically sound statistical studies were required.

We must therefore, give a 10 percent weight to the economists who upheld the money creed throughout the years of the ascendancy of Keynesian theory. Lloyd W. Mints, Clark Warburton and then with singular vigour, Milton Friedman and Karl Brunner and their associates, were writing in the monetarist tradition. It was this development and in the case of Brunner and Friedman their active participation,[2] which led to St. Louis Fed's Leonall Andersen and Jerry Jordan in 1968 to test three commonly held propositions.

These propositions held that the response of economic activity to fiscal actions relative to monetary actions is (I) greater (II) more predictable and (III) faster. Using small reduced-form equations, they found the opposite to be true. This set the stage for the St. Louis Model which brought even more fame and controversy to the St. Louis Fed.

The professional economists on the staff of the St. Louis Fed must also be given 10 percent weight in the development of its monetarist position. Keith Carlson, who worked with Leonall Andersen to develop the St. Louis Model, has had the opportunity to read this manuscript in first draft form. He complained to the author that credit must be given to the unnamed members of the Research staff who not only read and commented on the articles which have been cited in this paper, but through their own research and writings have made the Federal Reserve Bank of St. Louis Review required reading for most professional economists. That approximately 40,000 copies of each issue are mailed out, measures the competence of and interest in their work, and has helped spread the monetarist doctrine originally developed by Homer Jones, Leonall Andersen, Michael Keran, Jerry Jordan and Keith Carlson.

The remaining 10 percent must be given to the Chairmen, William McChesney Martin and Arthur Burns, and the members of the Board of Governors during this period - not for their active assistance - but rather for the fact they did not put too many roadblocks in the path of the St. Louis Fed. It must have been galling for them to have the St. Louis Fed, through its President at FOMC meetings and through its publications in the Review actively promoting a policy of control of the monetary aggregates which the majority believe to be a simplistic solution and unable to bring stability to the complex U.S. economy. Moreover, the implication was that monetary policy was being mismanaged by the Board of Governors and this mismanagement was the prime cause of the booms and contractions of the U.S. economy, past and present.

As well, espousal of monetarist doctrine led Presidents Francis and Roos to dissent frequently from the decisions of the majority at meetings of the FOMC. Thus Richard H. Puckett has written:

> The New York and St. Louis banks were the source of a large proportion of dissents, together accounting for 42 percent of all dissents by Bank presidents. Like dissents from the other banks, these were overwhelmingly on the tighter side ...of the four presidents representing the Federal Reserve Bank of St. Louis, two (Messrs. Francis and Roos) dissented on 16 occasions or about one-quarter of the time.[3]

It has been suggested that it was to the advantage of the Chairman to have one maverick amongst the twelve Reserve Banks in order that he could prove to Congress that the Federal Reserve System was not a monolithic organization. More likely, the attitude of the St. Louis Fed which said "Prove us wrong" - was more influential in allowing it to maintain its independent stance.

The St. Louis Model holds that changes in the money stock are the most important influence on nominal GNP. However, world events such as the OPEC oil cartel, wage and price controls, and the changing work force were pervasive in their influence on economic variables and had to be allowed for in the equations of the Model.

In answer to our second question - How has the St. Louis Model changed over the period 1970 - 1983 - we see two types of modifications.

From a statistical point-of-view four characteristics differentiate the 1982 Model from the original version published in 1970.

1. Most variables are entered in rate of change form rather than first difference form.

2. The demand slack variable is entered in real rather than nominal terms.

3. Where relevant, the model's equations have been corrected for serial correlation problems.

4. The addition of energy prices as an exogenous variable.

From an empirical point of view, the thrust of the Spending or GNP equation has not changed. It still asserts that monetary actions have a significant and permanent effect on nominal GNP growth, whereas fiscal actions exert no statistically significant or lasting influence. It is the Price Equation and the Unemployment Equation which have seen the most meaningful changes.

It is here that we see the St. Louis Fed carrying out President Francis' precept of May, 1973, namely "All the results of models must be examined to see if they are consistent with our accumulated evidence from history, theory and practical experience".[4] Because of the pervasive influence of energy costs and the quantum leaps in its price resulting from the actions of the OPEC cartel, a variable was added to the Price Equation based on the producer price index for fuels, related products and power. Moreover, potential output is now measured by the Rasche-Tatom method in order to take into account the fact that increased energy prices make some part of the industrial structure obsolete. As well, dummy variables have been added to allow for the Price and Wage controls of the Nixon administration.

The Unemployment Equation no longer adopts a constant 3.9 percent as the measure of 'full' employment - rather it changes with such things as the percentage of females and teenagers in the work force.

President Francis also advised, "When attempting to see into the future, it is useful to compare the results of more than one model".[5] As we have seen, staff economists John Tatom and Dallas Batten with R.W. Hafer, have been testing somewhat different equations in an attempt to make better forecasts. Moreover, the St. Louis Fed continues to compare the results obtained from its explicitly monetarist model against the large scale econometric models.[6]

Our third question asked, "Is the St. Louis Fed truly Monetarist?" In terms of the qualifications set out by Professor Thomas Mayer,[7] our answer must be a resounding yes! At the same time, I cannot help but have three nagging reservations.

1. The St. Louis Fed never explicitly faces up to the reasons why the FOMC varies the money stock. One gets the impression

that they appreciate the need for the FOMC to do so in order to validate cost-push increases of nominal GNP rather than cause greater unemployment, and as well, to accommodate changes in aggregate demand brought about by autonomous variations in consumer and/or investment spending.

When the FOMC then varies the money stock in response to such impulses, is not the money supply being accommodated to those requirements? In such cases, the causal connection surely extends from aggregate demand to money with the result that the money stock becomes an endogenous variable and not an independent source of disturbance in the economy. This is the argument which Arthur Okun makes in connection with the 1964 tax cut[8] and for me, it explains the success of that fiscal action.

Moreover, if the FOMC had not increased the money stock on that and other occasions, history tells that the people's ingenuity will find a way to provide a supply when it is required - witness the use of cigarettes as money in Allied prisoner-of-war camps during World War II. As Charles Kindleberger reminds us:

> Even when the growth of 'money' was limited to modest rates, financiers escaped the restraints with innovative financing methods - bills of exchange and bank notes in the nineteenth centry, later checking deposits and then today's C.D's 'repos', credit cards and even - in Kuwait, post-dated cheques.
>
> When the central bank gets a fix on Mi, once the market gets its bit in its teeth, it creates new financial instruments, a new money M_j.[9]

This problem came to the fore at the October 1982 meeting of the FOMC, when it decided to attach less importance to changes in M1 and increased significance to the broader, nontransaction-oriented measures such as M2 and M3. One of the main reasons for this decision was the fact that M1 was being distorted as new types of monetary instruments were brought into being as the result of financial deregulation.

It may be that Charles Kindleberger is correct when he writes:

> The Keynesian-monetarism framework is equally irrelevant today. It still assumes a neat continuity with a small number of variables and leaves out political factors, shocks and discontinuities.[10]

Perhaps we need another Lord Keynes, or even another Leonall Andersen and Keith Carlson partnership to inspire us.

2. The St. Louis Fed's position is that after five to fifteen years of reasonably stable monetary growth, discretionary changes would no longer be needed to bring about a stable economy because such a monetary policy would bring the economy to that point. But in practical, or perhaps one should say political terms - could Congress or the Board of Governors wait that long before taking fiscal and/or monetary action if unemployment or interest rates were unacceptably high? I think not.[11]

3. The St. Louis Model indicates that any fiscal action taken by the Federal government will have inconsequential effects on output and employment. On the other hand, Keith Carlson, one of its creators, tells us that automatic stabilization payments such as those for unemployment insurance, food stamps and welfare do maintain aggregate demand during recessions.[12]

My conclusion is that other than these transfer payments, fiscal measures are seemingly ineffective, not because of the St. Louis Fed's theoretical arguments, but rather because they are too difficult to organize in a timely manner.

For example, in September 1962, Congress passed an acceleratd public works program with an initial authority of $850 million. As Nancy Teeters points out:

> Although $152 million was obligated in that fiscal year (1962), only $62 million was spent then. The bulk of the money was obligated and spent in fiscal years 1964 and 1965, with vestiges of the program still in existence in 1971.[13]

That such expenditures in 1964 and 1965 were unnecessary in view of the then booming economy goes without saying. Moreover they undoubtedly 'crowded out' some private expenditures in those years and increased the rate of inflation. Nevertheless, the $62 million which was spent in 1962 would have contributed to aggregate demand by some $124 million in that year if we accept Blinder and Solow's multiplier of 2.[14] As I see it, the problem was not in the fiscal action as such, but rather that only so much as could have been spent during the emergency should have been allocated.

THE ST. LOUIS FED'S CONTRIBUTIONS

Our final question asks, what contributions has the St. Louis Fed made to monetary theory and policy? In my opinion, there are four answers:

1. The St. Louis Fed has done a remarkable service for economic theory and the country generally through the large range of monetary data which it makes available to interested parties. It is rightfully proud of the accuracy and reliability with which these figures are compiled.

2. The St. Louis Fed keeps up-to-date and the articles written by its Research staff and published in the Review reflect current monetary problems. For example, in March 1983, John Tatom had an article entitled "Money Market Deposit Accounts, Super-NOW's and Monetary Policy," which minimized the concern that these new accounts would distort the use of M1 in the conduct of monetary policy.

3. In my opinion, however, the most important contribution which the St. Louis Fed makes is its willingness to translate economic theory into statistical equations which they then test with actual empirical data. John Maynard Keynes puts the problem in his lucid style, saying:

> Too large a proportion of recent 'mathematical' economics are merely concoctions, as imprecise as the inital assumptions which they rest on, which allow the author to lose sight of the complexities and interdependencies of the real world in a maze of pretentious and unhelpful symbols.[15]

The St. Louis Fed makes its algebraic equations and their empirical results simple, understandable and applicable to current economic policy. For me, no higher praise can be given.

4. The Federal Reserve Bank of St. Louis has provided important contributions to the monetary debates at the meetings

of the FOMC. In the late 1960's and early 1970's the St. Louis Fed played an important part in convincing the Federal Reserve System that more emphasis should be placed on monetary aggregates as intermediate targets of policy. Thereafter the Federal Reserve Bank of Minneapolis emphasized the importance of rational expectations and in 1982 the Federal Reserve Bank of San Francisco developed an empirical money market model.

This book began by explaining how the Federal Reserve System was created to overcome any centralizing power in Washington. In 1980 the subcommittee on Domestic Policy of the House Banking Committee was considering a bill to remove Reserve Bank presidents from a role in the FOMC.

On September 8, 1980, Chairman Paul Volker wrote to the committee, opposing the bill and stating:

> From the beginning, the Federal Reserve System has been based on a combination of central and regional elements. It was Congress' intention that twelve Federal Reserve Banks should be established and given a significant role in the operations of the system in order to assume a proper consideration of viewpoints and needs from all sections of the country. The premise was that all wisdom does not reside in Washington and that some further insulation from short-term and partisan pressure would come from giving an important role to the Reserve Banks.
>
> The Reserve Bank presidents and their research staffs bring to the FOMC knowledge and informed opinion about regional interests and needs.

> They are closer to the nation's commerce, industry and agriculture than any Washinton-based organization can be.[16]

Needless to say the bill did not get out of Committee. We can appreciate that the Federal Reserve Bank of St. Louis has been eager to develop and to put forward the policies which they perceive to be in the best long-term interests of the United States. Undoubtedly their work was influential in defeating the bill.

WHAT ABOUT THE FUTURE?

When one thinks about the future of monetarism, two questions come to mind.

1. Will monetarist policies be adopted by the Administration, Congress and the Federal Reserve System?

2. Will the monetarist - Keynesian controversy be resolved?

History tells us that the answer to both questions must be in the negative. As we have seen, monetarist theory has been accepted in Congress and to a smaller degree by the Federal Reserve System. But monetarist policy has not been as successful. The reason is contained in an article printed in the Wall Street Journal of December 10, 1984, headlined "Money's Role". There were three somewhat smaller headlines:

1. Monetarists Succeed in Pushing Basic Ideas (but Not Their Policies).

2. Money Now is Widely Seen As Having a Big Impact; Fed Keeps Fine-Tuning.

3. A Few Bad Forecasts Hurt.

In the body of the article there are five short paragraphs which sum up the history of monetarism as recounted in these pages and depict its future. The authors, Lindley H. Clark, Jr. and Laurie McGinley say in part:

> (Economists) give monetarists much of the credit for a fundamental shift in the balance of economic and political forces away from the pro-expansion and pro-inflation tendencies of the 1960's and 1970's.
>
> The accomplishment is so great, contends Edward Yademi, the chief economist for Prudential-Bache Securites, that "monetarists could insist that we build statues to them on Main Streets across the country."
>
> But few statues are being built, and most monetarists aren't overjoyed at the widespread acceptance of their basic ideas. The reason is that their prescriptions for government economic policy haven't been accepted nearly as well. In fact, their clout is declining from the heady days of the late 1970's, when it looked as if they were about to become the dominant economic braintrusters of the U.S. and other Western industrial democracies.
>
> ...Milton Friedman complains, people still don't agree with the monetarists' principal recommendation: a requirement that the Fed

> produce slow, steady growth of the money supply at a set pace, year after year, (Friedman suggests that the money supply should grow 3% annually), regardless of fluctuations in prices, interest rates or employment.
>
> Instead of being adopted wholesale, monetarist ideas have been simply added to the eclectic kettle of theories - Keynesian, neo-Keynesian, supply side, rational expectationist, to name a few - that along with a hefty dollop of political expediency make up the mixed brew of economic policy in the U.S.[17]

For me, this puts the situation crisply and succinctly.

As far as the monetarist - Keynesian controversy is concerned Thomas Humphrey, the noted economic historian at the Federal Reserve Bank of Richmond, wrote an article in 1970 entitled "The Monetarist - Non-Monetarist Debate" and his conclusion is just as true now as it was then. Here is what he said:

> The longevity of the monetarist-non-monetarist controversy is remarkable. Despite two centuries of innovations in monetary thought, policy and institutions, the two sides argue over basically the same issues. One can only speculate as to why the debate has not long since been laid to rest. Maybe it is because some of the commentators have not been sufficiently aware of the work of their predecessors. Or perhaps it is because until very recently statistical analysis was not sufficiently advanced to permit rigorous

> testing of the opposing theories. More likely it is because neither side has a monopoly on the truth. If this is the case, it is unlikely that the controversy will be resolved in the near future. Even with sophisticated empirical techniques, it will take a long time to identify conclusively the valid elements of each positions [18]

Some fourteen years later, this book attests to the validity of Mr. Humphrey's prophecy as contained in his last three sentences.

REFERENCES

1 Quoted in The Atlantic Monthly for December, 1981.

2 Leonall Andersen and Jerry Jordan, "Monetary and Fiscal Actions, A Test of Their Relative Importance in Economic Stabilization," Federal Reserve Bank of St. Louis Review (November, 1968), footnotes on pp. 20 and 24.

3 Richard H. Pucket, "Federal Open Market committee Structure and Discussions", Journal of Monetary Economics (July, 1984), p. 99.

4 Darryl Francis, "The Usefulness of Applied Econometrics to the Policymaker", Federal Reserve Bank of St. Louis Review (May, 1973), p. 9.

5 Ibid.

6 For example, see Keith Carlson and Scott Hein, "Four Econometric Models and Monetary Policy: The Longer-Run View," Federal Reserve Bank of St. Louis Review (January, 1983), pp. 13-23.

7 Thomas Mayer, The Structure of Monetarism, (New York: W.W. Norton, 1978), p. 2.

8 see Chapter six, reference 4.

9 Charles Kindleberger, "Ten Lessons for Today" Challenge (March/April, 1983) p. 58.

10 Ibid.

11 An example is the Nixon administration in 1969. See W. Philip Gramm "Inflation: Its Cause and Cure", Federal Reserve Bank of St. Louis Review (February, 1975), p. 4.

12 Keith Carlson, "Large Federal Deficits, Perspective and Prospects," Federal Reserve Bank of St. Louis Review (October, 1976), p. 5.

13 Nancy Teeters, "The 1972 Budget: Where It Stands, Where It Might Go," Brookings Papers on Economic Activity (I: 1971), p. 232.

14 See Chapter four, Reference 40.

15 John Maynard Keynes, <u>The General Theory of Employment, Interest and Money</u>, (London, The MacMillan Press Ltd., 1936), p. 298.

16 John J. Balles "The Role of Reserve Banks" <u>Journal of Money, Credit and Banking</u>, (February, 1984), pp. 111-112.

17 Wall Street Journal, December 10, 1984, p.1.

18 Thomas Humphrey, "The Monetarist-Non-Monetarist Debate," <u>Essays on Inflation</u> 2nd ed., (Richmond, Va. Federal Reserve Bank of Richmond, 1980). p. 206.

APPENDIX A

CHECKLIST OF PERIODICALS AND REPORTS
THE FEDERAL RESERVE BANK OF ST. LOUIS
AUGUST 1971

CHECKLIST OF PERIODICALS AND REPORTS

Available from the Research Department

Federal Reserve Bank of St. Louis
P. O. Box 442
St. Louis, Missouri 63166

Name of Publication or Report	When Issued
PERIODICALS	
☐ Review Comments on the current financial and business situation; contains articles on the national and international economy, particularly monetary aspects; analyzes various sectors of the economy of the Eighth Federal Reserve District. (Quantity mailings monthly can be obtained for classroom use.)	*Monthly*, about the 15th of the month.
☐ U.S. Financial Data Presents some analyses of weekly financial conditions; includes charts and data.	*Weekly*, Thursday covering data for week ended Wednesday.
FINANCIAL REPORTS	
☐ Monetary Trends Some analytical comment on the national monetary situation, including charts and tables.	*Monthly*, about the 13th of the month.
GENERAL ECONOMIC REPORTS	
☐ National Economic Trends Analytical comment on national business situation, including charts and tables.	*Monthly*, about the 22nd of the month.
☐ Selected Economic Indicators, Central Mississippi Valley Presents raw and seasonally adjusted data for eight metropolitan areas and five states. The metropolitan area series include employment, unemployment check payments, bank deposits, and bank loans. The data for states include employment, unemployment, personal income, and farm cash receipts. Check payments for some medium-size cities in the district are also presented.	*Quarterly*, about the 30th of the month.

continued...

Name of Publication or Report	When Issued
☐ **Quarterly Economic Trends** Review and outlook for total spending, real product and prices, plus analysis, charts, and rates-of-change tables for national income accounts data and related series.	*Quarterly*, about the 15th of the second month following the quarter for the data reported.
☐ **Federal Budget Trends** Analytical comment on the Federal Budget, including charts and rates-of-change tables.	*Quarterly*, about the 8th of the second month following the quarter for the data reported.
☐ **U.S. Balance of Payments Trends** Analytical comment on the balance of payments, including charts and rates-of-change tables.	*Quarterly*, about the 15th of the month following the quarter for the data reported.

RATES-OF-CHANGE DATA RELEASES

☐ **Annual U.S. Economic Data, Compounded Rates of Change 1951-1970**	*Annual*, preliminary about February 15, revised in May.
☐ **Rates of Change in Economic Data for Ten Industrial Countries** Includes data on Money Supply, Price Indices, Employment, Measures of Output, and International Trade.	*Quarterly*, about the 15th of the second month following the quarter for the data reported. *Annual*, about July 15.

To order, simply indicate which releases you desire, sign your name, address, and ZIP CODE below, tear the page from the *Review*, and mail to Research Department, Federal Reserve Bank of St. Louis, P. O. Box 442, St. Louis, Missouri 63166.

PLEASE SEND THE ITEMS CHECKED ABOVE TO:

Name______________________________

Organization__________________________

Address_____________________________

____

(City, State and Zip Code)

Date_______________________________

Note: All of the above publications are available without charge. However, if ordered in bulk quantities the bank may charge for costs of printing.

APPENDIX B

ANDERSEN-JORDAN'S REGRESSION OF CHANGES IN GNP ON CHANGES IN MONETARY AND FISCAL ACTIONS

Regression of Changes in GNP on Changes in Monetary and Fiscal Actions

First Differences	(Equation 1.1) ΔM	Δ(R-E)	(Equation 1.2) ΔM	ΔE	ΔR	(Equation 1.3) ΔM	ΔE	(Equation 1.4) ΔB	ΔE	ΔR
t	1.57*	—.15	1.51*	.36	.16	1.54*	.40	1.02	.23	.52
	(2.17)	(.65)	(2.03)	(1.15)	(.53)	(2.47)	(1.48)	(.49)	(.67)	(1.68)
t-1	1.94*	—.20	1.59*	.53*	—.01	1.56*	.54*	5.46*	.37	.02
	(3.60)	(1.08)	(2.85)	(2.15)	(.03)	(3.43)	(2.68)	(3.37)	(1.36)	(.07)
t-2	1.80*	.10	1.47*	—.05	—.03	1.44*	—.03	6.48*	—.21	—.17
	(3.37)	(.55)	(2.69)	(.19)	(.10)	(3.18)	(.13)	(4.10)	(.84)	(.64)
t-3	1.28	.47*	1.27	—.78*	.11	1.29*	—.74*	3.05	—.93*	.14
	(1.88)	(1.95)	(1.82)	(2.82)	(.32)	(2.00)	(2.85)	(1.54)	(3.10)	(.39)
Sum	6.59*	.22	5.84*	.07	.23	5.83*	.17	16.01*	—.54	.51
	(7.73)	(.45)	(6.57)	(.13)	(.32)	(7.25)	(.54)	(5.67)	(.89)	(.67)
Constant	1.99*		2.10			2.28*		1.55		
	(2.16)		(1.88)			(2.76)		(1.22)		
R^2	.56		.58			.60		.53		
S.E.	4.24		4.11			4.01		4.35		
D-W	1.54		1.80			1.78		1.71		

Central Differences	(Equation 2.1) ΔM	Δ(R-E)	(Equation 2.2) ΔM	ΔE	ΔR	(Equation 2.3) ΔM	ΔE	(Equation 2.4) ΔB	ΔE	ΔR
t	1.50	—.24	1.58*	.53	.32	1.54*	.63*	.61	.28	.87*
	(1.84)	(.91)	(2.01)	(1.52)	(1.05)	(2.45)	(2.21)	(.28)	(.73)	(2.55)
t-1	2.11*	—.23	1.57*	.60*	—.04	1.63*	.59*	5.42*	.50	—.07
	(3.61)	(1.16)	(2.78)	(2.44)	(.17)	(3.57)	(2.61)	(3.16)	(1.87)	(.27)
t-2	1.89*	.15	1.41*	—.15	—.11	1.43*	—.16	6.87*	—.27	—.33
	(3.18)	(.81)	(2.45)	(.60)	(.47)	(3.16)	(.71)	(3.92)	(1.04)	(1.31)
t-3	1.06	.52	1.26	—.96*	.18	1.13	—.86*	3.51	—1.26*	.35
	(1.36)	(1.90)	(1.72)	(3.15)	(.48)	(1.71)	(3.07)	(1.71)	(3.65)	(.87)
Sum	6.56*	.21	5.80*	.02	.34	5.74*	.19	16.41*	—.75	.82
	(8.16)	(.47)	(7.57)	(.04)	(.54)	(8.45)	(.77)	(6.95)	(1.37)	(1.16)
Constant	2.02*		2.00*			2.30*		1.24		
	(2.48)		(2.14)			(3.55)		(1.14)		
R^2	.66		.72			.73		.67		
S.E.	3.35		3.03			2.97		3.26		
D-W	.88		1.14			1.13		1.05		

Note: Regression coefficients are the top figures, and their "t" values appear below each coefficient enclosed by **parentheses.**
The regression coefficients marked by an asterisk (*) are statistically significant at the 5 per cent level. R^2 are adjusted for degrees of freedom.
S.E. is the standard error of the estimate, and D-W is the Durbin-Watson statistic.

Source: Leonall Andersen and Jerry Jordan, "Monetary and Fiscal Actions: A Test of Their Relative Importance in Economic Stabilization". Federal Reserve Bank of St. Louis Review (November, 1968), p. 17.

APPENDIX C

THE 1982 MODEL AND IN-SAMPLE ESTIMATION

I/1960 - IV/1980

The Model

(1) $\dot{Y}_t = C1 + \sum_{i=0}^{4} CM_i(\dot{M}_{t-i}) + \sum_{i=0}^{4} CE_i(\dot{E}_{t-i}) + \epsilon 1_t$

(2) $\dot{P}_t = C2 + \sum_{i=1}^{4} CPE_i(\dot{PE}_{t-i}) + \sum_{i=0}^{5} CD_i(\dot{X}_{t-i} - \dot{XF}^{*}_{t-i})$

$+ CPA(\dot{PA}_t) + CDUM1(DUM1)$

$+ CDUM2(DUM2) + \epsilon 2_t$

(3) $\dot{PA}_t = \sum_{i=1}^{21} CPRL_i(\dot{P}_{t-i})$

(4) $RL_t = C3 + \sum_{i=0}^{20} CPRL_i(\dot{P}_{t-i}) + \epsilon 3_t$

(5) $U_t - UF_t = CG(GAP_t) + CG1(GAP_{t-1}) + \epsilon 4_t$

(6) $Y_t = (P_t/100)(X_t)$

(7) $\dot{Y}_t = ((Y_t/Y_{t-1})^4 - 1)\,100$

(8) $\dot{X}_t = ((X_t/X_{t-1})^4 - 1)\,100$

(9) $\dot{P}_t = ((P_t/P_{t-1})^4 - 1)\,100$

(10) $GAP_t = ((XF_t - X_t)/XF_t)\,100$

(11) $\dot{XF}^{*}_t = ((XF_t/X_{t-1})^4 - 1)\,100$

Y = nominal GNP
M = money stock (M1)
E = high employment expenditures
P = GNP deflator (1972 = 100)
PE = relative price of energy
X = output in 1972 dollars
XF = potential output (Rasche/Tatom)
RL = corporate bond rate
U = unemployment rate
UF = unemployment rate at full employment
DUM1 = control dummy (III/1971-I/1973 = 1; 0 elsewhere)
DUM2 = post control dummy (I/1973-I/1975 = 1; 0 elsewhere)

In-Sample Estimation: I/1960-IV/1980 (absolute value of t-statistic in parentheses)

(1) $\dot{Y}_t = \underset{(2.15)}{2.44} + \underset{(3.38)}{0.40}\,\dot{M}_t + \underset{(5.06)}{0.39}\,\dot{M}_{t-1} + \underset{(2.18)}{0.22}\,\dot{M}_{t-2} + \underset{(0.82)}{0.06}\,\dot{M}_{t-3}$

$- \underset{(0.11)}{0.01}\,\dot{M}_{t-4} + \underset{(1.46)}{0.06}\,\dot{E}_t + \underset{(0.63)}{0.02}\,\dot{E}_{t-1} - \underset{(0.57)}{0.02}\,\dot{E}_{t-2}$

$- \underset{(0.52)}{0.02}\,\dot{E}_{t-3} + \underset{(0.34)}{0.01}\,\dot{E}_{t-4}$

$R^2 = 0.39$ $SE = 3.50$ $DW = 2.02$

(2) $\dot{P}_t = \underset{(2.53)}{0.96} + \underset{(0.75)}{0.01}\,\dot{PE}_{t-1} + \underset{(1.96)}{0.04}\,\dot{PE}_{t-2} - \underset{(0.73)}{0.01}\,\dot{PE}_{t-3}$

$+ \underset{(1.38)}{0.02}\,\dot{PE}_{t-4} - \underset{(0.18)}{0.00}\,(\dot{X}_t - \dot{XF}^{*}_t) + \underset{(1.43)}{0.01}\,(\dot{X}_{t-1} - \dot{XF}^{*}_{t-1})$

$+ \underset{(4.63)}{0.02}\,(\dot{X}_{t-2} - \dot{XF}^{*}_{t-2}) + \underset{(3.00)}{0.02}\,(\dot{X}_{t-3} - \dot{XF}^{*}_{t-3})$

$+ \underset{(2.42)}{0.02}\,(\dot{X}_{t-4} - \dot{XF}^{*}_{t-4}) + \underset{(2.16)}{0.01}\,(\dot{X}_{t-5} - \dot{XF}^{*}_{t-5}) + \underset{(10.49)}{1.03}\,(\dot{PA}_t)$

$- \underset{(1.02)}{0.61}\,(DUM1_t) + \underset{(2.71)}{1.65}\,(DUM2_t)$

$R^2 = 0.80$ $SE = 1.28$ $DW = 1.97$ $\hat{\rho} = 0.12$

(4) $RL_t = \underset{(3.12)}{2.97} + \underset{(5.22)}{0.96} \sum_{i=0}^{20} \dot{P}_{t-i}$

$R^2 = 0.32$ $SE = 0.33$ $DW = 1.76$ $\hat{\rho} = 0.94$

(6) $U_t - UF_t = \underset{(11.89)}{0.28}\,(GAP_t) + \underset{(6.31)}{0.14}\,(GAP_{t-1})$

$R^2 = 0.63$ $SE = 0.17$ $DW = 1.95$ $\hat{\rho}_1 = 1.43$ $\hat{\rho}_2 = 0.52$

Source: K.M. Carlson, "A Monetary Analysis of the Administration's Budget and Economic Projections". Federal Reserve Bank of St. Louis Review (May, 1982), p. 14.

APPENDIX D
THE 1983 MODEL AND IN-SAMPLE ESTIMATION
I/1955 - IV/1981

The Model

(1) $\dot{Y}_t = C1 + \sum_{i=0}^{4} CM_i\,(\dot{M}_{t-i}) + \sum_{i=0}^{4} CE_i\,(\dot{E}_{t-i}) + \varepsilon 1_t$

(2) $\dot{P}_t = C2 + \sum_{i=0}^{4} CPE_i\,(\dot{PE}_{t-i}) + \sum_{i=0}^{5} CD_i(\dot{X}_{t-i} - \dot{XF}^{*}_{t-i})$

$+ CPA\,(\dot{PA}_t) + CDUM1\,(DUM1)$

$+ CDUM2\,(DUM2) + \varepsilon 2_t$

(3) $RL_t = \sum_{i=0}^{20} CPRL_i\,(\dot{P}_{t-i}) + \varepsilon 3_t$

(4) $RS_t = \sum_{i=1}^{2} CPERS_i\,(\dot{PE}_{t-1}) + CMRS\,(\dot{M}_t)$

$+ \sum_{i=0}^{16} CXRS_i(\dot{X}_{t-i})$

$+ \sum_{i=0}^{16} CPRS_i\,(\dot{P}_{t-i}) + \varepsilon 4_t$

(5) $U_t - UF_t = CG\,(GAP_t) + CG1\,(GAP_{t-1}) + \varepsilon 5_t$

(6) $\dot{PA}_t = \sum_{i=1}^{21} CPRL_i\,(\dot{P}_{t-i})$

(7) $Y_t = (P_t/100)\,(X_t)$

(8) $\dot{Y}_t = ((Y_t/Y_{t-1})^4 - 1)\,100$

(9) $\dot{X}_t = ((X_t/X_{t-1})^4 - 1)\,100$

(10) $\dot{P}_t = ((P_t/P_{t-1})^4 - 1)\,100$

(11) $GAP_t = ((XF_t - X_t)/XF_t)\,100$

(12) $\dot{XF}^{*}_t = ((XF_t/X_{t-1})^4 - 1)\,100$

Y = nominal GNP
M = money stock (M1)
E = high employment expenditures
P = GNP deflator (1972 = 100)
PE = relative price of energy
X = output in 1972 dollars
XF = potential output (Rasche/Tatom)
RL = corporate bond rate
RS = commercial paper rate
U = unemployment rate
UF = unemployment rate at full employment

In-Sample Estimation: I/1955–IV/1981 (absolute value of t-statistic in parentheses)

(1) $\dot{Y}_t = \underset{(3.11)}{2.81} + \underset{(6.91)}{1.13} \sum_{i=0}^{4} \dot{M}_{t-i} - \underset{(0.06)}{0.01} \sum_{i=0}^{4} \dot{E}_{t-i}$

$\bar{R}^2 = 0.40 \quad SE = 3.72 \quad DW = 2.13$

(2) $\dot{P}_t = \underset{(3.27)}{1.12} + 0.06 \sum_{i=1}^{4} \dot{PE}_{t-1} + \underset{(5.00)}{0.08} \sum_{i=0}^{5} (\dot{X}_{t-i} - \dot{XF}^{*}_{t-i})$

$+ \underset{(11.44)}{1.13}\,\dot{PA}_t - \underset{(1.33)}{0.80}\,DUM1_t + \underset{(2.79)}{1.72}\,DUM2_t$

$\bar{R}^2 = 0.76 \quad SE = 1.28 \quad DW = 2.00 \quad \hat{\rho} = 0.16$

(3) $RL_t = \underset{(3.50)}{0.87} \sum_{i=0}^{20} \dot{P}_{t-i}$

$\bar{R}^2 = 0.12 \quad SE = 0.32 \quad DW = 1.76 \quad \hat{\rho} = 1.00$

(4) $RS_t = 0.05 \sum_{i=1}^{2} \dot{PE}_{t-i} - \underset{(2.84)}{0.08}\,\dot{M}_t + \underset{(3.22)}{0.77} \sum_{i=0}^{16} \dot{X}_{t-i}$

$+ \underset{(5.62)}{0.97} \sum_{i=0}^{16} \dot{P}_{t-i}$

$\bar{R}^2 = 0.32 \quad SE = 0.90 \quad DW = 1.83 \quad \hat{\rho} = 0.89$

(5) $U_t - UF_t = \underset{(14.85)}{0.29}\,GAP_t + \underset{(6.84)}{0.14}\,GAP_{t-1}$

$\bar{R}^2 = 0.70 \quad SE = 0.19 \quad \hat{\rho}_1 = 1.33 \quad \hat{\rho}_2 = -0.44$

Source: K.M. Carlson and Scott Hein, "Four Econometric Models and Monetary Policy: The Longer-Run View", Federal Reserve Bank of St. Louis Review (January, 1983), p. 24.

BIBLIOGRAPHY

Boyle, Anthony. Montague Norman. London: Cassell, 1967.

Buchanan, James and Richard Wagner. Democracy in Deficit: The Political Legacy of Lord Keynes. New York: Academic Press, 1977.

Commission on Money and Credit. Stabilization Policies. Englewood Cliffs, New Jersey: Prentice-Hall, 1963.

Corry, John. Money, Investment and Saving in English Economics 1800-1850. London: Macmillan, 1962.

Culbertson, John. Full Employment or Stagnation. New York: McGraw-Hill, 1964.

Eckstein, Otto. The Great Depression with a Postscript on Stagflation. Amsterdam: North Holland Press, 1978.

Fisher, Irving. The Purchasing Power of Money. New York: Macmillan, 1911.

Friedman, Milton, ed. Studies in the Quantity Theory of Money. Chicago: University of Chicago Press, 1956.

Friedman, Milton, A Program for Monetary Stability. New York: Hordham University Press, 1960.

Friedman, Milton and Anna Schwartz. A Monetary History of the United States. Princeton, New Jersey: Princeton University Press, 1963.

Friedman, Milton. Dollars and Deficits. Englewood Cliffs, New Jersey: Prentice-Hall, 1968.

Friedman, Milton and Walter W. Heller. Monetary vs. Fiscal Policy. New York: W.W. Norton, 1969.

Friedman, Milton. The Counter-Revolution in Monetary Theory. London: Institute for Economic Affairs, 1970.

Heathfield, David. Perspectives on Inflation. London: Longman, 1979.

Heller, Walter. Perspectives on Economic Growth. New York: Random House, 1968.

Humphrey, Thomas M. Essays on Inflation. Richmond, Va. Federal Reserve Bank of Richmond, 1980.

Keynes, John Maynard. The General Theory of Employment, Interest and Money. London: The Macmillan Press, Ltd., 1936.

Lekatchman, Robert. The Age of Keynes. New York: Random House, 1966.

Maisel, Sherman. Managing the Dollar. New York: W.W. Norton, 1973.

Mayer, Thomas. The Structure of Monetarism. New York: W.W. Norton, 1976.

Mayer, Thomas, James S. Duesenberry and Robert Z. Aliber. Money, Banking and the Economy. New York: W.W. Norton, 1981.

Mints, Lloyd W. Monetary Policy in a Competetive Society. New York: McGraw-Hill, 1951.

O'Bannon, Helen, David Bond and Robert Shearer. Money and Banking, Theory, Policy and Institutions. New York: Harper and Row., PUblishers, 1975.

Okun, Arthur. The Political Economy of Prosperity. Washington, D.C.: The Brookings Institution, 1970.

Sraffa, Piero, ed. Works and Correspondence of David Ricardo. Cambridge: Cambridge University Press, 1952.

Stein, Jerome, ed. Monetarism. New York: North Holland Publishing Company, 1976.

Teigen, Ronald, ed. Readings in Money, National Income and Stabilization Policy, Fourth Edition. Homewood, Illinois: Richard D. Irwin, Inc., 1978.

Warburton, Clark. Depression, Inflation and Monetary Policy Selected Papers, 1945-1953. Baltimore: The Johns Hopkins Press, 1966.

Wonnacott, Paul. Macroeconomics. Homewood, Illinois: Richard D. Irwin, Inc., 1978.